The Story of Ethics
Fulfilling Our Human Nature

KELLY JAMES CLARK
Calvin College

ANNE POORTENGA

Prentice
Hall

Upper Saddle River, NJ 07458

Library of Congress Cataloging-in-Publication Data

Clark, Kelly James
   The story of ethics : fulfilling our human nature /
   Kelly James Clark, Anne Poortenga.
     p. cm.
   Includes bibliographical references and index.
   ISBN 0-13-097840-X
   1. Ethics—History. I. Poortenga, Anne. II. Title.

BJ71 .C58 2003
170'.9   2002016964

Acquisitions editor: Ross Miller
Production editor: Laura A. Lawrie
Manufacturing
  and prepress buyer: Brian Mackey
Copy editor: Laura A. Lawrie
Editorial assistant: Carla Worner
Cover design: Bruce Kenselaar
Cover art: © by Walter Lopez/Corbis

This book was set in 10.5/12 Bembo by
NK Graphics, and was printed and
bound by Courier Stoughton. The cover was printed by
Phoenix Color Corp.

 © 2003 by Pearson Education, Inc.
Upper Saddle River, New Jersey 07458

Printed in the United States of America

10 9 8 7 6 5 4 3 2 1

ISBN 0-13-097840-X

Pearson Education LTD., *London*
Pearson Education Australia PTY, Limited, *Sydney*
Pearson Education Singapore, Pte. Ltd
Pearson Education North Asia Ltd, *Hong Kong*
Pearson Education Canada, Ltd., *Toronto*
Pearson Educación de Mexico, S.A. de C.V.
Pearson Education--Japan, *Tokyo*
Pearson Education Malaysia, Pte. Ltd.
Pearson Education, *Upper Saddle River, New Jersey*

To our families

Susan, Will, Emily, and Evan Clark

and

Doug, Sam, Kate, and Maria Poortenga

CONTENTS

ACKNOWLEDGMENTS

We would like to thank those who have read drafts of this book, in part or in its entirety, for helpful comments and insightful criticisms: John Hare, Alfred Freddoso, Lee Hardy, Rebecca Konyndyk DeYoung, Simona Goi, Ruth Groenhout, Christine Yalda, and the omnipresent anonymous reviewers. We would also like to express our gratitude to our students at Notre Dame, Calvin College, and St. Andrews University, Scotland, who, through their enthusiasm, questions, and insights, have helped us to make some of the greatest thinkers of the Western world more accessible. We are grateful to those who have taught us moral philosophy for their clarity and inspiration. We also appreciate the help of Cheryl Bridges, Leonard Siddarta, Will Jensen, Jackie Tao, Heather Hillstrom, and especially Donna Kruithof in preparing the manuscript for publication. Finally, we are grateful to our families for their constant and concrete expressions of support and encouragement and, even more profoundly, for their insights into human flourishing: for the ways in which they bring us closer to it, and for their occasional reminders of how far we have yet to go.

Grateful acknowledgment is hereby made to the following for permission to use material reprinted in this volume: Excerpt from G. E. M. Anscombe, "Modern Moral Philosophy," *Philosophy* 33 (January 1958), 1–19, reprinted with the permission of Cambridge University Press; excerpt from Richard Rorty, *Contingency, Irony, and Solidarity,* reprinted with the permission of Cambridge University Press; University of Notre Dame Press, Notre Dame, Indiana, for material from Alasdair MacIntyre, *After Virtue* (1984); Plato, *Republic* 2nd ed., trans. Grube/Reeve (1992), reprinted by permission of Hackett Publishing Company. All rights reserved.

INTRODUCTION

"Do you think it a small matter to determine which whole way of life would make living most worthwhile for each of us?"—Plato

You walk through the streets of a big city and a dirty, smelly person wearing moth-eaten clothing begs for your money: "Can you spare some change?" Judgments or questions rush through your mind. About this person's moral character: Does she lack ambition? Is she an alcoholic? Is she sincere or is she a scammer? About the benefits to her and to society of giving her money: Will it encourage laziness? Foster drug addiction? Or will your kindness allow her room to gather herself so that she can get a job? About yourself: Will generosity somehow benefit you by building your character, that is, by making you the kind of person that you think you want to or ought to be? Will your act of kindness serve to create the kind of society that you wish to live in? Hard questions all; ethical judgments all.

Perhaps you are a college student and face the question "Why are you in college?" You don't have a good answer to that question ("It beats flippin' burgers at McDonald's") and your lack of a good answer plagues you during finals week. Just when you most need to be motivated to study, your lack of a goal or a vision makes you wonder whether it is really worth all the trouble. You look around enviously at those premed or preengineering students whose lives are entirely planned out; you see that their clearly perceived goals keep their minds alert and their bottoms stuck to their chairs when you are tempted to run off to a party. Why ARE you in college? Because it's the next thing to do after high school? Because it's good to get away from home and parental authority? Because it's a good place to make new friends and, perhaps, snag a mate? Because you will get a more interesting and higher paying job? Because it's good to get an education? Maybe your answer is simply and painfully, "I have no idea."

Going to college, most of us believe, makes some sort of contribution to a good life. Of what does that good life consist? Knowing lots of things? Earning lots of money? Having lots of friends? Creative self-expression? Sex and booze interspersed with sleep? A spouse and children? Big houses and fast cars? Serving the community? Working at an interesting job? Loving God? Again, these are all ethical questions. And again, these are all hard questions.

We are all familiar with straightforward cursory "Dos and Don'ts" answers to ethical questions: Don't murder, steal, or lie. Do cultivate your talents, be faithful to your spouse, kind to friends, and generous to the poor. Should we settle for the "Dos and Don'ts" answers to these questions? Will, for example, faithfulness, generosity, and truthfulness really make us happy? Will such a life satisfy us as persons? If not, why be faithful, generous or trustworthy?

Ethical or moral theories[1] help answer such questions. They do so, in part, by answering two other questions: What kind of persons are human beings? And, What kind of life should we live to fulfill ourselves as persons? Answers to these questions enable us to more deeply understand and evaluate the role "Dos" and "Don'ts" are to play in our lives.

Some people answer the question about the nature of human beings by claiming that we are totally self-absorbed. They consider the sorts of rules involved in typical "Dos and Don'ts" morality a constraint on their self-interest. Suppose, for example, that I want more than anything lots of money. Generosity constrains or is opposed to my desire. So generosity will frustrate, not satisfy, my deepest desire. It should be noted, of course, that if people are generous to me (and I would like to encourage that kind of behavior), *their* generosity will satisfy my desires. But the demand that *I* be generous runs contrary to my deepest desire to accumulate wealth.

Great moral thinkers like Plato and Aristotle did not believe that morality constrained or frustrated our deepest desires. Indeed, they believed that given our nature, morality is the primary contributor to a good, satisfying, and fulfilling life. This conviction was echoed by medieval thinkers such as Augustine and Aquinás, enlightenment thinkers such as Kant, late modern thinkers such as Marx, Mill, and Kierkegaard, and contemporary thinkers such as Rawls, Hare, and MacIntyre. In contrast, revolutionaries such as Nietzsche and Sartre claimed that human nature is such that the usually accepted moralities do run contrary to our deepest desires and frustrate our attempts at fulfillment. They sought to replace traditional morality with a radically new morality. Despite their differences, this diverse batch of thinkers holds in common the view that morality (traditional or radical) and the good life are intimately related. The connection between morality and human fulfillment is human nature. The moral life is the most fulfilling life for human beings given human nature. One simply cannot answer questions about the nature of morality and the good life without also, perhaps first, answering the question, What makes human beings essentially human?

If you think humans are basically and irredeemably selfish, you might opt for the moral views of Thrasymachus, the Sophists, or Hobbes. If you suppose that humans are initially selfish yet capable of obtaining the divine grace necessary for moral transformation, you may embrace the views of Augustine, Aquinás, Kant, or Kierkegaard. If you conclude that our finer nature can be trained by proper education for virtuous activity and selfless pursuits or for contemplation, you may prefer the moral teachings of Plato or Aristotle. If you judge that human beings are by nature good and social, you may prefer the views of Marx. And if you believe that humans are animal-like in their need for power and dominion, or

---

[1.] "Ethics" and "Morality" are sometimes distinguished in various ways. The distinctions are not important for our text; we will use the terms interchangeably.

godlike in their need for creative self-expression, you may find the moral views of Homer, Nietzsche, or Sartre attractive.

This text takes us on a journey through the history of ethics, placing the various ethical theories in the context of judgments about human nature. Most of these great thinkers will defend (roughly) traditional morality—kindness, moderation, wisdom, justice, and generosity. Yet, their differing views of human nature will require radically different justifications of traditional morality and the good life. Others defend more revolutionary approaches to morality, valuing power, domination, pride, and enmity. Again, their different views of human nature entail different views of morality and the good life.

Some 20th-century thinkers have challenged this entire approach to ethics, and our journey would not be complete without a look at their revolutionary views. Thinkers such as Moore, Ayer, and Rorty have severed ethics from the philosophy of human nature. Rorty, for example, argues that there is no such thing as an essential human nature and so moral philosophy must proceed very differently than it has in the past. It is not a matter of discovering the best way to fulfill out essential nature but, rather, a matter of radically free self-creation.

Our journey would also not be complete without a look at the feminist challenge to moral philosophy. Feminists such as Wollstonecraft and Gilligan claim that the study of the good life for man has been just that—the study of the good life for *man*.[2] They argue that woman, no less than men, are capable of moral excellence and human fulfillment.

At times, the theories in this book may strike the reader as strange or extravagant, possibly even outdated. It is important to remember that often times moral philosophers offered elaborate theories in response to challenges, both practical and theoretical, which threatened to undermine morality. The very real attraction of immorality as well as some highly persuasive arguments in its favor led Plato, for example, to develop and elaborate a grand anthropological and metaphysical system within which his views of morality safely fit. Big problems require big solutions. Seen as responses to the specific challenges he faced, Plato's solutions are not as extravagant as they might appear at first glance. Situating each of the thinkers within his historical context, at times including the political, religious, and cultural challenges as well as the philosophical challenges, will lead to a more sympathetic and fuller understanding of their moral theories. It may also enable us to find in their thought much that is relevant today.

This text is necessarily selective. There are a few major thinkers in the history of Western thought with which every educated person should be acquainted.

[2.] Regrettably, we must use the term "man" when discussing many of these views in this book. Women were often downgraded in these societies and their characteristic (and stereotypical) virtues were not prized like the "manly" virtues. Indeed, alleged deficiencies in strength, intelligence, and social status often were considered detrimental to women's pursuit of a full and rich life. These issues will be discussed more fully in the discussions of Mary Wollstonecraft (Ch. 3) and Feminist Ethics (Ch. 5). We will use the term "man" when it seems necessary for historical accuracy. We will use gender-inclusive language when it is appropriate.

Not everyone will agree with all of our choices, but most people will agree with most of our choices. This is all that could be expected. In our limited space, we have tried to present the most central views of each of the thinkers as clearly as possible. This means we have had to omit a great deal of the peripheral (but often important) positions of the various thinkers; we also have had to avoid the complex (but often important) debates about more subtle points including matters textual interpretation.

We hope this journey will help the reader understand the answers some of the Western world's greatest thinkers have given to the questions, What are human beings like? How should we live? How are we fulfilled? In coming to understand their answers, we hope the reader is better able to formulate and frame his or her decisions, both large and small, within the all-important context of what it means to flourish as a human being.

1
The Ancient World

Introduction

The three dominant moral philosophers of the Ancient world were Socrates (470–399 BC), Plato (c. 427–347 BC), and Aristotle (384–322 BC). Their moral theories were not developed in a sociohistorical vacuum. Like any other philosopher, each of them was responding to a set of problems raised within his culture. Socrates, Plato, and Aristotle lived in Athens, a budding democracy. They walked through the marketplace, discussing ideas with ordinary and extraordinary men each of whom held firm opinions about what it means to be a good man. They knew men who yearned for pleasure and power, who sought wealth and fame, and who longed to perform heroic actions that would be remembered by succeeding generations. These men were able to justify their desires and pursuits within moral traditions that valued power, pleasure, wealth, fame, and heroism. It seemed to be the case in the ancient world no less than today that whatever one desires, some moral thinker has elaborated a theory claiming that those desires are worthy of pursuit. Socrates, Plato, and Aristotle believed it to be part of their task as moral philosophers to critically examine and respond to these various traditions.

In this chapter, we will look briefly at two of the most prominent traditions, those belonging to Homer and to the Sophists. When viewed in isolation, the views of Socrates, Plato, and Aristotle sometimes seem extravagant. Seen against their sociohistorical background, they make more sense. We will have a fuller understanding of their views if we recognize that they developed in response to the strengths and weaknesses of the Homeric tradition and as antidotes to the skepticism, relativism, and egoism of the Sophists.

The Homeric Tradition

There are two urns at the threshold of Zeus,
One filled with good fates, the other with bad ones. . . .

Homer (c. mid-8th century BC) captured a several hundred years old oral tradition in his collected stories, *The Iliad* and *The Odyssey*.[1] He did not provide a systematic excursus on courage or perseverance or a manual on how to love; rather, he showed the courageous Achilles, the persistent Ulysses, and the faithful Penelope. In reading these stories, we see the kinds of moral virtues that Homer's heroic society endorsed as well as the vices that they scorned. The ideally good man, according to Homer, is the noble warrior and wise ruler. He has the physical prowess, skills, and character traits of the domineering soldier: for example, strength, cunning, and courage. And he is a wise counselor for his community in times of both war and peace. The noble warrior is courageous and cunning; he fights hard and rules well. He requires sufficient leisure time and wealth to practice his skills, and he should be rewarded with honor and money for his victories both in battle and in court.

Those who are not able to attain this ideal may still be good to a lesser extent if they fulfilled their functions in society. So the carpenter is good if he builds well, the cobbler is good if he makes plentiful and high quality shoes, the wife is good if she is faithful, and the slave is good if he obeys without question. But the further one is removed from the ideal of the noble warrior, the less ideally good one may be. Women and slaves, the furthest removed, can only be good in an impoverished sense of the term. Bad persons fail to attain even this level of goodness. They are cowardly, stupid, and lacking in both the kingly qualities of the good man as well as the qualities required to be good to a lesser extent.[2] Later, in the section on Aristotle, we shall see to what extent he was influenced by the Homeric picture of virtue.

Homer's stories also included tales of the gods in relation to each other and to human beings. These gods often times seemed like human emotions writ large and they held the fate of human beings in their capricious hands. While they demanded that human beings act appropriately toward them and each other, the gods themselves often times acted in ways that were less than what we might consider godly or virtuous.

The earliest moral training for the Greeks focused on the Homeric poems, the *Odyssey* and the *Iliad*. For several hundred years, children learned morality by example from Homer's heroes. Homer's poems were memorized and playacted partly because books were a rare and expensive luxury in the ancient world, but

---

[1.] *The Iliad of Homer*, trans. Richard Lattimore (Chicago: University of Chicago Press, 1987) and *The Odyssey*, trans. Robert Fagles (New York: Penguin, 1999).

[2.] Joseph M. Bryant, *Moral Codes and Social Structure in Ancient Greece* (Albany: SUNY Press, 1996), 18.

more importantly so that the student might acquire the heroic virtues by imitation, so that the virtues might permeate the learner from the inside. Much of the moral instruction of our own children proceeds by way of example, memorization, singing, and playacting. We instruct our children long before they learn to read. We read them fairy tales, constructing an imaginary world in which good people triumph over wicked people. And children are encouraged to act out the parts. We teach them catchy and unforgettable rhymes and tunes with moral overtones. And we sometimes refer to these when our children fail to be generous or kind. We shall see later that Plato objected both to the Homeric picture of the gods as well as to this sort of instruction.

The Sophists

Man is the measure of all things.

The Sophists flourished during the time of Plato; they were skilled and successful practitioners and teachers of rhetoric, traveling from city to city plying their wares. Although they were not typically citizens of Athens, their skills were valued by members of this democracy who were eager to persuade others through the spoken word. In a democracy, power is gained by the ability to sway the masses, and the Sophists were superb teachers of oral persuasion. Protagoras, one of the most famous Sophists, declares his purpose as a teacher; a student will learn: "The proper care of his personal affairs, so that he may best manage his own household, and also of the state's affairs, so as to become a real power in the city, both as a speaker and man of action."[3] The Sophist Gorgias contends that rhetoric is not intended for the acquisition and communication of the truth about right and wrong; rather, one uses clever rhetoric to persuade and thereby gain control over other people (Gorgias, *Plato's Dialogues* 451d–459e).

   In their zeal to win a debate, however, the Sophists often deliberately misconstrued arguments with the sole intention of vanquishing their opponents. They became quite infamous for their lack of concern for the truth. In Greek society, the Sophists were considered commonly deceptive in speech and interested in their own financial gain as a result. They were such skillful orators that they could make any argument, weak or strong, look good. And they were not attracted only to strong arguments (that is, to the truth), they were attracted to their own gain. Truth, according to the Sophists, is not a virtue to which the cunning

---

[3]   As quoted in Plato, *Protagoras,* 318e–319a. The quotations from this section on the Sophists come from various dialogues of Plato in *Plato: The Collected Dialogues,* eds. Edith Hamilton and Huntington Cairns (Princeton, NJ: Princeton University Press, 1961); hereafter cited in the text by name of dialogue, *Plato's Dialogues,* and textual reference.

person aspires in speech. Instead, the Sophists instructed men to win over their opponents with flattery, promises and half-truths.

During the time of the Sophists, increase in travel produced a growing awareness of vastly different religious, moral, and social standards. These competing beliefs led people to wonder about the certainty of their accepted beliefs and about the possibility of a single, universal standard of morality. Different cities have different moral codes; so the question was raised: Is morality merely a local, conventional social practice or is there a transcendent, absolute moral standard by which such local conventions and people themselves may be judged?

The Sophists embraced and capitalized on the moral diversity among various cultures and the apparent lack of a universal moral standard. Protagoras, for example claimed that "Man is the measure of all things" (Theatetus, *Plato's Dialogues* 152a). Human conventions are the measure of things, not some transcendent, universal standard. Humans are the measure, and they are not in turn measured by some scale of justice or truth that stands outside of and above them. Throwing off the shackles of moral absolutes, local and earthbound customs are the ultimate standards of justice. And what is right for one culture may not be right for another culture. In rejecting absolute moral standards, the Sophists instructed their students to adapt to the local customs. They should do so, not because they are right or true, but because following local customs is most often the way to become successful in a given society. They encouraged their students to assume the traditional morality as a means to the end of securing what they really desired: pleasure, power, and a variety of self-interested goals.

Thrasymachus, one of Plato's greatest sophistic interlocutors, believed that justice was actually an obstacle to the satisfaction of the desires of (power-, wealth-, and pleasure-hungry) people.[4] He did not consider these desires base or animal, indeed he considered them, as Nietzsche later did, noble like the desires of a young lion. It looks then like moral conventions are obstacles to the fulfillment of human nature. But, since ostracism or punishment may result from the public rejection of conventional values, and rewards, praise, and honor are bestowed on those who are virtuous, Thrasymachus suggested that conventional morality should be worn like a pretty garment that conceals the noble yet egoist motives hidden deep within.

Let us turn to the views of Thrasymachus in Plato's *Republic*[5] to see the force of the Sophist's defense of egoism. In Book I, Thrasymachus offers at least three views of justice. There is no attempt on his part to relate them and it is not clear that they can be held together in any consistent fashion. He attempts to deal with two related questions: What is justice? And Does justice pay? One thing is clear,

---

4. It is not clear that Thrasymachus actually existed. He may have simply been Plato's imaginative construction of a typical Sophist.

5. All references to Plato's *Republic* are from *The Republic/Plato*, translated by G. M. A. Grube, revised by C. D. C. Reeve (Indianapolis, IN: Hackett Publishing Company, 1992); hereafter cited in the text as *Republic*.

however, his answers to these questions constitute an outright attack on ethical absolutism.

First, What is justice? Thrasymachus maintains that *Justice is merely the advantage or interest of the stronger.* In other words, *Might Makes Right.* He writes:

> Each makes laws to its own advantage. Democracy makes democratic laws, tyranny makes tyrannical laws, and so on with the others. And they declare what they have made—what is to their own advantage—to be just for their subjects, and they punish anyone who goes against this as lawless and unjust. This, then, is what I say justice is, the same in all cities, the advantage of the established rule. Since the established rule is surely stronger, anyone who reasons correctly will conclude that the just is the same everywhere, namely, the advantage of the stronger. (*Republic* 338d–339a)

According to this view, justice is brought into being and held in existence by the power of the stronger. There is no binding force for morality other than the power and whim of those who make the laws. Rulers, according to Thrasymachus, are not selfless public servants but, rather, relentless and ruthless egoists. They make laws simply to obtain their own interests. They do not make laws according to some transcendental standard of justice. Justice is a mere convention. If those in power say that slavery is just, slavery is just. One cannot compare the laws enacted by those in power to some higher, absolute standard; there is no basis on which one could say, for example, that those laws are unjust. For those not in power, justice is a matter of obeying those laws, whatever they may be.

The challenge to morality is clear. Justice is no more than the arbitrary preferences of the powerful. Justice protects their interests but ignores the interests of the powerless and vast majority. If one wishes one's interests to be protected, one cannot appeal to some absolute standard of morality, one must gain power and then lord it over the less fortunate. A more cynical view of justice can scarcely be imagined.[6]

Thrasymachus compares this view of justice and the character of rulers to a shepherd caring for sheep. He says to Socrates:

> You think that shepherds and cowherds seek the good of their sheep and cattle, and fatten them and take care of them, looking to something other than their master's good and their own. Moreover, you believe that rulers in cities—true rulers, that is—think about their subjects differently than

---

6. Although we might disapprove of Thrasymachus' cynicism, there is ample evidence that those in office often enact laws that advance only the interests of those in power. The financial, social, and sexual rewards extended to those in power are inestimable. Some members of political office enter as members of the middle class and leave millionaires. Some are reelected not because of their self-sacrifice in securing the national interest but because of their ability to make laws that gain them favor. As Lord Acton so correctly observed, "Power tends to corrupt."

one does about sheep, and that night and day they think of something besides their own advantage. You are so far from understanding about justice and what's justice, about injustice and what's unjust, that you don't realize that justice is really the good of another, the advantage of the stronger and the ruler, and harmful to the one who obeys and serves. (*Republic* 343b–c)

The naive subject will believe, like a sheep led to slaughter, that she is being fattened for her own good, that justice is to her own advantage. The psychological effect of the realization of the actual nature of justice is obvious. Either one gains power, so that justice works in one's favor, or one becomes demoralized, recognizing that justice is unconcerned with and even hostile to one's own interests. This leads to Thrasymachus's answer to the second question, Does justice pay?

The challenge to morality involved in Thrasymachus's view is perhaps even more evident in his answer to this question, for he maintains that justice benefits another, whereas injustice benefits oneself. According to his egoistic view, *justice doesn't pay*. "Justice," he writes, "is really the good of another" (*Republic* 343c). Justice makes another happy, but not oneself. Consider the demands of justice to see whose interests are protected. Suppose I see Tony's wallet on the table with $1,000 inside. I need $1,000 and consider stealing it. Assume that I can easily steal it and get away with it. Whose interests are protected by morality? Tony's, not mine. Morality is his good, not mine. Suppose I get angry at Mary and wish to strike her on the nose. Assume I can punch her with impunity. Again, whose interests are protected by morality? Hers, not mine. The list of examples abound. It looks as if morality protects the interests of the other and is not (if I can be immoral and not get caught) in my own interest.

Thrasymachus multiplies examples to support his claim that the person of power, the one who is unafraid to defy moral convention, always gets the better deal. In the fulfillment of contracts, when the partnership ends, the unjust person has more than the just person. The scrupulously just person will always pay more taxes. The just person will also receive fewer benefits from the city; the unjust person will learn how, through deceit, to gain more. And unjust holders of public office will see their treasures multiply while the just will see theirs dwindle. The examples clearly suggest that it is injustice that pays.

Thrasymachus assumes in these examples that one is unjust and gets away with it. Surely if one is unjust, gets caught and is punished, it is not to one's advantage. So the most powerful person is the one clever enough to conceal his injustice, perhaps under the guise of justice, and get away with it. One gains the material rewards of the injustice as well as the social rewards of being renowned for justice. The person most admired, according to Thrasymachus, is the one who can pull off the moral charade on the grandest of scales. Petty thieves are easily caught and punished. But to gain the power necessary to rule the land, no doubt through the cagey wiles and silky tongue taught by the Sophists, is most prized:

But when someone, in addition to appropriating their possessions, kidnaps and enslaves the citizens as well, instead of shameful names he is called happy and blessed, not only by the citizens themselves, but by all who learn that he has done the whole of injustice. Those who reproach injustice do so because they are afraid not of doing it but of suffering it. So, Socrates, injustice, if it is on a large enough scale, is stronger, freer, and more masterly than justice. (*Republic* 344b–c)

Injustice pays.

Before one simply dismisses Thrasymachus' views as cynical and false, one needs to examine one's own moral psychology. We all are wicked (on occasion). Why do we choose injustice? Why lie, cheat, steal, break promises, or commit adultery? Surely because we have judged that it is, in this case, in our best interest to lie, cheat, steal, break promises, or commit adultery. No one would make this calculation: I can see clearly that it is not in my best interest to steal this money, so I shall. No one voluntarily chooses to be wicked unless one judges it to be to one's own advantage. Will the moral life really satisfy our nature as humans or is it an obstacle to human happiness? This last question is the one that Socrates and Plato must face squarely. As we will see, both maintain that if we understand the true nature of justice, we will see that it does in fact pay, that the just man is the happy man. In making this claim, they must take on the relativism and immoralism of the Sophists.

Socrates

Are you not ashamed that you give your attention to acquiring as much money as possible, and similarly with reputation and honor, and give no attention or thought to truth and understanding and the perfection of your soul?

Socrates (470–399 BC) was an extremely influential figure in Athens, but he never founded a school and he never wrote anything. He referred to himself as a "midwife" because he claimed never to teach anyone anything but merely to bring their thoughts to birth and then examine them to see if they were good or mere windbags. The method he used is referred to as *the Socratic Method:* a search for truth by discussion, or by question and answer, rather than by lecture. In the process, faulty views would be exposed so that they might be improved. He acted primarily as a critic of established but erroneous beliefs rather than as a teacher of his own substantive views. Unlike the Sophists, he never accepted any payment for his services. Socrates was also sometimes referred to as the "Gadfly of Athens," because he was a constant source of irritation to many of its citizens, cornering them and questioning them about their beliefs, often making even the most prominent of men look foolish. The people that he questioned were typically ones who claimed to have some sort of special and important knowledge of the gods, truth, justice, or beauty. Rather than let them get away with their ignorance, obstinacy, and presumption, Socrates questioned these leaders in public until their folly was exposed. You can imagine that publicly insulting leaders, even in so progressive a city as Athens, did not endear him to those leaders who eventually put him on trial on trumped-up charges and sentenced him to death.[7] Socrates was a clever, brave, and honest man, committed to the pursuit of truth until the very end. His role was not unlike that of a Hebrew prophet, sounding the judgment of God to a people resistant to the demands of truth and justice. And he met the same fate as many a Hebrew prophet.

Socrates seemed to believe that he was called by God to proclaim to Athens the folly of pursuing wealth, fame, and honor at the expense of goodness. He warned the rulers of Athens of the folly of disregarding self-criticism, claiming that the unexamined life is not worth living. Fulfillment of our humanity, Socrates believes, is not found in the beauty of our garments, the size of our bank accounts, or in the garnering of praise. What makes us distinctively human, what distinguishes us from the animals, is our ability to reason and to rationally rule our desires. The life of pigs—one that is dominated by desire—is not worth living. We can see, from his self-defense during the trial, his passionate commitment to righteousness that he desired more than life itself: "You are mistaken, my friend, if you think that a man who is worth anything ought to spend his time weighing up the prospects of life and death. He has only one thing to consider in performing any action— that is, whether he is acting rightly or wrongly, like a good man or a bad one" (Apology, *Plato's Dialogues* 28b). It is more important and much harder, Socrates claimed, to avoid unrighteousness than to avoid death. And it is only in the righteous life that one is truly happy.

Furthermore, Socrates seemed to believe, the righteous will be rewarded in the afterlife. In his self-defense at his trial, Socrates talks of an afterlife in which true justice reigns. He warns his accusers that in the next life, he (and they) will be justly judged. His own fear of death is diminished because he believes that philosophers routinely pursue death—they seek wisdom and virtue that can be glimpsed only briefly in this life but may be seen face to face in the next. He is unafraid of death because he believes that what he has sought all his earthly life will be found in the next. Contra the Sophists, Socrates believed that there is an absolute standard of justice against which we will all be judged. Those who seek righteousness rather than self-interested advancement will receive their just reward.

[7.]   Socrates also may have been punished as a convenient scapegoat for his and his students' antidemocratic views.

Plato

Virtue seems, then, to be a kind of health, fine condition, and well-being of the soul, while vice is disease, shameful condition, and weakness.

Plato was Socrates' most famous pupil. Unlike Socrates, he developed his own systematic views of philosophy. He wrote a number of dialogues featuring Socrates as the main character.[8] We will look at his best developed treatise on morality, the *Republic,* which is clearly a response to the challenge to morality posed by the Sophists. Plato is dearly concerned with the sophistic view that the life of the unjust person is preferable to the life of the just. He encourages the reader to stick with his elaborate and lengthy argument because "the argument concerns no ordinary topic but the way we ought to live" (*Republic* 352d). How can we live in such a manner as to fulfill our human potential and attain human happiness? We might be inclined to answer that we attain human fulfillment by a life of virtue: only by being moral can a human being be happy. But Thrasymachus has posed a potent challenge to that answer. We are more likely, Thrasymachus argues, to satisfy our desires if we are immoral; morality is an obstacle to human happiness because it systematically thwarts the satisfaction of human desire. The *Republic* is Plato's response to Thrasymachus' challenge to morality. It constitutes his most thorough answer to the question, "Why be just?"

Before looking in some detail at his answer, we should note that the subject of Plato's discussion is broader than our more modern concept of "justice." The Greek term that is commonly translated "justice" is *dikaiosune*. In our time, we understand "justice" in terms of the appropriate treatment of other people—for example, being fair to others, treating equals as equals, obtaining appropriate outcomes in court, or distributing material goods in certain ways. But that is not exactly what Plato has in mind with *"dikaiosune."* For the Greeks, justice concerned both the individual and the communal. According to the former, *dikaiosune* means something like being moral, being a just kind of person, having the right kind of character. This is what it fundamentally means in Plato, although he does not intend to slight the political sphere. Consonant with this usage is the New Testament translation of *dikaiosune*—righteousness. So, roughly and depending on the translation, the term "justice" = *"dikaiosune"* = "righteousness." So, although we will continue to use "justice," the common translation of Plato's term, we will understand *"dikaiosune"* in the deeper sense of personal morality or righteousness that finds proper expression in communal interaction.

There are two responses one might give to the question, "Why should I be moral? One might answer in terms of the consequences attached to being moral or immoral. Or one might try to give an answer that shows morality to be

---

8. Plato's writings on ethics include *Republic, Apology, Protagoras, Gorgias, Meno,* and *Laws.*

intrinsically valuable, that is something desired for its own sake, regardless of the consequences. Plato uses both responses. He maintains that justice is something that is desirable both for its own sake and for its consequences. Let's look at each of these.

We often attempt to motivate people to be moral with various punishments and rewards. The punishments and rewards can be of the milder sort we offer children. "If you tell a lie, you will have to go to your room." "If you behave, I'll give you a piece of candy." "If you share with your friends, they will share with you." Or they might be of the grander sort offered adults. "If you murder, you will spend the rest of your life in prison." "If you are brave in battle, you will receive a medal of honor." "If you are kind, you'll have many friends." The grandest punishments and rewards are heaven and hell. One might be enticed to pursue virtue just to gain an eternity of bliss and to shun vice just to avoid eternal torment. Human beings, most of whom desire pleasure and wish to avoid pain, can understand and appreciate these sorts of reasons. So, if true, these would be good answers to the question, "Why be moral?"

Part of Plato's answer to the question "Why be moral?" is in terms of rewards and punishments. In Book X of the *Republic* he acknowledges that just men typically receive rewards from other people in this life. For example, they may obtain high office, they often marry whomever they want, and they typically receive all sorts of honors and privileges. By contrast, the unjust man, even if he escapes detection while he is young, will eventually be scorned and suffer various punishments. Plato also thinks that the just and unjust will receive their due in the afterlife. He recounts the Myth of Er (*Republic* 614b–c) in which Er is granted a vision into the next life in which everyone is judged according to his or her deeds; the righteous go upwards into heaven and the wicked drop down into Hades. Plato endorses the vision of Er: "His story wasn't lost but preserved, and it would save us, if we were persuaded by it, for we would then make a good crossing of the River of Forgetfulness, and our souls wouldn't be defiled" (*Republic* 621b–c). Plato believes that our souls are immortal and that there is a judgment in the next life in which the just are rewarded and the unjust are punished. Clearly, justice is desirable for its consequences, both in this life and the next. This might be enough to motivate one to pursue a life of justice. Plato writes:

> If we are persuaded by me, we'll believe that the soul is immortal and able to endure every evil and every good, and we'll always hold to the upward path, practicing justice with reason in every way. That way we'll be friends both to ourselves and to the gods while we remain here on earth and afterwards—like victors in the games who go around collecting their prizes—we'll receive our rewards. Hence, both in this life and on the thousand-year journey we've described, we'll do well and be happy. (*Republic* 621c–d)

This sort of reasoning can appeal to someone as selfish as Thrasymachus. If the long-term satisfaction of desire is best served by short-term self-denial, then the most reasonable course of action is to be just. The thoroughly selfish person is not oblivious to benefits attainable through delayed gratification. We might find such motivation crassly self-interested and inadequate as moral motivation. We tend to think that people who are moral for these sorts of external reasons are motivated by the wrong, or at least inferior, reasons. While Plato seemed to believe that one could reap eternal benefits by acting justly, for whatever reasons, he thought these external reasons were peripheral to the main reason to be just. Indeed he discusses the external reasons in the outside books of the *Republic* (Books I and X). It is Plato's intention, however, to take us deeper inside the moral life and he does so, fittingly, in the inside books of the *Republic* (II–IX).

While allowing that it is legitimate to be moral in order to gain rewards, Plato clearly endorses a more suitable, interior answer to the question "Why be moral?" Once we understand what justice is, Plato maintains, we will see that it is desirable for its own sake, regardless of the consequences it brings. If we are persuaded by him, we'll "[practice] justice with reason in every way" (*Republic* 621c). So let us turn to the internal arguments of the *Republic* and see if he can persuade us.

Plato divides goods in the following way. There are goods that are desired only for their consequences but are undesirable in themselves; for example, physical training, treatment when ill, a trip to the dentist. There are goods that are desired for their own sakes, regardless of the consequences; for example, joy and pleasure. Finally, there are goods that are desired both for their own sake and for their consequences; for example, knowledge, sight, and health. Plato intends to show us that justice belongs to the class of goods that are desirable in themselves and also for their consequences.

We already saw that justice is desirable for its consequences (e.g., it keeps one out of prison and secures one a decent reputation as well as a place in Heaven). The task remains for Plato to show that justice is desirable in itself. To do so, he must overcome the popular notion that justice is desirable *only* for its consequences, like jogging or a trip to the dentist that we despise but know that they can do us some good. So, too, many believe that justice is a necessary hardship worth enduring only because, for example, people will like them better and may even honor them for their good deeds. If Plato is successful in his argument, we will see that justice is something we would desire regardless of its consequences. Indeed, he hopes we will see that justice is something we should desire even if we had to suffer bad consequences.

In Books II–IV of the *Republic,* Plato presents his view of the nature of justice. Here is his peculiar strategy: once we see what justice is, we will know that it is good for us, and we will pursue it. He paints a word-picture of justice that in the end will, if we are so constituted, capture us with its beauty.

Before looking at justice in the individual, Plato looks at justice in the city. He does so because he believes that it will be easier to see JUSTICE writ large in a city and, if cities and people are similar, what we learn about justice in the city will help us understand justice in the individual. So, a large portion of the *Republic* is Plato's description of the ideally just society. Although we will discuss Plato's views of justice in the city for the next several paragraphs, we must not forget that his interest is primarily personal morality.

Before he introduces the ideally just society, Plato discusses how a city arises. With the birth of a city, we can see the beginnings of justice and injustice. People enter into society because of need. We are not self-sufficient, but need many things such as food, shelter, clothes, and shoes. So, for a more efficient satisfaction of needs, we enter into a society with other people who are skilled at raising sheep and growing wheat, constructing houses, and making clothes and shoes. For the most efficient division of labor, each person must perform that service to which he or she is most naturally suited. The farmer must spend his time farming, the carpenter constructing buildings, the cobbler making shoes, and so on. Each person is born with a proclivity for a certain task. If everyone were to do what they wanted, rather than that for which they are naturally suited, the maximal satisfaction of human needs would be diminished. So, to provide more plentiful and higher quality goods, there is a specialization of labor based on natural ability.

The maximal satisfaction of human needs will result if people are permitted to do exactly that for which they are suited. The farmer will serve society best if he is allowed to farm and doesn't need to stop and make or fix plows or distribute his harvest. So cities need metal workers, a marketplace with merchants, sailors to trade on the seas, even servants "whose minds alone wouldn't qualify them for membership in our society but whose bodies are strong enough for labor" (*Republic* 371d–e). And farmers will serve better if they can, say, specialize in growing olives; so there will be a need for shepherds and cowherds. Plato develops this city until it becomes increasingly specialized and, hence, increasingly large. The result is the construction of an efficient, communal, tranquil society devoted to the mutual satisfaction of basic human desires.

Some people, however, won't be content with this idyllic city and will wish for things that aren't necessities. They want more "civilized" comforts and other delicacies. They want fine houses, fine furniture, perfumed oils, incense, jewelry, embroidery, paintings, entertainment, prostitutes, and (of course) pastries. So Plato develops a luxurious city replete with hunters, artists, musicians, poets, actors, dancers, beauty parlors, bakeries, and so on. This city will grow, so it must seize land from its neighbors; thus, we have the beginnings of war. For that, the city will need an army of men naturally suited to the task of fighting.

The luxurious city may be more exciting, but its vices are evident: greed, vanity, pride, and envy. Plato calls this a sick city, a city with a fever, an untrue city. This luxurious city is not the ideally just city that Plato set out to discover. The ideally just state develops from the purging process that rids the luxurious city of all that is unhealthy. This purging process begins with the proper education of the guardians. The guardians must be high-spirited yet gentle, wisdom-loving, swift, and strong by nature. How can people be brought up to have qualities of good rulers? Plato begins a lengthy discussion of the education of the guardians, an illustration of the highest development of human reason.

For Plato, education involves the total training of a person: physical training for the body and training in the arts for the soul. He is not primarily concerned with the acquisition of information or the learning of a skill. Education is most fundamentally moral education. The purpose of education is to produce people who find the good appealing and evil repulsive (see *Republic* 401b–402a). When children are properly educated, they develop the right tastes and distastes. Morality is inculcated in children in such a manner that when they grow older they are naturally attracted to the good and welcome it as their friend. They will later recognize the good because "of its kinship" with them. They will find evil ugly, vulgar, shameful, and hateful and therefore easy to resist. Little children are too young to understand why this is good and why that is bad. So they are taught to develop the right attitudes and, when they are older, reason can help them understand what, as children, they simply accepted.

In order to raise children properly, nurses and mothers, who "shape their children's souls with stories" (*Republic* 377c), should be instructed to tell the stories that the Guardians have approved. Children should hear stories that incline them to virtue. What sorts of stories should and shouldn't be told? Here we must remember that children in Athens were educated through the works of Homer. Consider stories of the gods. The classical Greek gods seemed to be little more than extremely powerful and huge human beings. Take any human emotion and write it large on the heavens and you have a Greek god. Proper conduct included relating well to these capricious, quasi-divine beings who ruled on a whim. First Socrates and later Plato attacked this conception of divinity. Poets must write, Plato argues, that God is good and never the cause of evil. In addition, God cannot change (or lie). Why is Plato so concerned about the behavior of the gods? Surely if it is okay for the gods to be overcome by emotion, bitter and warring, spooking around the world in human shapes, deceiving, scaring, and seducing women, then it is okay for humans to behave in such a manner. Both Socrates and Plato felt that the Homeric gods set a bad example for people. People need to learn that justice is embraced by God, that ultimate reality undergirds their pursuit of justice. If people are persuaded that ultimate reality is indifferent to or contrary to either justice or their welfare, they will order their lives accordingly. Plato defends a universe that is at bottom just so people will order their lives around this fact.

Plato also focuses on stories about heroes. Recall the Homeric ideal of the good man as the noble warrior. Plato rejects the excesses of the heroic virtues—people who are more foolhardy than courageous, lamentations of famous men (he leaves this excess of emotion to women and cowardly men), people who lack self-control, money-lovers, kidnappers, and so on. And children should never hear stories, even if they are true, in which injustice is profitable. Plato writes: "We must put a stop to such stories, lest they produce in the youth a strong inclination to do bad things" (*Republic* 392a). Finally, the heroes must value truth and practice moderation with respect to the pleasures of drink, sex, and food. In the education of children, it is especially important to think about what sorts of ideals are made attractive by the heroes and heroines of their stories.

Why does Plato focus on poetry? Recall that poetry was the foundation of Greek education. Poetry was "narrative through imitation" (*Republic* 392d); it was often recited or sung. Plato worried that if children memorized and then acted or sung certain parts of a Homeric poem, they would take cowardice, excessive emotion, and wickedness inside themselves, into their souls. By imitation, they might become cowardly, excessively emotional, and wicked. Plato warned that children must not imitate wickedness, "lest from enjoying the imitation, they come to enjoy the reality" (*Republic* 395c).

Since poetry in Greek times was often word allied with music, Plato also was concerned about the effects of music on its hearers. He believes that we need the rhythms of an ordered, harmonious, and brave life. Music, Plato believes, appeals directly to the emotions and when attached to words allows the words, unchecked by reason, easy access into one's soul. Music has the power to override the rational part of our nature. Since music is so powerful, it must be used to positively reinforce the appropriate moral feelings and right beliefs. If children's passions are allowed to get out of control or are misdirected, they may never come to exercise right reason. In other words, they may never come to see the good. If their passions are completely excised, rather than brought into harmony with reason, they may never come to love the good. A contemporary defender of Plato's views of music puts the issue succinctly:

> . . . education is the taming or domestication of the soul's raw passions—not suppressing or excising them, which would deprive the soul of its energy— but forming and informing them as art. The goal of harmonizing the enthusiastic part of the soul with what develops later, the rational part, is perhaps impossible to attain. But without it, man can never be whole. . . . Hence, for those who are interested in psychological health, music is at the center of education, both for giving the passions their due and for preparing the soul for the unhampered use of reason.[9]

The guardians, when properly educated, will rule the city well. Their character permeates the entire city and purges it of its previous excesses. So, by the end of Book III, we start to see justice emerging in the city. The just society has three classes of people. We have already briefly discussed the Guardians; they rule the city, always keeping before them the interest of the whole. Another class is the Auxiliaries or Soldiers. These are people who were training to be Guardians but who were excessively spirited and failed the tests of making decisions for the good of the whole. Their job is to protect the city. Finally, there is the productive class or Workers. Plato contends that just as the city has three parts, so a person has

---

9. Allan Bloom, *The Closing of the American Mind* (New York: Simon & Schuster, 1987), 71–72.

three parts:—reason, spirit, and appetite. Reason is the part that desires and pursues knowledge and cares for the interest of the whole person. Spirit is honor and victory-loving and is rather assertive. The appetitive part includes our desires for food, drink, sex, money, and sleep. The appetitive part seeks to satisfy its own particular desires and is unconcerned about the good of the whole person.

Plato believes that the lessons gleaned from the just city apply to the just person because of this tripartite analogy between cities and persons. The just city will have the four virtues of wisdom, courage, moderation, and justice (*Republic* 427e); so, too, the just person will exemplify these four virtues.

Wisdom (*Republic* 428b–429a) is sound judgment about the good of the whole. The city is wise, not because of the knowledge of the carpenters or farmers or the soldiers, but because of the deliberation of its smallest class, the Guardians, who deliberate about the city as a whole (*Republic* 428c). The Guardians' education ensures that they will disregard their own interests and consider the interests of everyone involved. If the Auxiliaries were allowed to rule, they might be so interested in personal valor, they would put the entire city in danger. If a merchant were allowed to rule, his zeal for money may corrupt the city. Only the Guardians make decisions for the good of the whole.

Wisdom in the individual is defined similarly: "And we'll call him wise because of that small part of himself that rules in him and makes those declarations and has within it the knowledge of what is advantageous for each part and for the whole soul, which is the community of all three parts" (*Republic* 442c). If spirit were allowed to rule in the individual, he might place too much value on honor. If appetite were allowed to rule, he might become out of control in his pursuit of money or bodily pleasure.

Courage (*Republic* 429a–430c) is the particular province of the Auxiliaries. It is right and lawful preservation of belief regarding what is to be feared and not feared in the face of pain (*Republic* 429c–d). The city is brave when the members of the army, the Auxiliaries, are brave. Bravery is not fearlessness; it consists in knowing what should and should not be feared, a knowledge inculcated in them by their education and the laws designed by the rulers. Courage also involves sticking to one's beliefs in the face of temptations and coercions. The soldiers have habit and opinion, not knowledge like the rulers. So, for example, they may not understand fully why slavery is to be feared more than death, but they will preserve the belief and will stand fast in the face of death.

An individual is courageous when he "preserves through pains and pleasures the declarations of reason about what is to be feared and what isn't" (*Republic* 422c). Like the soldier taking orders from the rulers, preserving their teachings, and aiding them, spirit listens to reason, holds to its teachings even if tempted, and helps control the appetites.

Moderation (*Republic* 430d–432b), often translated "temperance," refers to self-controlled behavior. It is a certain orderliness. Moderation in the city occurs when the Guardians rule and the Auxiliaries and Workers defer to this rule. The entire city is functioning properly when the parts are in their places and are pleased to be ruled by the Guardians and are doing what they do best. The self-controlled person is the one in whom reason harmoniously controls the spirited and appetitive parts. A person is moderate "because of the friendly and harmonious relations between these same parts, namely, when the ruler and the ruled believe in common that the rational part should rule and don't engage in civil war against it" (*Republic* 442c).

Justice (*Republic* 432b–434d) seems an odd virtue if one interprets justice strictly communally as we moderns do. But recall that Plato is concerned with justice = *dikaiosune* = righteousness, which is both individual and communal. In the city, justice is "doing one's own work and not meddling with what isn't one's own" (*Republic* 433a); each person performs the task to which he or she is naturally suited and does so for the common good. Plato believes that if society were ordered justly, happiness would be distributed appropriately to each of society's members (*Republic* 420b–421c).

A person is just when reason rules, spirit supports reason, and the appetites are pleased to be ruled by the other two. According to Plato, justice is more the internal state of a person than how we behave toward others:

> It [justice] isn't concerned with someone's doing his own externally, but with what is inside him, with what is truly himself and his own. One who is just does not allow any part of himself to do the work of another part or allow the various classes within him to meddle with each other. He regulates well what is really his own and rules himself. He puts himself in order, is his own friend, and harmonizes the three parts of himself like three limiting notes in a musical scale—high, low and middle. He binds together those parts . . . and from having been many things he becomes entirely one, moderate and harmonious. Only then does he act. (*Republic* 443c–e)

Harmony, one, order, friend . . . these terms describe the soul of a person that is healthy, integrated, fully functional, and fulfilled. There is a psychological harmony in which each part functions properly. The person flourishes because all of the parts are allowed their harmonious and proper expression.[10]

The unjust person, by contrast, has a sick soul. He is unharmonious, the parts meddle, interests compete for supremacy, and civil war ensues. One desire may take over and enslave the rest. Consider the following example. Suppose your desire for money, say, takes over and begins ruling. You spend all of your time devising strategies for obtaining as much money as possible. Reason becomes a slave to your desire for money. Eventually, you may decide that you can acquire more money by dishonest means than by honest ones. You hate your job, your house, your car, you live in fear of getting caught, you fail to develop other talents, your

---

10. According to Plato, your happiness also depends on the community. You can't be happy in a cave and you can't be happy in an unjust society. Justice in the individual requires membership in a just community.

relationships suffer. You are in turmoil and various parts of your personality are unfulfilled because the desire for money rules. The same state of turmoil and enslavement could be produced when any number of desires (for honor, fame, food, sex, drugs, etc.) is allowed to rule.

Plato has been painting a word-picture of the just and the unjust person. Virtue is a kind of health of the soul and vice a sickness. So we come back to Plato's question: Why be moral? Why not be wicked if we can get away with it? The answer:

> This inquiry looks ridiculous to me now that justice and injustice have been shown to be as we have described. Even if one has every kind of food and drink, lots of money, and every sort of power to rule, life is thought to be not worth living when the body's nature is ruined. So even if someone can do whatever he wishes, except what will free him from vice and injustice and make him acquire justice and virtue, how can it be worth living when his soul—the very thing by which he lives—is ruined and in turmoil? (*Republic* 445a–b)

Plato's reply is simple: now that we have seen what justice is, we can see that it is good for us. His answer to the question "Why be moral?" is simply his picture of the just person. When faced with this picture, we are expected to desire justice like we desire health, as something good in itself and for its consequences. The virtuous person may secure honor, friendship, and, perhaps, a blessed eternity. But, he is also the only one who is fulfilled in all levels of his personality—rational, spirited, and appetitive. The vicious person necessarily represses or enslaves parts of his soul, allowing a particular desire to rule for its own satisfaction and not for the good of the whole person. An unjust person cannot flourish. Plato's argument is that only in the just person are the parts of the soul ordered so that he can flourish and be fulfilled. Justice is not instrumental to happiness, justice IS happiness.

No reasonable person, once shown a healthy and a sick person, would choose sickness. So, too, no reasonable person, once shown a just and an unjust person, would choose injustice. Yet, people still choose injustice. If Thrasymachus were to see Plato's picture, he would likely reject it. The deficiency, however, may not be in Plato's argument, but in Thrasymachus' character. Plato believes that we sometimes reach the bottom of an argument and can go no further than the attitudes that people bring to the argument. Others, Plato hopes, will see his picture and be so constituted that they find it attractive and choose the life of virtue. This is why moral education is so important. Only through proper education can we create a society in which everyone rationally chooses virtue.

Suppose we are persuaded by Plato that the life of virtue is worthy of pursuit. We might still ask, which virtues? Why not Homer's or Sparta's? We might claim, with the Sophists, that virtue varies by location in space or time. In contrast, Plato maintains that a universal standard of goodness exists in a world beyond the world of our senses. This heavenly world is more real than the world we experience with our senses. In the "Myth of the Cave" (*Republic* 514a–518d), Plato describes our earthly existence as like people trapped inside and forced to look at the back of a cave:

> Imagine human beings living in an underground, cavelike dwelling, with an entrance a long way up, which is both open to the light and as wide as the cave itself. They've been there since childhood, fixed in the same place, with their necks and legs fettered, able to see only in front of them, because their bonds prevent them from turning their heads around. Light is provided by a fire burning far above and behind them. Also behind them, but on higher ground, there is a path stretching between them and the fire. Imagine that along this path a low wall has been built, like the screen in front of puppeteers above which they show their puppets. . . . Also imagine that there are people along the wall, carrying all kinds of artifacts that project above it—statues of people and other animals, made out of stone, wood, and every material. And, as you'd expect, some of the carriers are talking, and some are silent. (*Republic* 514a–b)

All the prisoners can see are shadows cast by the statues. Since they have never experienced anything but this shadow world, they take it to be the real world. Education, according to this metaphor, is being released from our chains, turning around, walking out of the cave and into the sunlight. The sunlight dazzles and dispels the darkness, but it also hurts our eyes that are so accustomed to the dark. Some find this experience so painful, they quickly return to the familiar comfort of the cave. Others will persevere and may also return to the cave to attempt to lead people out of the darkness and into the light.

What is Plato trying to teach with the metaphor of the cave? Since we are accustomed to our impoverished, earthly existence, we take it to be real. However, we need to be set free from our conventions, prejudices, and senses to see what is really Real. The sun, in the Myth, corresponds to the Good, the highest standard or form of goodness. But, enjoying our usual prejudices, few are liberated from unrighteousness. The courageous few who are willing to have their lives exposed to the sun will come to understand the truth both about themselves and about goodness. What we see, that is grasp, with our mind, in making true judgments of virtue is the standard or Form of the Good. It is not simply up to individuals or societies to decide what is a virtue and what is a vice. In fact, Plato argues in another section of the *Republic* that relativism undermines society and can lead a free society into tyranny. The Good is fixed, eternal and absolute. And the process of education can lead us from moral darkness into the light of the Good.

When reason comprehends the Good and rules the other parts of our soul, when spirit assists reason, and when our appetites are pleased to be so ruled, then we flourish as human beings. The way we flourish does not vary from society to society as the Sophists maintained; it is not up to us to determine, it is built into our very nature. Plato's view of human nature provides the rails on which his idea of human flourishing runs. This track is made of steel that can be altered only within the limits set by the nature of the metal. Our character, likewise, is only malleable by proper education within the limits set by human nature. And just as the train runs properly on the tracks only when there is a good fit among all of the working parts, so, too, the human "machine" will function properly only when there is a "good fit" among all of its working parts.

Although there is much to admire in Plato's moral views, there are some elements that are less admirable. Plato believes that we can only flourish as human beings within the kind of society that he describes. But this society is ruled by an elite aristocracy with what we would consider totalitarian tendencies: it practices censorship of artists, allows very little educational freedom, institutionalizes the oppression of women, slaves, and noncitizens, and looks down on the productive class. In addition, it is justified by a lie. The Guardians, who are supposed to be educated to love the truth, are licensed to lie for the good of the people (*Republic* 414–415).

In addition, as we saw, Plato's view of morality depends on his view of human nature. If he is wrong about human nature—if, for example, our nature is satisfied when spirit rules (when we attain glory and honor) or when our desires rule (when we are true to ourselves, satisfying our various needs and wants, whatever those might be) or when we exercise our will in freely choosing a way of life— then Plato is wrong about the nature of morality. If we are chiefly glory- or pleasure- or freedom-seekers and only secondarily rational, then Plato's recipe for human flourishing is doomed.

Aristotle

Happiness requires both complete virtue and a complete life.

Aristotle was Plato's finest student and although there are important differences in their philosophies, the influence of Plato on Aristotle is striking. Both, for example, emphasize the importance of the virtues and moral education. Both think that the happy life is the virtuous life and that such a life involves the exercise of reason. We will look at how Aristotle develops these views in his *Nichomachean Ethics* (*NE*).[11]

In order to illustrate some points Aristotle is making in the first chapter of that work, we ask you to imagine the following conversation. You are reading a book and your roommate asks, "Why are you reading that?" You reply, "Because

---

[11.] Aristotle, *Nichomachean Ethics,* trans. Terence Irwin (Indianapolis, IN: Hackett Publishing Company, 1985); hereafter cited in the text as *NE.*

it's an assignment for my philosophy class." Your roommate responds, "But you don't always do your assignments; why are you doing this one?" "Because I have a paper to write." "Can't you just use your class notes?" your roommate asks. "No," you say, "I want to do well in this class." "Why?" asks your roommate. You're starting to get a little frustrated, but you answer, "Because I've decided to apply to graduate school in English, and my grades are important." "Why are you going to do that?" You think your roommate is acting like a three-year-old, but you respond, "Because I want to be an English professor." Again, "Why?" Finally, you say, "Because I think it will make me happy." The questioning will probably end. Your roommate could ask, "Do you think teaching English will really make you happy?" But, if he says, "Why do you want to be happy?," you walk away. Your roommate is just trying to bug you, you think, or he's gone crazy.

This imaginary conversation helps illustrate a number of observations Aristotle makes on the nature of human action. First, human actions have ends or purposes. If it is a human action, there is always an answer to the question, "Why are you doing that?" If there isn't an answer to this question, then it does not qualify as a human action. In characterizing human action, we look at the ends or purposes the agent is trying to achieve; which brings us to Aristotle's second observation. Our ends or purposes are hierarchically ordered. As we saw in the conversation above, one was reading the assignment in order to write the paper in order to do well in class in order to go to graduate school, and so on. Aristotle provides his own examples: the goal of going to the doctor is health; of carpentry, a house; of running for office, elective victory. Is there an ultimate end, a highest good, some ultimate goal, toward which all human actions are directed? According to Aristotle, most people identify the highest good with happiness. As we saw above, the questioning usually stops here. We do not ask people why they want to be happy. Finally, knowledge of this good helps direct our lives, says Aristotle, like archers who have a target to aim at; or like one who knows teaching English will help make him happy. But, while all persons, the wealthy and the poor, the knowledgeable and the uneducated, the Sophist and the Platonist, agree that happiness is the highest good, they disagree about what happiness is. Your roommate, for example might be just like you in seeking happiness, but he might think that it is found not in hitting the books but in crashing parties.

Before going any further in our discussion of the nature of happiness, we ought to note that the Greek term that Plato and Aristotle use that is typically translated "happiness" is *"eudaimonia."* But that is a concession to the limitations of translation; there is no precise English translation of *"eudaimonia."* Let us approach the term first by looking at what it is not. *Eudaimonia* is not a state of giddiness that might be attained by watching comedians or getting tickled. Nor is *eudaimonia* a state of constant pleasure that might be attained by regular consumption of cocaine. Aristotle is not a hedonist. *Eudaimonia* might be translated as human flourishing or fulfillment, proper and full human functioning, or inner peace. The Hebrew term *"shalom,"* usually translated "peace" but better translated "wholeness," is a close equivalent. The attainment of *eudaimonia* means that a person is fulfilled in every aspect of his or her being. No parts of one's personality or nature are repressed and each part is allowed its proper expression. So, while we will follow many translators in primarily using the term "happiness," the reader should keep this richer meaning in mind. In what does happiness consist? Aristotle rejects pleasure, honor, and wealth. Pleasure would make us slaves to our desires and more like animals than humans: The "vulgar" choose "a life for grazing animals" (*NE* 1095b, 19–20). Honor depends too much on others' willingness to recognize the significance of our actions. And wealth is simply a means to some other end.

Aristotle discerns the nature of human happiness by reference to our special function as human beings. If something has a function, its good depends on its function. For example, what we call a good car depends on what a car is used for. Similarly, whether or not someone is a good flautist or sculptor or carpenter depends on what their functions are. What constitutes a good human being will depend on what the unique function of a human being is. What could this be? It's not simply living, the life of nutrition and growth; that's shared with plants. It's not a life of sense-perception; that's shared with all animals. What then does distinguish humans from animals and plants? What makes us essentially human? It is, says Aristotle, "the soul's activity that expresses reason" (*NE* 1098a, 5–10). The special function of humans is reason; so, happiness for humans consists in the excellent use of reason, which is virtuous activity. This is the end or goal toward which all other goals should ultimately be directed. Human fulfillment, since it is based in our human function, is the same for all men everywhere. It is not, as the Sophists seemed to hold, relative to a given society, a matter of mere convention.

If human happiness is the life of virtue, what is virtue? Aristotle defines virtue as "(a) a state that decides, (b) [consisting] in a mean, (c) the mean relative to us, (d) which is defined by reference to reason, (e) i.e., to the reason by reference to which the intelligent person would define it. It is a mean between two vices, one of excess and one of deficiency" (*NE,* 1107a). Let us look more closely at what is often referred to as Aristotle's *doctrine of the Mean.*

Virtue is the mean between the vices of deficiency and excess. Consider behavior appropriate to battle or when in danger. The deficiency in these sorts of situations is cowardice. The coward lacks what is necessary to respond appropriately to danger. The excess in these sorts of situations is foolhardiness or rashness; fools rush in where reason prescribes caution. The virtue, the mean between these excesses, is courage. A courageous person is disposed to respond appropriately to danger and threats: to hold back or to charge ahead according to the situation.

Let us briefly consider some other Aristotelian virtues. With respect to the enjoyment of pleasures, licentiousness is the excess and insensibility (the inability to enjoy pleasure) is the deficiency; the mean between these extremes is temperance or moderation. The moderate or temperate person is not one who denies herself pleasure but who is disposed to go to just the right length in the enjoyment of pleasure. With respect to the use of money, the excess is prodigality and the deficiency is miserliness; the mean is generosity. Concerning one's desires for making a mark in the world, the excess is ambition, the deficiency is laziness, and the mean is aspiration. Wittiness, according to Aristotle, is a virtue, the mean between buffoonery and boorishness. Modesty is the mean between bashfulness and shamelessness. Friendliness is a virtue with obsequiousness and quarrelsomeness the extremes. Justice is a curious virtue in which both the excess and deficiency are the same, namely, injustice.

A second portion of the definition states that virtue is a mean relative to us. When considering what kind of person one ought to be, one needs to consider one's natural abilities, tendencies, strengths, weaknesses, and especially the circumstances. Consider the virtue of temperance. For the sake of illustration, let us consider a single pleasure, the eating of food. Consider Andrea, a skinny athlete with low cholesterol and no family history of heart disease. Now consider Eric, a couch potato who is overweight, has high cholesterol, and a family history of heart disease. Eric is considerably more likely to be adversely affected by the large consumption of food than Andrea. If Eric were to reflect on the virtue of temperance, he might reasonably decide not to eat any rich or fatty foods at all. Andrea, by contrast, might be temperate and eat as she pleases. The point is this: with respect to the consumption of food the mean relative to Andrea is different from the mean relative to Eric.

In trying to cultivate virtue we must think about the particular extreme toward which we tend. In trying to become courageous, for example, I must know if I tend to be rash or if I tend to be cowardly. In order to attain the mean, I will have to drag myself in the contrary direction. Regarding the virtue of temperance, Aristotle says that we should recognize that the tendency toward insensibility is rare, and he offers this sound advice: "We must beware above all of pleasure and its sources; for we are already biased in its favour when we come to judge it" (*NE* 1109b, 5–10).

But surely this focus on virtues and vices is insufficient to account for all of morality. Aren't there some actions that are just plain wrong? Aristotle acknowledges as much:

> But not every action or feeling admits of the mean. For the names of some automatically include baseness, e.g., spite, shamelessness, envy [among feelings], and adultery, theft, murder, among actions. All of these and similar things are called by these names because they themselves, not their excesses or deficiencies, are base.
>
> Hence, in doing these things we can never be correct, but must invariably be in error. We cannot do them well or not well—e.g., by committing adultery with the right woman at the right time in the right way; on the contrary, it is true unconditionally that to do any of them is to be in error. (*NE* 1107a, 10–15)

So, according to Aristotle, certain actions such as adultery, murder, and theft are always wrong as are certain feelings such as spite, shamelessness, and envy. No virtuous person could ever perform these actions or have these feelings. And this, again contra the Sophists, is the case for all persons everywhere.

We know that happiness is the life of virtue and what virtue is. How is virtue acquired? The simple answer: practice, practice, practice. We become virtuous by performing virtuous actions. By repetition, virtue becomes a habit; it becomes part of our character. We develop good and bad habits by our actions. We become good harpists if we practice well; we become bad harpists if we constantly play poorly. Building well makes good builders; building poorly makes bad builders. Likewise with the virtues. In dealing with others, some persons become just, other unjust. A person's actions in terrifying situations and the acquired habit of fear or confidence make some brave and others cowardly. It is the same for situations involving appetite. We become temperate by performing temperate actions, intemperate by performing intemperate actions. This emphasis on habit led Aristotle to believe that the moral education of children is of the utmost importance since once persons reach a certain age, their habits, good or bad, are completely fixed.

Like Plato, Aristotle believes that moral training involves more than simply learning the right actions; we also must develop the right likes and dislikes, attractions and repulsions. To be virtuous, we must have the appropriate feelings. If you deny yourself some bodily pleasure yet find the moral demand burdensome, you are not yet temperate. If you give alms but begrudge the impudence of the person in need, you are not generous (*NE* 1104b, 5–15). What we find pleasant and painful can tell us a lot about our characters. The desires and passions of the virtuous person have been brought into line with right reason so that the virtuous person takes pleasure in right actions and finds wickedness painful. His feelings are an expression of his reason.

All of this makes it look as if the virtuous life is sufficient for happiness. But might something be missing? In order to understand how Aristotle answers this question, we should consider the distinction between *having* and *leading* a good life. We might say someone has a good life if he has certain material comforts, a thriving family, good friends, and has not suffered any serious misfortune. Someone leads a good life if he is honest, just, temperate, generous, and compassionate. Which sort of life—having or leading—will make one happy? Is leading a good life sufficient to make a person happy? Are all of the resources for happiness contained within one's soul regardless of one's external circumstances? Aristotle contends that a person who suffers many miseries and misfortunes cannot be happy. He thought the happy life consisted in both—having and leading a good life. Although he thought that leading a good life is more important than having such things as food, shelter, clothing, health, family, and friends, he contends that we also require external comforts for happiness: "Happiness evidently also needs external goods . . . since we cannot, or cannot easily, do fine actions if we lack the resources" (*NE* 1099a, 32–34). We require certain external conditions—including good birth, beauty, and friends—that allow us to lead a good life and count ourselves truly happy.

One of those conditions is sufficient leisure for both virtuous acts and for contemplation. Both forms of activity involve the use of reason, and both are required for full flourishing. But Aristotle maintained that the finest expression of reason is the contemplation of unchanging truths. Since God is unchanging, reason's highest expression is contemplation of God. The greatest virtue of the human life, and hence the most pleasant life, is the theoretical study of the timeless and unchanging God. The most complete happiness will include the leisure to understand God as well as the exercise of the other virtues mentioned above.[12]

While this may be an attractive picture of the fulfilling life, it is important to note that Aristotle excludes both women and what he believed to be natural slaves from the happy life. He maintained that neither class of persons had sufficient rational capacities to fully participate in the life of moral and intellectual virtue. Furthermore, there seems to be a significant lack of concern for those who do not qualify for the happy life, for those who are viewed as less than full human beings, or merely as outsiders. Aristotle does not seem to have anything like what we would consider an adequate account of justice. And there are other problems with his ideal as well.

If you were to become an Aristotelian good man, would people today like you? Our immediate answer to this question might be: "Who wouldn't appreciate a person who is temperate, just, generous, witty, and honest?" We have, however, omitted discussion of some apparently odd characteristics of the Aristotelian good man. Aristotle says, for example, that a man can't be happy unless he walks slowly and proudly, speaks well and is good looking, has money, and is of noble birth. Ugliness and a lack of material things and status, Aristotle believes, can mar our happiness. We might be inclined to judge Aristotle harshly here, yet perhaps there is something to these claims. Aristotle contends, far more so than Plato, that external conditions are in some measure important to happiness. And, in the face of evidence to the effect that rich, witty, slim, tall, and handsome men get better jobs, more promotions, higher salaries, and prettier wives than short, fat, poor, dull-witted, and ugly men, it is hard to disagree with Aristotle's claim that these superficial traits contribute to a complete life. Furthermore, the fact that we spend far more time trying to improve our external circumstances (our looks, coiffure, social status, income, etc.) than we do developing our moral life and contemplating God indicates that we may go even farther than Aristotle on this point. An examination of the ends we pursue might suggest that we think such things do not merely contribute to happiness but actually constitute the whole of happiness. Still, supposing that we agree with Aristotle that external conditions play some important part in human flourishing, this seems to leave a great deal of human flourishing to luck. Most of us can't control whether or not we are ugly, women, slaves, citizens of a Greek *polis,* brilliant, or witty. Likewise few of us have or could

---

12.   Aristotle's God, it should be noted, has little to do with most people's beliefs in God. Aristotle's God is the first and unmoved mover but is not the creator of the world. Indeed, Aristotle's God is unconcerned about the imperfect world and only contemplates perfection, that is, himself.

obtain sufficient financial resources to allow for time for contemplation. We tend to think that fulfillment is attainable and within our control; but, Aristotle's understanding of human flourishing seems to leave too much to chance and seems to place it beyond the grasp of nearly every human being.

Our discomfort with Aristotle's ideal may not be limited to the endorsement of apparently shallow traits; his "Magnanimous Man" manifests virtues that, following the Homeric tradition, were revered in Aristotle's day but are repugnant to most morally sensitive people today (NE 1123b, 1 ff). Magnanimity is the virtue of rightly thinking you are worthy of great things. The greatest reward the Magnanimous Man deserves is honor. He accepts honor from excellent people but from others he disdains it. The Magnanimous Man tries to display his greatness to other excellent people but holds back around ordinary people. He is openly disdainful of "lesser" people. People cannot do good things for the Magnanimous Man because "doing good is proper to the superior person, and receiving it to the inferior" (NE 1124b, 10). We are likely to view such a person, not as the epitome of virtue, but as proud, conceited, disrespectful, self-centered, and improperly motivated. Our discomfort with such an ideal Man is perhaps due in part to our implicit acceptance of the medieval view of virtue that values humility, self-sacrifice, and love for others, especially the vulnerable. In the next chapter we look not at the Magnanimous Man but at Christ, who humbled himself by living a life of service and dying as the ultimate sacrifice for those who are lower than he.

Conclusion

There is much to be admired both in Aristotle and Plato: the emphasis on character and the need for the development of moral sensitivities or feelings—the proper moral tastes and distastes, and the importance of the moral education of children. They defend human excellence, hence human flourishing, primarily in terms of the cardinal virtues (courage, temperance, prudence, and wisdom) rather than in terms of the Homeric virtues of success and power. Their attempt to find a rational means for determining what is virtuous and what is vicious would, if successful, refute the relativist implications of the Sophists. Yet, there also are some things subsequent thinkers have found difficult to accept. Plato's view of another world in which perfect Goodness and Justice reign and are seen face-to-face seems to some to be metaphysically extravagant. Still others have found Aristotle's "Magnanimous Man" morally objectionable. In addition, the apparent lack of an adequate conception of justice which includes all human beings simply because they are human beings has prompted others to make justice toward all human beings a central ethical concept. Finally, others have maintained that human beings are not primarily rational creatures. Various thinkers have focused not on reason, but on our appetite, spirit, or will in deriving very different conceptions of morality and human fulfillment. Still others have kept a central place for reason, but developed a different sort of morality from it, one which focuses on rules rather than virtues.

This brings us to an important issue in the understanding of ethical theories. Before studying ethics, you might have thought the primary subject matter was rules or duties like "You shall not kill" or "You should keep your promises." According to such a conception of morality, as long as you follow the rules you are fulfilling all of your ethical responsibilities. Good rule-keepers are good people. Plato and Aristotle, however, believe that being good is not simply a matter of being good rule-keepers. According to them, ethics is primarily about the formation of character. The primary question is not, What rules should I follow?, but What sort of person should I be? Their answer is: A temperate, courageous, truthful, just, and self-controlled one. Such virtues are character traits; and although they do not precisely specify any actions, they are dispositions to feel and to act in certain ways in certain situations. When a just person is put in a situation that demands justice, she will act justly. And, in the proper situation, the temperate person will act temperately. Out of a good character will flow good and right actions as well as appropriate feelings. Virtue is a strong, inner moral strength that helps one to respond appropriately to the challenges in life. As we shall see in later chapters, still other thinkers set the primary focus on neither rules nor character but on the consequences of an action. For such thinkers, actions are right and persons good insofar as they bring forth good consequences.

In spite of these disagreements, the subject matter, vocabulary, and style of argument for a history of Western ethics have been set. Attempts to overcome threats of egoism and relativism like those facing Plato and Aristotle have been made time and time again, at times producing grand elaborate theories of human nature, human morality, and human fulfillment.

Suggested Readings

W. K. C. GUTHRIE, *A History of Greek Philosophy* Vol. III (Cambridge: Cambridge University Press, 1962).

GEORGE KERFERD, *The Sophistic Movement* (New York: Cambridge University Press, 1981).

TERENCE IRWIN, *Plato's Moral Theory* (New York: Clarendon Press, 1977).

JULIA ANNAS, *The Morality of Happiness* (New York: Oxford University Press, 1995).

SARAH BROADIE, *Ethics with Aristotle* (New York: Oxford University Press, 1991).

MARTHA NUSSBAUM, *The Fragility of Goodness* (New York: Cambridge University Press, 1981), Ch. 9–10.

WILLIAM JORDAN, *Ancient Concepts of Philosophy* (New York: Routledge, 1990).

2

The Medieval World

Introduction

The biggest influences on the development of medieval moral theories were religious: Jewish, Christian, and Muslim. This chapter will focus on the influence of Judaism and Christianity on moral thinking. The conversion of Emperor Constantine (306–337 AD) ushered in the official religion of the Roman Empire; Christianity's influence spread undeterred. Persecution gave way to proselytism and civil rejection to social acceptance. The Roman Empire became, curiously, "Holy." Many of the greatest thinkers of the medieval world were Christians who attempted to develop a consistent and thorough Christian ethical theory.

The early medieval period was a time of astonishingly varied theological reflection. Out of the fire of disagreement about the nature of Christ, the extent of the canon, the necessity of grace, the attributes of God, God and evil, and the plan of salvation was forged orthodoxy or right belief. Gradually, "consensus" emerged about basic Christian doctrines and dissent was quelled. The difficulty, however, is that, in many cases, there is simply not enough information in scripture to settle matters one way or the other. So these early religious thinkers found intellectual support in the secular—typically Greek and Roman—philosophies of their day. In particular, the early thinkers were deeply influenced by Platonism and its heir, Neoplatonism, as well as stoicism. In this chapter, we will briefly look at these secular philosophies in order to understand their influence on the moral thinking of Augustine.

Aristotle's works were not readily available to these early Christian thinkers from the 7th to the 12th centuries but were rediscovered in the late medieval period. It would be difficult to overestimate the subsequent influence of Aristotle, especially on the greatest philosopher of the medieval world, Thomas Aquinás. For Aquinás, Aristotle was *the* Philosopher, accorded the same high stature as *the* Theologian, Augustine. In the final portion of this chapter, we will show how Aquinás "baptizes" the moral views of Aristotle in a synthesis of Aristotelian philosophy and scriptural reflection. But, before looking at these Greco-Roman influences on Christian thought, let us first turn to the Bible itself for the Judeo-Christian view of morality.

31

Christianity

And what does the Lord require of you?
To act justly and to love mercy
and to walk humbly with your God.

The Bible does not present a systematic discussion of the nature of morality like those we might find in some ethics textbooks. Christianity was based on the teachings of Jesus in the gospels and the writings of St. Paul, which often were more practical than theoretical. But, although there is little that would qualify as a systematic, theoretical treatment of ethics in the Bible, there are many pieces of a puzzle that, when put together, make a coherent picture of the good life for human beings. This picture of the good life was sufficiently compelling that it dominated Western thought for nearly two millennia. Let us look at some of those pieces of the puzzle as found in both the Old and New Testaments.

The Jewishness of Jesus has been oft-ignored but his connection to his Hebrew tradition is evident. Jesus's intellectual background, and therefore Christianity's, is the Hebrew scriptures. The Bible begins with Genesis, which teaches that prior to the creation of the world, only God existed. God created the world—the heavens, the earth, and all they contain—and the world is entirely dependent on God. Although the author(s?) of Genesis was not a philosopher and didn't have Platonic Forms or abstract objects in mind, if he had been pressed, he would likely have contended that everything—including goodness—depends on God for its existence. God is the absolute creator and sustainer of everything that is not God. So God is the ultimate source of goodness.

God, self-named "Yahweh," established a covenant with his chosen people that they should, like him, be holy. A covenant is an agreement between two parties (in this case between two unequal parties). Yahweh imposed a series of moral, dietary, and ceremonial demands on the Hebrews; in return, he promised to be their god. This covenant, established with Abraham, was not intended simply for a small Middle Eastern tribe; rather, through Abraham's descendants, all of the nations would be blessed. So, Yahweh is no mere tribal or nature deity who exercises his limited powers only for the welfare of a small community of people; he is the Almighty, Lord over all of the earth. The Hebrews were given the responsibility of extending the covenant to the entire world. More general covenantal demands, which are applicable to all peoples, were given to Moses on Mt. Sinai and came to be called "The Ten Commandments." The Ten Commandments specify proper relations between people and God as well as between people and other people. One version of the commandments is briefly listed as follows:

1. You shall have no other gods before me.
2. You shall not make idols and worship them.
3. You shall not misuse the name of God.

4. Keep the Sabbath holy.
5. Honor your father and mother.
6. You shall not murder.
7. You shall not commit adultery.
8. You shall not steal.
9. You shall not give false testimony against your neighbor.
10. You shall not covet.

These commandments are not considered arbitrary demands on the part of God but are essential guidelines for proper human functioning. If persons violate these commands, they cannot flourish as human beings. In addition to the commandments, a major ethical concern, especially for the prophetic writers, is justice. God seems especially concerned for the plight of the weakest in society: children, orphans, widows, and the poor. The severest pronouncements of prophets such as Isaiah, Jeremiah, and Amos are against injustice. Satisfaction of the basic human needs for food, shelter, clothing, equitable treatment, and so on, secure the social conditions necessary for the flourishing of human beings.

Jesus is sometimes portrayed as rejecting the ethical tradition of the Old Testament. It is important to note, however, that he claimed to be establishing the Law and the Prophets; he came not to abolish them, but to fulfill them. In the time of Jesus, the Pharisees declared themselves prime examples of covenant fidelity. Jesus, however, condemned the Pharisees for failing to understand the import of the law. The Pharisees, to use the language of the previous chapter, were superb rule-keepers. They prayed, they tithed, and they fasted (often in view of other people). Jesus denounced the Pharisees for failing to understand that mere external behavior, without inner moral and spiritual transformation, is empty. The ancient Hebrews, for example, practiced circumcision as an outward sign of their covenantal relation with God. While the Pharisees focused on the outward signs, they neglected the inward commitment that God prized: circumcision of the heart. So Jesus, noting their outward righteousness but inner wickedness, called the Pharisees "whitewashed tombs" that were beautiful on the outside but inside were filled with dead men's bones and ungodliness (Matthew 23:27).

A large portion of Jesus' moral teaching was in parables—brief and memorable moral stories that indicated the importance of inner righteousness that manifests itself in the just and kind treatment of others. And, in the Beatitudes (Matthew 5), Jesus proclaims that blessedness (fulfillment) is reserved for the poor in spirit, the meek, those who hunger for righteousness, the merciful, and the pure in heart. He later condemns those who believe that they are righteous simply because they have not committed murder or adultery: anger, which we carry within, may betray our unrighteousness as much as our actions. Finally, this inner righteousness, which is to be manifest in our treatment of others, is to include all others, not simply our friends but even our enemies.

The Apostle Paul, whose writings fill up nearly half of the New Testament, develops Jesus' emphasis on inner moral transformation and treatment of others.

He commends love, joy, peace, patience, kindness, goodness, faithfulness, gentleness, and self-control (Galatians 5:22). He implores persons to "serve one another in love," and claims, "The entire law is summed up in a single command: 'Love your neighbor as yourself'" (Galatians 5:13–14).

Central to the teaching of Christianity is the messianic role of Jesus. On our own, we are incapable of fulfilling the commandments and acquiring the virtues necessary for human flourishing. We require a savior to atone for our sins. Gratitude for divine forgiveness becomes the foundation for the redemption of the moral life. By grace, we desire change; by grace, we are made capable of transforming our lives from vice to virtue. The moral transformation of Christ's followers is the foundation of the redemption of the wicked world.

Christians are sometimes accused of "otherworldliness," of focusing so much on the life to come that they are of no good in this life. Yet, the Bible is clear in its teaching that Christians are called to transform this world, in the here and now, rather than simply awaiting God to right everything in heaven. According to the Christian religion, there is a transcendent being, the source of reality who has come down into this world to redeem it. God's immanent redeeming activity is the only basis for this worldly transformation. Christians are called not to wait for the kingdom of God but to work for the kingdom of God in their daily lives.

Before we consider the ethical views of Augustine, the first major Christian philosopher and theologian, we will look at stoicism and Neoplatonism, which had a great impact on his ethical beliefs.

The Stoic Influence

Nothing is miserable, except when you think it is so.

Stoicism exercised a tremendous influence on Christian moral theories in the early medieval world. While stoicism began about 300 BC, it was influential for the next six or seven centuries. It received its name from the porch (*stoa*) of the Athenian acropolis where its original members met for discussion. Stoicism developed during a time of political uncertainty and upheaval. People were anxious about their life prospects and stoicism provided a means for maintaining tranquility amid the struggles of life. Some of the most famous Stoics are Epictetus, Epicurus, and Marcus Aurelius.[1]

Stoicism was a decidedly rational approach to the vicissitudes of life. It sought the development of self-control as the means to the attainment of tran-

[1]. Some of the principle texts include Epicurus, *The Epicurus Reader: Selected Writings and Testimonia,* trans. L. P. Gerson (Indianapolis, IN: Hackett Publishing Company, 1994; Marcus Aurelius, *Meditations,* trans. Maxwell Staniforth (New York: Viking Press, 1987); and Epictetus, *The Art of Living: The Classic Manual on Virtue Happiness, and Effectiveness,* trans. Sharon Lebell (San Francisco: Harper San Francisco, 1995).

quility. Consider fame, fortune, and health. We want these and when we lack them, we get upset. But we cannot control what others think of us, we often have little influence on the accumulation of our wealth, and a microbe has more power over our health than we do. Many things in life are just not up to us. The Stoic solution: Eliminate desire for things that are not up to us. Epictetus (c. 50–c. 130 AD) writes, for example, "So detach your aversion from everything that is not up to us."[2] Because we cannot control the world outside of us, we need to readjust our attitudes within. What upsets us is not what happens to us but our attitude toward what happens to us: "What upsets people is not things themselves but their judgments about the things" (Epictetus, *Handbook,* c. 5). So, in order to secure inner peace, the Stoic advises adjusting our attitudes to accord with whatever happens to us: "Do not seek to have events happen as you want them to, but instead want them to happen as they do happen, and your life will go well" (Epictetus, *Handbook,* c. 8). We need to control what we can control: our attitudes. Again, Epictetus:

> Some things are up to us and some are not up to us. Our opinions are up to us, and our impulses, desires, aversions—in short, whatever is our own doing. Our bodies are not up to us, nor are our possessions, our reputations, or our public offices, or, that is, whatever is not our own doing. The things that are up to us are by nature free, unhindered, unimpeded; the things that are not up to us are weak, enslaved, hindered, not our own. So remember, if you think that things naturally enslaved are free or that things not your own are your own, you will be thwarted, miserable, and upset, and will blame both gods and men. (Epictetus, *Handbook,* c. 1)

If we can reform our attitudes, accepting what comes without emotional disturbances, we can be at peace. The person who adjusts himself to the way things are can accept whatever is his position in society (beggar or ruler), lack of honor or prosperity, being crippled, illness, and even death *without loss of tranquility.* "Illness," Epictetus writes, "interferes with the body, not with one's faculty of choice, unless that faculty of choice wishes it to" (Epictetus, *Handbook,* c. 9). Again, adjust your attitude. Here is the path to peace: despise "what is not up to us" (Epictetus, *Handbook,* c. 19).

Stoics typically were materialists who believed that all that exists is matter and motion and that the world is governed by fate or providence.[3] Everything is destined to happen as it happens and there is nothing we can do about it; things happen whether we want them to or not. As Epictetus writes: "The most important aspect of piety toward the gods is certainly both to have correct beliefs about

---

2. *The Handbook of Epictetus,* trans. Nicholas White (Indianapolis, IN: Hackett Publishing Company, 1983, Ch. 2); hereafter cited in the text as *Handbook.*
3. Many Stoics considered God a sort of fine matter.

them, as beings that arrange the universe well and justly, and to set yourself to obey them and acquiesce in everything that happens and to follow it willingly, as something brought to completion by the best judgment" (Epictetus, *Handbook,* c. 31). Our task is simply to want whatever "the gods" have providentially fated or ordered, then we will never be disappointed. The Stoic sought to rid himself of the disturbing passions of hope or fear. If you hope for something and it doesn't come to pass, you will be disappointed. If you fear something and it occurs, you will be disappointed. The Stoic wills to accept everything that occurs gladly as part of the overall good, even perfection, of the universe as a whole.

The Stoics criticized the passions (*pathos*)—desire, fear, pleasure, and pain—considering them disturbances in the soul. They thought the influence of the passions needed to be reduced by rigorous self-control. Some Stoics thought that the wise person would seek to rid him or herself of these nonrational impulses entirely. The virtuous life is the life led entirely by reason. Since we can control neither external affairs nor the actions of others, we should be indifferent or apathetic (*apatheia*—without passions) toward them.

It is perhaps worth noting here that a stoic moral education would proceed very differently than an Aristotelian one. For Aristotle, educators should attempt to cultivate the child's appetites and passions to be attracted to what is good and repulsed by what is bad. The goal is a person whose appetites and passions are in agreement with right reason, someone who not only understands the good, but is passionate in his pursuit of it. For the Stoics, educators should attempt to rid the child of appetite and passion. The goal is not a passionate attachment, but a form of apathy. It is a debate that persists even today. In cultivating right reason, should children be led by their passions or should they be taught to minimize them?

The stoic sage, hope and fear banished, would attain to a certain level of fulfillment; he has rid his life of the *disturbing* passions. But, while the life of virtue is the life free from disturbing passions, the Stoics allowed that such a life includes the undisturbing passions of joy, wishfulness, and caution. The Stoics believed that *whatever* happened to one, as long as one was virtuous, one could still be counted happy.[4] The stoic sage has seen the folly of letting his fulfillment depend on Fortune: what Fortune gives, Fortune can also take away. He has turned her attention to what he can control, namely his own soul. Hear Epictetus' description of the moral progress of a lover of wisdom (a philosopher):

> The position and character of a nonphilosopher: he never looks for benefit or harm to come from himself but from things outside. The position and character of a philosopher: he looks for all benefit and harm to come from himself.

[4.] It is worth noting that the Stoics believed that people should delight in their own goodness. They also developed and endorsed the notion of philanthropy, that is, the love of humanity as such (and not simply the members of one's community).

Signs of someone's making progress: he censures no one; he praises no one; he blames no one; he never talks about himself as a person who amounts to something or knows something. When he is thwarted or prevented from something, he accuses himself. And if someone praises him he laughs to himself at the person who has praised him; and if someone censures him he does not respond. . . . He has kept off all desire from himself, and he has transferred all aversion onto what is against nature among the things that are up to us. His impulses toward everything are diminished. If he seems foolish or ignorant, he does not care. In a single phrase, he is on guard against himself as an enemy lying in wait. (Epictetus, *Handbook*, c. 48)

The Stoic sage refuses to seek fulfillment from external comforts and instead finds it within. He is self-contained and has attained to equanimity. He is freed from his attachments to this world and is fully reconciled to the way the world is, it can bring him neither grief nor excessive delight. He is serene. We will see in our discussion of Augustine how attractive this Stoic ideal initially appears in the face of life's great disappointments.

Neoplatonism

And the author and principle of what he [man] is and holds is the Supreme, which within Itself is the Good but manifests Itself within the human being.

A second major influence on medieval ethical theories was the philosopher Plotinus (205–270 AD), considered the founder of Neoplatonism.[5] Plotinus' grand metaphysical scheme was both exciting and stimulating; it was the product of a great mind grappling with the ultimate nature of reality. Many, including Augustine, have found Plotinus' antimaterialistic views religiously and intellectually satisfying. And so, his Neoplatonism had a tremendous influence on the development of religious doctrines from the early medieval period to the 17th century and still exerts some influence today.

The distinctive doctrine of Neoplatonism is that of the transcendent One or Good, a single being on whose Intelligence the rest of reality depends. The transcendence of this supreme being is stressed with an emphasis on God's ineffability (that God's ultimate nature is unknowable by humans). Human intelligence is incapable of attaining knowledge of what this being is and is, therefore, largely limited to negative theology—to saying what God is not. God is not this or that (not finite, not limited in power, not limited in knowledge, without sin); he is superior to any concept that we humans could understand or apply.

[5.] Plotinus, *Enneads*, trans. Stephen MacKenna (New York: Penguin, 1991).

According to Plotinus, all of reality is generated by the One in levels according to each thing's participation in perfection. According to Neoplatonism, human beings are essentially dualistic with a godlike soul, a "real self" in which intelligence resides, temporarily trapped in an earthly body. The human project is to free oneself from the confusing world of the senses and return in spirit to the divine intelligible world to which we really belong, a world infinitely superior to the physical world.

One can see in Neoplatonism much that early Christian thinkers might welcome. Neoplatonism emphasized the importance of the wise turning away from a transient world in their quest for God, a rejection of the life of the flesh for the life of the spirit. It was quite other-worldly in its focus. Although some relief may be offered to individual sufferers, it was felt that little could be done to improve social conditions which perpetuate the suffering; therefore, the religious quest must turn inward.

Augustine

You have made us for yourself, and our heart is restless until it rests in you.

In addition to his many philosophical and theological writings, Augustine wrote a spiritual autobiography entitled, *Confessions*.[6] *Confessions'* rich ethical reflection arises within the context of personal experience. It is a powerful autobiography, filled with universally human angst and hope, desire and frustration, and guilt and redemption. As we briefly reflect on some of the moral themes present in this work, what will emerge is a distinctly Augustinian combination of Scripture, Neoplatonism, and Stoicism. Some of the autobiographical details may seem more appropriate to a book on theology; but we include them because they help make sense of the medieval Christian and moral world that Augustine both inhabited and influenced.

The most famous quotation from the entire opus of Augustine, "You have made us for yourself, and our heart is restless until it rests in you," captures Augustine's own personal journey from restlessness to rest; from rebellion to peace with God (*Confessions,* I.i). This is Augustine's confession of both his moral shortcomings and of his hope and belief in a redeeming God. This prayer is, he believes, applicable to all people because the need for God is built into our human nature. He describes the false and seductive paths that carried him away from God. He followed those paths seeking peace, but none of them satisfied nor, he argues, could they. We are, after all, made for God and he alone can fill our empty hearts.

[6.] Augustine, *Confessions,* trans. Henry Chadwick (New York: Oxford University Press, 1992); hereafter cited in the text as *Confessions.*

Augustine begins by developing the doctrine of original sin. We are born with Adam's sin of rebellion against God and so cursed with Adam's guilt. And, although he can't recall his own infancy, he is reminded of his own reprehensible rebellion when he sees an infant's "jealousy and bitterness" while watching his mother feed his brother. The infant is "vehemently indignant" and, much worse than raging against his loving mother, he shakes his tiny fist at God (*Confessions,* I.vii). He recounts a number of his own childhood sins and rejects the notion of innocent youth: the child who cheats at marbles is doing the same, according to the capacities of his age, as the adult who cheats someone out of their vast estate.

Augustine's reflections on his "past foulness and carnal corruptions" are Platonic (*Confessions,* II.i). Like Plato and the Neoplatonists, Augustine views the soul as a higher, ruling part and the body as something lower that wreaks havoc if it is allowed to rule. He observes that he was not unified but is in a state of disintegration; he was hopelessly divided because he had allowed his base desires to have control over him. He sought delight, as we all do, in loving and being loved, but his loves were improperly directed. He wanted intimacy, to touch soul to soul, but settled for bodies clinging to bodies. "Clouds of muddy carnal concupiscence filled the air" (*Confessions,* II.ii). His view of the good was obscured by the dark impulses of his desires. He was trapped in an adolescent cave of his own appetites.

But Augustine did not see himself as merely a slave to his own appetites, he considered himself to have sunk even lower than this. In the recounting of his theft of some pears, Augustine's Christian worldview forces him to view what would normally be viewed as a gratuitous childhood prank as an incident charged with grave moral and spiritual implications. He did not steal the pears out of a desire for the pears or even out of a desire to be "one of the guys." He and his peers found pleasure in stealing the pears simply because it was not allowed. Because of this, Augustine believes himself worse than the villainous Catiline, a vicious and cruel man. At least Catiline murdered for a reason—to gain honors, power, and wealth. Augustine and his friends were wicked for no other reason than to be wicked.

Augustine's theological reflection in this section is crucial for understanding his views on the moral life. Augustine observed that in sinning, all humanity imitates something supremely good, namely God. Each person repeats the primordial sin, "Ye shall be as gods." How could a young boy strive to attain godhood? According to Augustine, in stealing the pears he was seeking absolute liberty and power; in making his own moral law, he sought to be his own moral authority. Absolute liberty, supreme power, source of morality: in short, he desired to be God.

The problem with vice is that it often appears under the guise of virtue. Excessive curiosity, for example, can be called "zeal for the truth"; licentiousness can be called "freedom"; and shamelessness, "courage." Think, for example, of the student who, experienced in drunkenness, drugs, and premarital sex, denigrates someone who is innocent of such pleasures: "She's such a Puritan. She hasn't experienced the world." The profligate turns his vices into a virtue.

Augustine's view of the nature of immorality is perhaps best understood as the problem of misplaced loves. This theme runs throughout the *Confessions:* If we love the creation, but not the creator, we will find misery because things of this world are temporary. Like Plato, Augustine thinks that the properly ordered soul has the right attractions and repulsions. The disordered soul of the unrighteous person is inordinately attracted to things like power, fame, honor, wealth, even human love, which is too often reduced to lust. Augustine satisfied these desires, but rather than find himself fulfilled, found himself empty and self-destructed. This consequence is inevitable because human beings are designed to find fulfillment not in the things of this world but in loving God, the creator of the world.

Love, properly ordered, desires God alone as the focus and fulfillment of the moral life. Human beings, however, have been granted the freedom to place our love of other goods above our love for God. This is disordered love or unrighteousness. The primary disordered love is nothing less than pride—the love of oneself above God and other human beings. But disordered love can take various forms, some more obvious than others. The wicked person debases him or herself by loving things inordinately and becoming their slave. Augustine thinks that even a deep love of another human being can be disordered if it is placed above love of God. Augustine's most dramatic description of the misery that accompanies misplaced love is his profound reflection on the death of his best friend and soulmate (*Confessions,* IV.iv–xii). His description of that friendship, of any friendship for that matter, is as fine as anyone has ever written: "It had been sweet to me beyond all the sweetness of life that I had experienced" (*Confessions,* IV.iv). Hear his statements of his grief:

> "Grief darkened my heart" (Lamentations 5:17). Everything on which I set my gaze was death. My home town became a torture to me; my father's house a strange world of unhappiness; all that I had shared with him [his friend] was without him transformed into a cruel torment. My eyes looked for him everywhere, and he was not there. I hated everything because they did not have him, nor could they now tell me "look, he is on the way," as used to be the case when he was alive and absent from me. I had become to myself a vast problem. (*Confessions,* IV.iv)

The beauty of the friendship and the misery of his friend's death are criticized by the mature Augustine as he writes his memoirs. Even though the depth of his feeling was profound and natural, Augustine denounces these expressions of sorrow, praying, "Cleanse me from these flawed emotions" (*Confessions,* IV.vi). This Stoic denunciation of upsetting emotions is further criticized through his lament to God: "I was in misery, and misery is the state of every soul overcome by friendship with mortal things and lacerated when they are lost. Then the soul becomes aware of the misery which is its actual condition even before it loses them" (*Confessions,* IV.vi).

Augustine's problem: his grief betokens misplaced love. His prayer: direct my eyes toward you. Again, the Stoic influence is clear. Augustine chastises himself for loving a human being that was sure to die: "How stupid man is to be unable to restrain feelings in suffering the human lot" (*Confessions,* IV.vii). Like the Stoics, he thinks we should not attach ourselves to the things of this world, since they will only bring emotional upheaval: "Things rise and set: in their emerging they begin as it were to be, and grow to perfection; having reached perfection, they grow old and die" (*Confessions,* IV.x). If one's loves are oriented around things that can be lost or die, unhappiness is certain. No matter how great the pleasure of temporal things, they are not the proper loci of human love. Only God is a good that cannot be lost: "Wherever the human soul turns itself, other than to you, it is fixed in sorrows, even if it is fixed upon beautiful things external to you . . ." (*Confessions,* IV.x).

Why are transient things sure to disappoint us? Here, Augustine's reliance on Neoplatonism seems most clear: unchanging goods are better than changing goods. The soul seeks rest in the objects of its love, but it cannot find repose in things that lack permanence. They will be lost. Transient things are intended to move us to God, in whom our soul can rest: "There is the place of undisturbed quietness where love is not deserted if it does not itself depart. . . . Fix your dwelling there" (*Confessions,* IV.xi). If you seek the good in the transient, sensible world, then frustration and misery are inevitable. Our only hope for the consistent and deep satisfaction of our desires is to attach to God who is unchanging, permanent, eternal. God is a good that cannot be lost. Fix your dwelling there.

While these reflections clearly demonstrate a Stoic influence (things of this world are transient and disappointing, we need to control our emotions by reason), we ought not think that Augustine went on to conclude, like many monks, that we ought to reject all earthly goods, including friendship, as potentially dangerous distractions from our love of God. Augustine did not deny the worth of earthly goods, but, he insisted that they be put in their proper place, that is, subordinate to love of God. In their proper place, they can be the source of great enjoyment and even increase our love of God, their creator. He writes: "Let these transient things be the ground on which my soul praises you (Psalms 145:2), 'God creator of all'" (*Confessions,* IV.x). And, "If physical objects give you pleasure, praise God for them and return love to their Maker lest, in the things that please you, you displease him. If souls please you, they are being loved in God; . . . The good which you love is from him. *But it is only as it is related to him that it is good and sweet*" (*Confessions,* IV.xii; emphasis added). If love of God is primary, all other genuine loves will gain true value and permanence. If we love God first, we will love the right things in the right way; our loves will be properly ordered and we will find fulfillment (*eudaimonia*).

Augustine says that his general skepticism and doubts about Christian belief were resolved through reading the books of the Neoplatonists.[7] The Neoplatonic philosophy taught that everyone can come to the vision of the truth by using his reason. They affirmed an intelligible, immutable, and noncorporeal God. In order to see unchanging truths, Augustine concurs with Plato and the Neoplatonists, we must look within. He describes reason's ability to grasp the truth: "I entered and with my soul's eye, such as it was, saw above . . . the immutable light higher than my mind" (Confessions, VII.x). By illumination he was able to see the transcendent One or the Good or Being and he claims that his skepticism left him as he embraced this philosophical view of God. Augustine believes that there is a realm of immaterial and unchanging ideas that can be grasped by reason with the assistance of divine illumination. Some access to truths, even moral truths, is possible by reason; but, in a Christian version of Platonism, access to truth is even more likely when God illuminates our reading of Scripture.

Augustine's intellectual conversion to Platonism, however, was insufficient for submitting to God; he still needed to be cured of pride. And illumination, the only resource available to the Neoplatonist, cannot redirect our loves to God. Divine assistance is necessary, according the Augustine, to rid us of vice, turn our hearts toward God, and enable us to acquire virtue. In describing the events prior to his conversion, Augustine writes "my old loves held me back" (Confessions, VIII.xi). Reason had failed to exercise its dominion over his appetites. He required, as we all do, assistance from God both to see the good but also to do the good. He required illumination and grace that came, for him, in the voice of a child saying "Pick up and read, pick up and read" (Confessions, VIII.xii). Interpreting the voices as a divine command, Augustine opened a Bible and read. Of the experience, he writes: "At once, with the last words . . . , it was as if a light of relief from all anxiety flooded into my heart. All the shadows of doubt were dispelled" (Confessions, VIII.xii).

Like Aristotle, Augustine believed that adult character hardens like cement into stone: it cannot be retrained in new habits. He writes, "By servitude to passion, habit is formed, and habit to which there is no resistance becomes necessity. . . . A harsh bondage held me under restraint" (Confessions, VIII.v). But, unlike Aristotle, Augustine believed in and experienced divine grace, a grace sufficient to soften one's hard heart and reorient one's will, a grace sufficient to free one from the bondage of sin. As with the other thinkers we have studied, Augus-

---

7. Earlier in his life, Augustine fell in with a philosophical and religious order called the Manichees. Their primary belief was that God is good but not all powerful (otherwise he would be responsible for evil in his creation). Furthermore, they believed in two coequal powers—good and evil or light and darkness. They endorsed a dualism of spirit and matter and betrayed a disgust with the physical world. They opposed procreation because it involved the trapping of a soul in a body. The Manichees believed that the human soul, like the Cosmos, is divided into a good soul that comes from God and an evil one that comes from the Prince of Darkness. This disunity cannot be overcome in spite of our finest moral effort. Through reading the Platonists, Augustine says that he was freed from the grips of the Manichees and led to the true knowledge of God.

tine's view of human nature informs his quest for the good life. Augustine maintains that human beings are trapped by sin in immorality and untruth. Illumination may assist humans in the recognition of some truth, but divine assistance is required to understand and attain the deepest truth—that true human fulfillment is found only in the love of God. We cannot understand this fully, nor live accordingly, without God's grace. For Augustine, unlike for Plato, seeing the good is not sufficient to motivate unregenerated human beings to be good. Our disordered loves require divine reorientation toward our only source of deep and lasting satisfaction—God himself. Why God? Because God has made us to find our fulfillment in him. We will never rest, according to Augustine, until we rest in Him.

The Euthyphro Problem

How ill they know divinity in its relation, Socrates, to what is holy or unholy.

The Judeo-Christian tradition seems to embrace the view that God is the source of morality; that is, that goodness is the will of God. Or, more precisely, the good is that which is willed by God and the bad is that which is forbidden by God. There is, however, a potential problem for such a divine command theory of ethics. The problem was first raised by Plato, in the dialogue *Euthyphro,* from which it has taken its name. The belief that goodness is the will of God may be taken in either of two ways: (a) Something is good because God wills it; or (b) God wills something because it is good.

The problem with (a), something is good simply because God wills it, is that it seems to make morality quite arbitrary. God has laid down a particular set of moral commandments for our lives, but God could have laid down a very different set. God happened to command us to tell the truth, but what if God had willed that we lie instead? Would that have made lying good? Suppose, even worse, that God had commanded the torture of innocent babies for fun. If God's will is the source of all goodness, it looks as if such an act would make it good to torture innocent babies for fun. But surely it is not good and never could have been good to torture innocent babies for fun. Indeed, it seems that if God *had* willed that, *God* would have been wrong. But that suggests that there is a standard of morality to which even God is subject.

The difficulty with (a) seems to lead the divine command theorist to accept (b) God wills something because it is good. If (b) is true, however, then God appears to be superfluous. If there is an independent standard of goodness that God recognizes and wills, then that standard is the source of morality, not God. The Euthyphro problem raises an important issue for the relationship between God and morality: How can goodness both depend upon God and not be arbitrary? In our section on Aquinás, we shall see how his synthesis of Aristotle and Christian belief is used to overcome this objection.

Thomas Aquinás

All desire their good to be complete.

When Thomas Aquinás, the greatest thinker of the medieval world, learned of the writings of Aristotle, he rewrote Christian theology. In his attempt to harmonize the Christian understanding of the virtues with Aristotle's ethics, Aquinás addressed two main questions: What is the good (life)? And how is the good (life) attained? We will focus on Aquinás's *Treatise on Happiness,* following the form of question and answer used there.[8]

Question 1: Is there an ultimate end for human beings? Human beings perform a variety of actions but only some are distinctly human. Those that are impulsive or coerced (like breathing, growing, or falling down when tripped) are actions *of a human being,* but those that are freely and deliberately chosen are *human actions.* All human actions, those undertaken deliberately (i.e., rationally desired), are for the sake of an end. Consider choosing to go to a dentist. You might be coerced to go to a dentist who drills your teeth down to the nerve to extract vital information. Or you might freely choose to endure the pain of the dentist's drill because you wished for healthy teeth. In the latter case, you deliberately acted for the sake of an end—healthy teeth. The former is the action of a human being and the latter is a human action. All *human actions* are purposive; they are freely chosen and done for the sake of an end or a goal.

Suppose you are attending college. You might be doing so to learn, to earn a degree, to get a good job, to find a spouse, or because you don't know what else to do. In all of these cases, you are acting for the sake of an end. There is, of course, a huge variety of ends. And some ends become means to other, higher ends. You might wish for a degree so that you can get a higher paying job. You might wish for more money so that you can attract a beautiful or handsome spouse, drive a nicer car, build a bigger house, and take extravagant vacations. Yet, no one wants piles of money, an attractive spouse, or bigger house, period. You want them because they contribute to a further end.

Is there some ultimate end or ultimate good toward which all humans strive? Is there something we desire more than spouses and houses, or, to put it another way, what is the end to which spouses and houses are intended to contribute? Is there something we desire simply for itself and not because it will help us attain something else? Is there some rational method for sorting through these various ends to see if some ends are more desirable than others? We need a supreme good to separate out or measure all the other goods. We need a final good for a standard. Aquinás believes that if we follow the chain of human ends or goals we will

---

[8.]   Saint Thomas Aquinás, *Treatise on Happiness,* trans. John A. Oesterle (Notre Dame, IN: University of Notre Dame Press, 1983); hereafter referred to in the text as *Happiness.*

end up with a single end that all humans desire: College for learning; learning for a better job; a better job for more money; more money for a better spouse and house; a better spouse and house for what? The ultimate end, Aquinás argues, is one's perfection, a maximally fulfilling life: "It is impossible for man's happiness [*eudaimonia*] to consist in a created good, for happiness is the perfect good which wholly brings desire to rest, for it would not be the ultimate end if something should still remain to be desired" (*Happiness*, Q. II, Art. 8). It should come as no surprise that the ultimate end for human beings is *eudaimonia*—human flourishing, completeness, fulfillment, peace, and contentment. As Aquinás puts it: "[Happiness], 'the complete and sufficient good,' excludes all evil and fulfills all desire" (*Happiness*, Q. V, Art. 3). Willful human action is always in search of human fulfillment. We desire what fulfills us as human beings (although we might be wrong about what fulfills us). The right understanding of and orientation toward human fulfillment is the foundation of morality.

Question 2: In what does human fulfillment consist? Aquinás first considers various "external goods" such as wealth, honor, fame or glory, and power. These cannot be the highest good because fulfillment is incompatible with evil, and wicked people can secure any of these goods. In addition, fulfillment is self-sufficient—the highest good satisfies all of our (well-ordered) desires and is not dependent on anything external. Honor, for example, cannot be the highest good, because it depends on other people to do the honoring. Second, "goods of the body," such as health, strength, fitness, longevity, good looks, and pleasure, are also not the ultimate good. Aquinás does not deny that these sorts of things are good, but, he believes that the goods of the body are obtained for the sake of something else—for the soul or for a rich human life. In addition, devotion to pleasure is a sign of a disordered soul and an unfulfilled, therefore, unhappy life. So, finally, he considers "internal goods" of the soul such as friendship, intellectual ability, moral virtue, artistic ability and appreciation, and knowledge. Goods of the soul are partial or limited goods and are incapable of giving us complete fulfillment. Human fulfillment, so defined, cannot consist in the possession of any finite good. Once again:

> It is impossible for man's happiness to consist in a created good, for happiness is the perfect good which wholly brings desire to rest, for it would not be an ultimate end if something should still remain to be desired. . . . This [universal good] is not found in any created thing but only in God. . . . Hence only God can satisfy the will of man. . . . Therefore man's happiness consists in God alone. (*Happiness*, Q. II, Art. 8)

Only an infinite good, God, can completely satisfy our desires; so God alone is sufficient for human fulfillment.

Question 3: What is fulfillment? We know that fulfillment has something to do with God and that only God can satisfy all of our deepest desires. But it is clear from experience that some ways of relating to God are more conducive to fulfillment than others. Aquinás tries to clarify exactly how humans should relate to God in order to attain fulfillment. Aquinás agrees with Aristotle that fulfillment is activity in accordance with complete virtue. And, again agreeing with Aristotle, he believes that the characteristic excellence of human beings is reason. Human fulfillment, therefore, includes the intellectual activity of the soul. The highest expression of reason is contemplation that finds rest only in God, the source and goal of all things. Therefore, our ultimate good is seeing God face to face, which is called the beatific vision.

Question 4: What are the prerequisites for attaining human fulfillment? If fulfillment is seeing God face to face, two problems arise. First, because we glimpse God only partially and sporadically in this life, complete fulfillment is attainable only in the next life: "Ultimate and complete happiness, which we look for in a future life, consists entirely in contemplation" (*Happiness*, Q. III, Art. 5). So we must, this side of the grave, settle for imperfect fulfillment that includes contemplation, just actions and proper passions. Second, fulfillment exceeds our natural abilities: we are morally and intellectually unable to perceive the divine essence. Like Augustine, Aquinás believes that we are morally incapable because our bondage to sin makes our loves disordered: we pursue finite ends as ultimate ends. Without rectitude of the will (righteousness) we cannot pursue the proper ends. Without moral reorientation, no one could see God, hence, no one could flourish as a human being.

Question 5: Can we attain fulfillment? Not by our natural powers alone. Righteousness, although necessary for fulfillment (seeing God face to face), cannot be obtained without divine assistance. Aquinás concedes that a rather imperfect (but Aristotelian) fulfillment is attainable through our natural human capacities in this life: activity in accordance with human virtue, adequate earthly comforts, and good friends to discuss speculative matters. But, we may be hindered in various ways from virtuous activity, we cannot entirely control our level of earthly comforts, we may not have the leisure for contemplation, and friends depart, disappoint, or die. Even imperfect happiness is rare. In this life and with these moral and intellectual capacities, we cannot eliminate all evil, fully satisfy our desire for the good, or adequately grasp the divine essence (*Happiness*, Q. V, Art. 3). Indeed, without divine assistance, no one can be happy except in the imperfect, Aristotelian, sense; our natural powers are incapable of attaining the vision of God. So we must know God in order to be happy but we, by our natural powers, cannot know God. And we must be righteous in order to know God but we, by our natural powers, cannot be righteous. The hope for the attainment of fulfillment lies not in our natural capacities, but must lie in supernatural grace to heal us and direct us toward God (*Happiness*, Q. V, Art. 7, reply 2).

Aquinás believes that the most important virtues—faith, hope, and charity—surpass our natural abilities. These theological virtues are necessary for the attainment of the beatific vision and require God's assistance both to make them known to us and to "infuse" them in us.[9] The moral and intellectual virtues are perfected by being subsumed under the theological virtues. Faith illuminates the intellect in its quest for moral, practical, and spiritual truths. Hope keeps our wills oriented toward our ultimate, other-worldly end, as something that is attainable. And charity creates in us a desire for our end of sharing in the divine nature.

The theological virtue of charity provides a remedy for part of the "dark side" of Aristotle. When the moral virtues are subsumed under the authority and direction of charity, they guide us to be just to every member of the kingdom of God (and not simply to fellow-citizens). In addition, the respect and honor due to every child of God forbids the arrogance that Aristotle praised. Finally, the possibility of divine grace remedies the problem of adult moral growth. With God, all things are possible, even the moral perfection of the most vicious of persons.

Aquinás's moral theory also provides a response to the Euthyphro problem. The good for human beings is that activity that fulfills them. This depends on our nature as human beings and is, therefore, not arbitrary, but objective and universal. Given our nature, some things or activities will help us function properly and some will not. We are so constituted that eating chocolate and nothing else will not lead to human flourishing. Nor will drinking gasoline. Nor will lying or committing adultery. Once God has created us, with a certain nature, it is not up to God to decide arbitrarily what is good or bad for us. So morality is not simply a divine command. Morality is a matter of proper human functioning, which is determined by our nature. Consider proper automobile functioning. Once an engineer makes an automobile, she can't just decide to fuel it with water; gasoline is good and water is bad for the proper functioning of cars. So, too, once God has created us as God has, God could not simply decide that gasoline, or lying, or adultery, is good for human beings. God could, however, have made these things good for us; but how? By creating us differently. God could have made us so that we thrive on gasoline or so that lying and adultery somehow fulfilled us. So morality is dependent on God in the sense that God created us with a certain nature that functions properly when it functions as God intended it to function, that is when we live lives of love for God and for our fellow human beings. But, God is also necessary for morality in another way. We may be able through reason to discover some of those activities that fulfill our nature and are, thus, good for us (Aristotle did a good job of that); but, since our will is disoriented and our intellect is limited, we need God to reveal certain moral and divine truths and to infuse us with virtue so that we are enabled to attain complete fulfillment.

Aquinás's ethics synthesizes divine law and virtue, both metaphysically and motivationally.[10] The metaphysical synthesis is this: If God creates human beings, then obeying God's law is conducive to our true fulfillment. That is, obeying God's

9.   We are following Aquinás's discussion in *Summa Theologica*, I–II Q. 62–63. See Thomas Aquinás, *Summa Theologica*, trans. Fathers of the English Dominican Province (Allen, TX: Thomas More Publishing, 1981).

10.   We are grateful to Alfred Freddoso for suggesting and clarifying this section.

law contributes to our being virtuous and thus to our leading lives that are as happy as they can be on earth and that serve as preparation for complete fulfillment in the next life by giving us rectitude of will. What's more, this virtuousness increases—and, indeed, is made possible—to the extent that we even now participate in eternal life through grace. The motivational synthesis resolves the apparent conflict between morality and fulfillment. Morality is often considered other-regarding and, therefore, an obstacle to the individual's pursuit of fulfillment; in other words, self-interest and morality are opposed. According to Aquinás, however, our true fulfillment lies in (often sacrificial) love of God and neighbor. To be motivated by a desire for fulfillment, therefore, is indistinguishable from desiring to love God above all things and to conform our wills to God's will. Obedience to God's law—"to love one another as I have loved you"—is the specific form that our desire for fulfillment (i.e., true friendship with God) takes.

Summary and Conclusion

Medieval thinkers are often ignored in contemporary philosophy simply because their religious commitments are considered by many scholars to be woefully out of fashion. If you are not a theist, you will no doubt be tempted to reject their views out of hand. Yet they raise views about morality which require careful consideration. What kind of creatures are we and what sorts of activities will fulfill us as human beings? If we are, as the medievals imagine, created for God, then it is not surprising that deep, human fulfillment is as elusive as it is in this life. If we were not created to be satisfied by houses and spouses, then the emptiness that we often feel when surrounded by abundance is to be expected. Augustine's frustration and misery will look all too familiar. If as Augustine and Aquinás thought, we were made to find ultimate satisfaction only in God, then we will not find fulfillment in any other way. But this seems to put fulfillment squarely in the next life. Flowers, fish, and frogs seem perfectly suited for their environments. Human beings, by contrast, seem a bad fit for this world. The medievals claim we were made for another world. Our ultimate goal is not attainable, except imperfectly, in this life. The quest for fulfillment points us toward the next life and union with God. This will lead some to reject the medieval view in favor of some other view which makes human happiness more easily attainable. Others will see it as confirmation of experience and an incentive to transform this world. They will be motivated to work, by God's grace, for the kingdom of God in this life, to strive for that level of fulfillment that can only come when we are in right relationship with God and neighbor.

Finally, theist and nontheist alike must address the question of the possibility of moral transformation. If we are by nature devoted to ourselves and to satisfying our more base desires, how can we alter this nature? Is such alteration possible later in life, or are our characters cemented, for good or bad, by the time we reach early adulthood? If there is no such thing as divine grace to keep us from endlessly expanding our egos, what can? Thomas Hobbes, our next major thinker, proposes a powerful, human sovereign to keep our natures in check.

Suggested Readings

BOETHIUS, *The Consolation of Philosophy* (New York: Penguin, 1969).

FREDERIC COPLESTON, *A History of Philosophy* Vol. II (Westminster, MD: Newman Press, 1950).

FREDERIC COPLESTON, *Aquinás* (New York: Penguin, 1955).

ETIENNE GILSON, *The Christian Philosophy of St. Augustine,* trans. L. E. M. Lynch (New York: Random House, 1960).

ETIENNE GILSON, *The Christian Philosophy of St. Thomas Aquinás,* trans. L. K. Shook (New York: Random House, 1956).

JOHN RIST, *Stoic Philosophy* (Cambridge: Cambridge University Press, 1969).

JOHN RIST, *Plotinus: The Road to Reality* (Cambridge: Cambridge University Press, 1967).

3

The Modern World

Introduction

The modern world that emerged from the medieval world was largely rooted in the criticism of authority. The Enlightenment, as this era is often called, elevated reason above authority with enlightenment thinkers seeking to reconsider the nature of religion, morality, learning, science, society, and the family. Each of these domains was subjected to the searching criticism of reason; whatever could not survive the scrutiny of reason was to be discarded. All that was fit for human belief was that which could be supported by reason alone, as distinct from the teachings of some established authority.

The revolutions and reformations of the 16th and 17th centuries created a situation unparalleled in medieval times; there was a bewildering variety of social, political, scientific, and religious options available. Dire consequences often were threatened and realized for making the wrong choice, yet there was no clear method for making these choices. Reason became the preferred method for settling matters. Unlike Augustine and Aquinás, Enlightenment thinkers such as Immanuel Kant, Thomas Hobbes, and David Hume do not justify their moral theories with appeals to divine or scriptural authority. In an increasingly pluralist society, appeals to divine authority become increasingly problematic: which God (the one of the Protestants, Roman Catholics, or Anabaptists) is the authority? And whose scriptural interpretation is true? As Hobbes writes, "If one prophet deceive another, what certainty is there of knowing the will of God, by other way than that of reason?"[1] Which way, indeed?

Hobbes, Hume, and Kant attempt to defend their ethical views by appeal to reason alone. Hobbes's argument is a thought experiment invoking his best judgments about human nature. Hume bases morality on the experience of our sentiments or feelings. And Kant's ethical argument involves an analysis of the nature and function of reason itself. Hobbes and Kant are not unconcerned with

---

[1.] Thomas Hobbes, *Leviathan,* ed. J. C. A. Gaskin (New York: Oxford University Press, 1998), Ch. 32; hereafter cited in the text as *Leviathan.*

scripture or the teachings of the church. Indeed, large portions of their defenses of morality refer to scripture and to God. However, the arguments in their writing that carry the most weight are not based on religious authority but on reason and experience.

Despite the Enlightenment's critique of authority, reason was typically used not to discard but to reinforce traditional beliefs and values. Reason and experience, rather than authority and scripture, now provided the justification for those beliefs and values. The early modern thinkers attempted to rationally justify a roughly or broadly Christian understanding of morality: tell the truth, keep your promises, be faithful to your spouse, do not murder, give to the poor, do not commit suicide, and so on. And they affirmed traditional virtues like courage, wisdom, temperance, justice, chastity, and benevolence, and denounced the various vices that correspond to these. This is especially clear in Kant, who explicitly defends Christian morality on the basis of reason. Hobbes offers his own unique defense of traditional morality. Hume is a bit further removed from the Christian tradition, but its influence is still present in his work. It is not until the 19th century that moral thinkers begin to defend entirely new and radical views of morality.

In this chapter, we will also consider the work of Mary Wollstonecraft, considered by many to be the first feminist philosopher. Like the other philosophers of this era, she rejects the constraints of unquestioned tradition and spurious authority. Unlike them, however, she challenges the traditional ethical and social understanding of women. She does not discard traditional conceptions of reason and morality; she boldly applies them to women, extending the full riches of the moral life to the other half of the human race. But, before we look at the views of Hobbes, Kant, Hume, and Wollstonecraft in more detail, we will briefly consider the revolutions and reformations that precipitated this reliance on reason, focusing on three objects of rational criticism: the absolute and unquestioned authority of the church, the commonsense authority of Aristotelian physics, and the conventional and divine endorsement of the medieval feudal system.

Revolutions and Reformations

In 1517, the disaffected monk Martin Luther posted 95 theses to the door of the Wittenburg church, thus setting off the Protestant Reformation, perhaps the turning point of modern history. Although it was called a reformation (Luther claimed to be interested merely in reforming the Roman Catholic Church), it was in reality a revolution, a revolution to reclaim the ancient authority of the Word of God as the sole foundation of true religion.

It would be difficult to state all of the religious, economic, social, and political factors that were brewing in the time of Luther. The Roman Catholic Church was certainly in need of reform. There were papal and priestly abuses of power that exploited the illiterate masses. An emphasis on works rather than faith made people uncertain of their eternal destinies and beholden to the clergy for absolution. The race to build bigger and more beautiful basilicas and cathedrals was paid for with the blood, sweat, and extorted tithes of peasants. Donations, for example, often were contributed out of fear for the release of deceased relatives from purgatory (thus the saying, "As soon as the coin in the coffer rings, a soul from purgatory springs"). The alliances of popes and kings lent divine approval to both an outdated feudal system and the amassing of civil and clerical wealth and power. The expanding middle class and the demand for social mobility put pressure on the religiously sanctioned, medieval social structure. The Reformation was a legitimate critique of an abuse of religious authority.

The Reformation ushered in new branches of the Christian religion based on the precepts *sola scriptura* and *sola fide*. Scripture alone is the final authority in all matters of faith and practice. This is in opposition to the Roman Catholic Church's insistence on the twin founts of authority—scripture and tradition. Salvation is acquired through faith alone, not, as the Roman Catholic Church taught, faith plus works. There were additional disagreements about church authority, the sacraments, the canon, and church structure.

In addition to disagreements with the Catholic church, Protestants disagreed amongst themselves. In no time at all, in Switzerland alone one could choose, to name just a few, to become a Calvinist, Lutheran, Anabaptist, and, of course, Roman Catholic. The choice one made was thought to determine both one's earthly and eternal destiny. The wrong choice could result in torture, death, and even damnation. The possibility of martyrdom and the yearning for eternal security demanded a method for choosing among the religious options.

The need for a method of rationally appraising options was not restricted to religious beliefs; the crisis of scientific authorities created a need for a rational method for determining scientific beliefs as well. On June 21, 1633, Galileo Galilei recanted his belief in the opinions of Copernicus. His *Dialogue on the Two Principal World Systems* was banned and he was placed under house arrest for the final eight years of his life. The issue before the Tribunal of the Inquisition was clear enough: whether the earth revolves around the sun or vice versa. The systems of Ptolemy and Copernicus were on trial. At stake were the traditions of well over a millennia: scriptural interpretation, papal authority, Ptolemaic cosmology, and Aristotelian physics. The issues involved were not merely science versus religion; they were science versus science as well. The commonsense physics of Aristotle implied that appearance is reality: because the sun, planets, and stars appear to move in uniform circular motion around the earth, they do; the earth appears to be stationary—neither revolving on its axis nor speeding around the sun, thus it is; things don't move unless moved by something else, therefore they don't. The implications of Aristotle's commitments were developed by Ptolemy and revised by Tycho Brahe into a sophisticated view of reality that harmonized well with a literalist interpretation of scripture: the earth (including man, the crown of creation) is the center of both cosmic and spiritual reality.

Copernicus, the intellectual prime mover of the scientific revolution, cautioned that appearance is not always reality and also that common sense and sense experience are not always reliable guides to comprehending the world. The sun does not rise and set; the earth rotates. Copernicus, in defending his views, caused the earth to shake. Galileo popularized Copernicus's views, writing in Italian, the vernacular, rather than Latin, the language of scholars. And, although his books were condemned, the threat to the privileged authority of the church and the received authority of Aristotle was delivered.

As if scientific and religious uncertainties were not enough, political unrest demanded an evaluation of the justification of the social order. In 1649, Charles I of England was executed while Thomas Hobbes, a royalist, found refuge in France. A king beheaded. By what right could someone kill a king? By what right did a king rule? How could anyone ask such questions when doing so might overturn more than a millennia of tradition? According to a synthesis of the work of Aristotle and medieval theology, every person was accorded a fixed role in a divinely instituted order. Kings ruled by divine right. Nonkings were required to obey their sovereign by the church. Every person had his or her natural place or role in a castelike society with little opportunity for social mobility. This rigid hierarchical system was endorsed by the church, tradition, and power that kept people in their places and maintained social control. But, in 1649 a king was killed; the event sparked the question, Who or what would take his place? How, without the support of divine right, can one justify an alternative political and moral system? Such questions were prominent in the thought of Thomas Hobbes.

Thomas Hobbes

Life is a race with no other good but to be foremost.

Thomas Hobbes (1588–1679) lived through revolutionary times. The English monarchy teetered on the precipice of revolutionary democracy. It would fall, Hobbes feared, into chaos. Without a powerful, central government to keep people's desires in check, anarchy would prevail. The sweet persuasion of reason or conscience could not inspire human beings to obey the law; Hobbes believed the clanging ego would overwhelm these timid voices. The only thing that could inspire people to obey the law is power and lots of it: the great LEVIATHAN. Hobbes defended the monarchy, or at least a powerful central government, but without appeal to divine right.

In defending the monarchy, Hobbes follows the strategy of a Galilean thought experiment: break complex things into their constituent parts and then see how the whole arises from the parts. What are the constituent parts of society? Society is nothing but a group of individuals, each of whom seeks to preserve, not the good of the whole, but his or her own interests. Here we see the influence of the Calvinist doctrine of total depravity. Hobbes's genius was his ability to mine this Calvinist understanding of the doctrine of original sin. Hobbes sees deep into the human heart: Underneath the thin veneer of human civility we are selfish, competitive, distrustful, and glory seeking. Our deepest desires are to dominate and to avoid death. How could society, where people like that live together with other people like that, possibly arise?

Hobbes's thought experiment begins with a question: What would life be like if there were no government authority? This so-called *State of Nature* is a state in which there are no laws and there is no one to enforce the laws. The only law that governs people in the state of nature is the law of self-preservation. According to Hobbes, persons in the state of nature are equal. Hobbes's understanding of equality may seem a bit odd: we are equal in our ability to kill. Some are quicker, some stronger, and some smarter, but these differences are not sufficient to ground inequality. The clever, small person is sufficiently cunning to kill the huge, musclebound but dumb person. This rough equality of ability provides us grounds for hope in attaining our chosen ends. Herein lies the problem: two people often desire the same end. Competition for the same things engenders a state of war because the only way to control scarce resources is to destroy or subdue the other.

Imagine Karl, a large but lazy brute, and Sarah, a small but smart lass, living nearby one another in the state of nature. Sarah plants her fields in the spring, prunes her fruit trees, cultivates the garden in the summer, and carefully stores her bounty for the winter. Karl spends the summer eating wild berries and fish and frolicking in the pond. But now it is getting colder and Karl is getting hungrier. He enviously eyes Sarah's foodstores, so he rushes in and forces her out. He gorges himself and drops off into a deep sleep, whereupon Sarah sneaks back and bashes his head in with a rock. Having taken care of the Karl problem, Sarah notices other hungry eyes staring earnestly at her food. She can either wait for another attack, which might cost her life, or she can make plans to attack them immediately. Only when her enemies are vanquished can she safely secure any peace for herself. But as word of her bounty spreads, her secure haven is threatened once again.

Given his view of human nature and the problem of the scarcity of goods and this distrust between people, one can see why Hobbes thinks the state of nature is a state of continual war. The uncertainty of the continued enjoyment of the spoils of one's labors and the perpetual threat of war dramatically decrease one's sense of well being. One can scarcely sleep for fear of having one's head bashed in, let alone leisurely partake of a meal. One must always be on guard. In such a state, there can be no security, and, thus, no enjoyment of the fruits of one's labor, no home improvement, no culture, and no time for the improvement of one's mind. In the state of nature, Hobbes writes, there is that "which is worst of all, continual fear, and danger of violent death; And the life of man, solitary, poor, nasty, brutish and short" (*Leviathan,* Ch. 13.9).

Before one dismisses Hobbes's conception of the state of nature as idle speculation (people are nicer than that, after all), consider what happens when civil authority breaks down. Shortly after the delivery of the Rodney King verdict, the police were ordered to evacuate south-central Los Angeles. A chaotic hell of every person for him or herself broke loose. No property, no life, was safe during this unhindered pursuit of self-interest. Consider also the behavior of soldiers during wartime; with their power they can (and do) rape, murder (noncombatants and children), and pillage with impunity. When a powerful authority is removed, lawlessness ensues. Hobbes's argument is no mere thought experiment. Indeed, Hobbes observes that our actions reveal our agreement with him:

> Let him therefore consider with himself, when taking a journey, he arms himself, and seeks to go well accompanied; when going to sleep, he locks his doors; when even in his house he locks his chests; and this when he knows there be laws, and public officers, armed, to revenge all injuries shall be done him; what opinion he has of his fellow-subjects, when he rides armed; of his fellow citizens, when he locks his doors; and of his children, and servants, when he locks his chests. Does he not there as much accuse mankind by his actions, as I do by my words? (*Leviathan,* Ch. 13.10).

Suppose that Sarah, when Karl stole her house and food, told Karl that he ought to give it all back because it's wrong to steal. According to Hobbes, such reasoning won't do, because no actions are unjust in the state of nature. In this state, there are no laws and, if no laws, no injustice. In order for something to be wrong, there must first be a law. To create laws, there must be a common power strong enough to make the law and to enforce it. In his description of the state of nature, Hobbes would appear to endorse Thrasymachus' claim that might makes right. He believes that in the state of nature it is our natural right to do as we please, especially for the preservation of our own life. If someone threatens us or is even perceived as a threat, we have the right to decide the best means to eliminate that threat. And, given that there is no injustice in the state of nature, there is no limit to our right to self-preservation—head-bashing as we please is our right.

Hobbes goes on to observe that life in the state of nature is so insecure that fear of death and hope for a more fulfilling life inclines people to seek peace. It is the fear of death and the desire for peace that compel people to organize a society. It is important to note that they do not form a society in order to help others; they do so in pursuit of their own individual interests; for persons, according to Hobbes, act in their own self-interest: "of the voluntary acts of every man, the object is some *good to himself*" (*Leviathan,* Ch. 14.8; his emphasis). Thus, Hobbes concludes the first part of his thought experiment, society arises out of individuals rationally pursuing their own interests.

But the choice to form a society is not as easy as it may sound, for persons in the state of nature are in a terrifying position. Their only protection is their right to defend themselves as they see fit, but their only hope for gaining peace may lie in giving up that right. How could any reasonable person give up his or her only defense from other selfish and potentially violent people even in the interest of peace? In simpler terms, how shall he or she sleep at night while fearing a head-bashing? If I give up my powers of self-protection, who will protect me? How can this reasonably be in my self-interest?

Hobbes argues that we ought to give up the right to do as we please by transferring that right to another. But it would not be reasonable to transfer your right if no one else were to do so—you'd become an easy target. Hobbes writes: "For he that should be modest, and tractable, and perform all he promises, in such time, and place, where no man else should do so, should but make himself a prey to others, and procure his own certain ruin, contrary to the ground of all laws of nature, which tend to nature's preservation" (*Leviathan,* Ch. 15.36). It is only reasonable to give up your rights on the condition that everyone else do so as well. When everyone agrees, for the sake of peace, to transfer his or her rights, a contract is established.

What are the terms of such a contract? What are the benefits and the costs for those who enter into this mutual agreement? Since the primary reason for entering into this contract is peace, the primary benefit of this contract should be peace. But peace cannot be obtained simply by renouncing one's right to defend oneself as one pleases and hoping that everyone else will do so as well. One thing that we have learned is that people cannot be trusted. Peace is ensured not by frail trust but by severe power. So, each person must agree to transfer his or her rights to a common power who will protect persons from one another. In the mutual transferring of that right, an individual or a group of individuals is granted sufficient power to compel obedience: "Covenants, without the sword, are but words, and of no strength to secure a man at all" (*Leviathan,* Ch. 17.2).

This common power, the sovereign authority, is "That great LEVIATHAN" (a huge and terrifying sea monster). By this endowed authority, he has the power (i.e., terror) necessary to keep peace. Here is the covenant that persons enact when forming a society:

> The only way to erect such a common power, as may be able to defend them from the invasion of foreigners, and the injuries of one another, and thereby to secure them in such sort, as that by their own industry, and by the fruits of the earth, they may nourish themselves and live contentedly; is, to confer all their power and strength upon one man, or upon one assembly of men, that may reduce all their wills, by plurality of voices, unto one will . . . as if every man should say to every man, *I authorise and give up my right of governing myself, to this man, or to this assembly of men, on this condition, that thou give up thy right to him, and authorise all his actions in like manner.* This done, the multitude so united in one person, is called a COMMONWEALTH, in Latin CIVITAS. This is the generation of that great LEVIATHAN, or rather (to speake more reverently) of that *Mortal God,* to which we owe under the *Immortall*

God, our peace and defence. . . . And in him [the Sovereign] consisteth the essence of the commonwealth; which (to define it,) is *one person, of whose acts a great multitude [subjects], by mutual covenants one with another, have made themselves every one the author, to the end he may use the strength and means of them all, as he shall think expedient, for their Peace and common defence.* (*Leviathan,* Ch. 17.13, emphasis his)

When the Leviathan is created, it will be reasonable, given our desire for peace, to keep our covenant with the subjects with whom we entered into the covenant. We gain peace and security but we must also—here the cost to self-interested people is dear—submit our wills to his will and our judgments to his judgments. He will tell us how to behave—do not kill, steal, or lie; keep your promises, pay your taxes, and keep your place in society. He also may tell us what to believe in matters of religion, politics, or social order. Hobbes's sovereign has absolute authority to keep the peace and to make and enforce laws as he sees fit. Justice comes into existence only when this absolute authority makes laws and has the power to enforce them. Injustice, therefore, is disobeying the sovereign.

Given the absolute authority of the monarch, the possibilities of abuse of power are tremendous. Surely the rule of the monarch will often be arbitrary, oppressive, even harmful. If you don't like the monarch, however, your only recourse is to return to the state of nature. But few burdens imposed by the sovereign can be as bad as life in the state of nature; no matter how bad things are in the commonwealth, you can still sleep in peace.

Hobbes maintains that we are obliged to the sovereign as long as the sovereign has the power to protect us. If the original impetus for entering the contract—fear of death—reoccurs within the commonwealth, the contract is dissolved. This implies that the contract is dissolved only if the commonwealth is as bad as the state of nature. Hobbes is no revolutionary; there have been few commonwealths as bad as the state of nature.

We have outlined Hobbes's important and original defense of the absolute authority of the sovereign. One might wonder, however, what this has to do with ethics. Hobbes's views are influential in recent thought not so much for his social contract defense of political authority but for his social contract defense of morality. Recall Hobbes's view of human nature—we are rational individuals who are driven by self-interested desires; so, human happiness is continual success at satisfying one's desires (*Leviathan,* Ch. 6.58). Recall also Hobbes's view that, in the state of nature, there is no justice or injustice. Hobbes defends morality as something that is in the best interest of rationally self-interested people. Since I will only heed matters that I deem in my best interest, Hobbes needs to argue that being moral, that is, being other-regarding, is in *my* best interest (at least being other-regarding toward people who are either friends or family members). To do so, he offers a *social contract defense of morality:* right and wrong are nothing more than the agreement among rationally self-interested individuals to give up the unhindered pursuit of their own desires for the security of living in peace. It is in my best interest to enter into a society where everyone's desires are constrained by an agreed-on morality. Hobbes argues as follows:

> *Good,* and *evil,* are names that signify our appetites, and aversions; which in different tempers, customes, and doctrines of men, are different. . . . the same man, in divers times, differs from himself; and one time praiseth, that is, calleth good, what another time he dispraiseth, and calleth evil: from whence arise disputes, controversies, and at last war. And therefore so long a man is in the condition of mere nature, (which is a condition of war,) as private appetite is the measure of good and evil: and consequently all men agree on this, that peace is good, and therefore also the way, or means of Peace, which, (as I have shewed before) are *justice, gratitude, modesty, equity, mercy,* and the rest of the laws of nature, are good; that is to say, *moral virtues;* and their contrary *vices,* evil. (*Leviathan,* Ch. 15.40)

Why, according to Hobbes, be moral? In the state of nature, my own desires and aversions measure good and evil. But it is not rational for me to remain in the state of nature. I desire peace, so I desire the means of peace—taking on the constraint of traditional morality. Hobbes contends that it is in *my* best interest to be moral (to constrain my desires). I should be moral, even though acting morally typically squelches my appetites, because that is the condition necessary for obtaining what I most deeply desire—peace. It is rational for me to give up the unfettered pursuit of some of my desires in order to satisfy my deepest desire, which is for peace and security. The benefit of living in peace with others is worth the cost of the unfettered liberty of satisfying my own desires as I see fit. Human flourishing, it seems, is always a compromise between our desire for the unfettered satisfaction of our desires and our desire for a secure peace.

We should note here that while Hobbes thinks that traditional morality often runs contrary to many of our self-interested desires, he thinks we have natural feelings of love and affection especially toward family and friends, which make acting for their good something we do in our own interest. If I have natural feelings of affection for my children, for example, it will be in my own interest to be kind to them. It is, therefore, rational for self-interested persons to be other-regarding, at least toward family and friends. Hobbes's view of human motivation leaves some room for the genuine desire for the good of another, and he can embrace the virtues of charity, generosity, pity, benevolence, and love.

A problem arises, however, when the requirements of morality cannot so easily be incorporated into our self-interest. Hobbes has said that it is actually in our self-interest to obey these requirements because they are necessary for the maintenance of society and so for the peace that is our deepest desire. But, what if my violating a certain moral requirement will do little or nothing to jeopardize society and my peace? Hobbes recognizes this problem of defections from the social contract. Won't it be reasonable (i.e., in one's own interest) in certain situations to disobey the sovereign? He writes:

The fool hath said in his heart, there is no such thing as justice; and sometimes also with his tongue; seriously alleging, that every man's conservation,
and contentment, being committed to his own care, there could be no reason, why every man might not do what he thought conduced thereun-
to: and therefore also to make, or not make; keep, or not keep covenants,
was not against reason, when it conduced to one's benefit. (*Leviathan,*
Ch. 15.4)

If one reasonably judges that one can violate the social contract and get away with
it, won't that be in one's best interest? If, for example, you can speed, cheat on
taxes, or submit an inflated claim to your insurance company and get away with
it, wouldn't it be more reasonable to violate the social contract? Surely such actions
would not result in the destruction of the commonwealth.[2]

One solution to this problem unites Hobbes's moral philosophy and his religious beliefs. Although Hobbes contends that he has deduced his theory from
consideration of human nature, he also writes a great deal about the relationship
of law and God.[3] While he was accused of atheism in his lifetime, one simply cannot ignore the fact that over half of *Leviathan* is a positive theological exploration
of this topic. Hobbes argues that one reason for not violating the social contract
when one can get away with it is that God sees what you do and will judge you
accordingly (*Leviathan,* Ch. 38). "Might makes right," according to Hobbes, especially when it comes to the Omnipotent. God's commands must be obeyed because he has the power to cast violators into eternal torment and to reward the
righteous with eternal life. God's vastly greater powers to reward and punish violators of the Law entail that it would always be irrational to defect from the covenant. Such an answer is unlikely to satisfy nontheists (perhaps even some theists),
however, and the problem of defection remains at the heart of many contemporary social contract theorist's defenses of morality.[4]

One final point is worth raising. The sovereign in a Hobbesian commonwealth can compel obedience to the law, but he cannot work an inner transformation of character. He can make people give money to the church, but he
cannot make people generous. He can prevent people from killing one another,
but he cannot make them love each other. He can make people wait for benefits
from the state, but he is unable to make them patient. The point is this: Hobbes's
defense of morality focuses more on external obedience to the law than on creating certain kinds of persons. Governmental powers can only ensure rule-keeping,
they cannot cultivate virtue. During the modern period, we see the beginnings of
a shift toward law rather than virtue as the focus of ethics. Qualities of character
and education of the passions will become increasingly less emphasized while natural laws, natural rights, and their enforcement come to the fore. We cannot see

---

[2] The question arises, however, as to how many such violations society can sustain.
[3] Indeed he suggests that Law, *properly understood,* is delivered in the word of God (*Leviathan,* Ch. 15).
[4] See David Gauthier, *Morals By Agreement* (New York: Oxford University Press, 1986).

inside a person nor can we control a person's feelings; we can, however, ensure that people are relatively obedient to the law. Moral thinking begins to shift from an emphasis on attitude toward an emphasis on behavior.

According to Hobbes, humans are by nature driven from desire to desire. The competition for desired goods makes human beings threats to one another. Given the insistence of our self-regarding desires and the necessity of competition, we must erect a common terror to ensure the enjoyment of our chief desire—not to live in fear. We give up our right to live as we please and enter into a social contract in order to live in peace. On such an account, morality is at least partly a necessary evil. It, with the assistance of Leviathan, compels us to act in opposition to many of our own interests. Contrary to the teachings of Plato, Aristotle, Augustine, and Aquinás, morality is often not our friend. Nonetheless, it is a burden that all rational persons should bear to secure peace.

David Hume

Reason is, and ought only to be, the slave of the passions, and can never pretend to any other office than to serve and obey them.

Although David Hume (1711–1776) is widely considered a skeptic about matters of metaphysics (God, freedom, immortality, the self, and causality), he is not a skeptic about morality. A witness to the decline of religion in his day, he was himself an agnostic or atheist. Yet, he believed that morality could survive the loss of its religious backing; morality could get along quite well without God.

Hume's philosophy is a response both to a materialistic view of the world (that everything is just matter and motion) and to moral rationalism. A materialistic view of the world does not seem to leave room for good and bad as objective properties. Science can discuss the shape, position, motion, and so on of physical objects, and that is all. Science cannot study good and evil, since they are not sensory properties of objects. But if good and evil are not "out there" then they must be "in here," inside human beings, perhaps in the mind. *Moral rationalists* maintained that reason could discover moral truths by examining the furniture of the mind. According to the rationalists, there are clear and invariant moral principles in our minds that are discoverable by reason. Theistic rationalists claimed that these principles were placed there by God.

Although Hume is not a rationalist, he believes that good and evil exist and locates the source of morality within human beings. By looking at Hume's *An Enquiry Concerning the Principles of Morals,*[5] we will see how he bases morality not on God or on reason but on human feelings or affections.

[5.]   David Hume, *An Enquiry Concerning the Principles of Morals,* ed. Jerome Schneewind (Indianapolis, IN: Hackett Publishing Company, 1983); hereafter cited in the text as *Enquiry.*

Hume rejects moral rationalism because he believes that reason alone cannot motivate any action. This is not hard to see given his definition of reason. According to Hume, there are only two kinds of reason: mathematical or logical reasoning ("relations of ideas") and empirical reasoning about the properties of material objects ("matters of fact") (*Enquiry,* p. 84). Neither of these sorts of reasons can impel us to act. Hume writes:

> The end of all moral speculations is to teach us our duty; and, by proper representations of the deformity of vice and beauty of virtue, beget correspondent habits, and engage us to avoid the one, and embrace the other. But is this ever to be expected from inferences and conclusions of the understanding, which of themselves have no hold of the affections or set in motion the active powers of men? They discover truths: But where the truths which they discover are indifferent, and beget no desire or aversion, they can have no influence on conduct and behaviour. (*Enquiry,* 14–15)

Reason can assist our impulses and guide our actions, but only our desires and aversions can actually move us to action. He completes the above quotation: "What is honourable, what is fair, what is becoming, what is noble, what is generous, takes possession of the heart, and animates us to embrace and maintain it" (*Enquiry,* 15).

Consider a person—Debbie—standing on railroad tracks with a train fast approaching. Debbie may make all sorts of rational judgments about the momentum of the train, expected time of arrival, displacement of body parts upon impact, quantity of blood loss, and so on. None of these judgments, however, is sufficient to compel Debbie to move off the tracks. If Debbie wished to die, she would stay and use her reason to secure her morbid end. If Debbie wanted to live but experience a close brush with death, she would use her reason to calculate how to ensure this thrilling experience. The point of this illustration is that only one's desires compel one to act; reason alone, as Hume defines it, cannot compel action. Those things that move us to act, things Hume calls *propensities and aversions,* are emotions or passions that are in themselves not reasonable or unreasonable.

Reason cannot motivate us to act, nor can it discover virtue and vice. Recall that as Hume defines it, reason concerns relations of ideas and matters of fact. Virtue and vice fall under neither class. Virtue and vice do not involve logical or mathematical relations. Nor are they matters of fact: look as intently as you wish, you can't *see* (or hear, touch, taste, or smell) virtue or vice in an action or a person. Suppose you see someone getting shot in the head and you try to describe it with all the properties that you can sense. You describe the velocity of the bullet, the retort of the gun, the impact on the skin and skull, the size of the entry wound, and the exit wound, and so on. Turn it over, view all sides, describe it as fully as you like and something morally important is still missing: goodness or badness. You cannot observe goodness, argues Hume. Nor is goodness a logical or mathematical relation.

So where is the powerful impression of goodness or badness? Hume argues that we have a certain feeling when we make a moral judgment. When we think of an innocent person being shot, one feels strong disapproval. The badness is located not in the act itself but within one's heart. Hume writes: "The vice entirely escapes you, as long as you consider the object. You never can find it, till you turn your reflexion into your own breast, and find a sentiment of disapprobation which arises in you toward this action. Here is a matter of fact; but tis the object of feeling, not of reason. It lies in yourself, not in the object."[6] "Morality," Hume concludes, "is more properly felt than judg'd of."[7]

Moral judgments are not unlike aesthetic judgments in this way (*Enquiry*, 86ff). While on sabbatical in Scotland, I took my family to a festival. We were standing next to a group of bagpipers while they were tuning up. Out of the chaos of individual tuning came the serene sounds of "Amazing Grace." When my son Will heard it, he gasped. Bagpipes are emotionally powerful instruments and "Amazing Grace" is a passionate tune. Will's reaction to the combination of pipe and tune aroused the appropriate aesthetic response; the beauty was in his heart. This visceral aesthetic response is similar to Hume's understanding of moral judgments. Moral properties are not outside of the visceral responses of a person; they are in a person's heart. So, Hume defines *virtue* as "whatever mental action or quality gives to a spectator the pleasing sentiment of approbation; and vice the contrary" (*Enquiry*, 85).

At first glance, Hume's moral theory seems to reduce morality to autobiography. I have certain aversions and desires and you have different aversions and desires (I prefer bagpipes, you prefer rock and roll). And, since reason is incapable of reorienting our desires toward the good, it looks as if we may each have our own morality, dependent on the particular desires we happen to have, whether those happen to be desires to serve others, to accumulate wealth, or even to consume human flesh. Sentimentalist moral theories like Hume's have a strong tendency toward subjectivism (right and wrong are up to each individual; there is no higher standard than the individual). The problem is that if virtue and vice float free of objective states of affairs (either actions or character), then they are simply matters of subjective whim. Let's see how Hume tries to avoid this.

Hume avoids subjectivism by locating the *source* of morality in states of affairs not in the mind. He claims that virtue and vice are analogous to secondary qualities like color and sound.[8] Color and sound are universal qualities, perhaps not of objects proper but of the effect of an object on us. Consider the color of an apple: light reflects off the surface of the apple, some of it is absorbed and some of it is passed on, it impinges on our retinas, stimulates our rods and cones, and produces a sensation of red in our minds. The apple itself may or may not be

---

6. David Hume, *A Treatise of Human Nature*, ed. L. A. Selby-Bigge (London: Oxford University Press, 1888), Bk. III, Sec. 1, 468.

7. Hume, *Treatise*, Bk. III, Sec. 2, 470.

8. Hume, *Treatise*, Bk. III, Sec. 1, 469.

colored (it may be made up of colorless particles such as atoms); nonetheless, apples are so constructed that when light reflects off of them they effect a sensation of red in their viewers. The apple has the objective properties that cause a particular sensation in its observers. So, the color red is in our minds but was not produced on its own (by the observer) independent of the apple. One need not deny that there is an objective property in objects that causes the nearly universal experience of, for example, seeing red when looking at an apple or hearing a loud bang when watching a gun being shot off; but, color and sound, properly speaking, are not qualities in the objects themselves but are the effect of the objects on our sensory receptors. But colors and sounds are not figments of our imagination, nor are they whimsical human creations. They arise in our minds due to the causal powers of the objects in question: that object has a tendency to produce that effect. Although they "occur" in the subject, there is an objective element to secondary qualities.

Likewise, there is a certain objectivity to moral qualities. Hume maintains that just as nearly all of us have the experience of seeing green when confronted with grass, we nearly all have the same experience when confronted with certain moral situations. We all have feelings of moral aversion, for example, when confronted with the killing of innocent persons, and we all have feelings of moral attraction when confronted with someone coming to another's aid.[9] And we nearly all have the same experience when confronted with certain character traits. Such feelings are built into each person's nature; they are, as Hume writes, transfused "into each beholder" (*Enquiry*, 18), so that everyone approves and disapproves of similar traits of character. There are qualities, according to Hume, that are useful or agreeable to ourselves and qualities that are useful and agreeable to others. The former include, for example, such virtues as discretion, industry, strength of mind, cheerfulness, and tranquility; the latter include benevolence, wit, justice, cleanliness, and decency. But the greatest of these is benevolence.

The most important sentiment Hume believes to be universal is the sentiment of benevolence. Contra Hobbes, Hume believes we are all attracted by actions that benefit others. He writes:

> It may be esteemed, perhaps, a superfluous task to prove, that the benevolent or softer affections are ESTIMABLE; and wherever they appear, engage the approbation, and good-will of mankind. The epithets *sociable, good-natured, humane, merciful, grateful, friendly, generous, beneficent,* or their equivalents, are known in all languages, and universally express the highest merit, which *human nature* is capable of attaining. (*Enquiry,* 16–17)

---

9. There is another similarity to be drawn between secondary qualities and moral qualities. In both cases, we tend to "project" our subjective experience onto the object itself. So, we talk as if the grass is itself green or as if the action is itself good or bad.

According to Hume, benevolence motivates us to act to relieve the suffering and promote the happiness of other human beings, and reason judges the best means for attaining this end. Thus, moral judgments may attain a certain level of objectivity.

Contra Hobbes, Hume maintains that benevolence, not self-interest is the (almost divine) sentiment in human nature that is the foundation both of right action and society. "In all determinations of morality," Hume writes, "this circumstance of public utility is ever principally in view; and wherever disputes arise, either in philosophy or common life, concerning the bounds of duty, the question cannot, by any means, be decided with greater certainty, than by ascertaining, on any side, the true interests of mankind" (*Enquiry*, 19).

According to Hume, sympathy (the capacity to be affected by the happiness and suffering of others) and utility (the tendency to promote the good of the whole) work together to create moral feelings as well as to bring moral feelings in line with genuine benevolence. We may find that we are required, Hume writes, to "retract our first sentiment, and adjust anew the boundaries of moral good and evil" (*Enquiry*, 19). Sympathy can help us to see, for example, that tyrannicide that was praised in ancient times because it eliminated monsters and kept people in line, conduces toward cruelty and should not be valued. Likewise, it can help us see that incautious almsgiving can create idleness and help us learn the proper limits of generosity.

Hume's suggestion that morality keeps considerations of public utility ("its tendency to promote the interests of our species, and bestow happiness on human society" [*Enquiry*, 20]) constantly in view influenced the development of utilitarianism that we will examine in later chapters. Hume thought that by coming together and dialoguing in sympathy with people of varying desires and aversions, we could develop a better moral standard: "The intercourse of sentiments, therefore, in society and conversation, makes us form some general unalterable standard, by which we may approve or disapprove of characters and manners" (*Enquiry*, 49).

It is not difficult to construct a Humean picture of the fulfilled human being. First, "frame the model of a praise-worthy character, consisting of all the most amiable moral virtues" (*Enquiry*, 41). Second, place that person in a society where everyone works to secure the happiness of the species. In such a society, benevolence reigns, happiness is maximized and unhappiness minimized. The benevolent person dialogues and labors to realize such a society in which she and everyone manifests qualities useful and agreeable to themselves and others.

Hume grounds morality not in some supersensible Platonic realm but in the sentiments of human beings. We are so constructed, he believes, that the appropriate moral feelings well up within our breasts and we are moved, not by reason, but by sentiment, to act for the good of others. But what if Hume is unduly optimistic? What if nature, unguided by the hand of God, is not capable of "transfusing" the appropriate moral feelings into each and every human being? Observation should tell us that too often it is Hobbes who seems closer to the

truth with his sometimes frightening account of our selfish nature. If our sentiments vary from person to person or are corrupt, they cannot provide a secure
foundation for morality. We must look elsewhere. Immanuel Kant looks to reason
to supply the foundation for morality and the corrective for our corrupt sentiments.

Immanuel Kant

*If we look more closely at our thoughts and aspirations, we everywhere come upon the
dear self.*

We move from Hume, the sentimentalist, to Immanuel Kant (1724–1804), the rationalist. Kant's view of human nature is more like Hobbes's than Hume's: persons
have an innate tendency to prefer their own good. Lurking behind even the most
apparently benevolent action is "the dear self." We are likely to deceive others and
even ourselves about our self-love. Contra Hobbes, Kant argues that we do not
need to harness this tendency, we need to overcome it if morality is to be possible. He seeks a rational standard that can be used to guide our actions and correct
our feelings or inclinations. How can Kant defend the profoundly other-regarding
nature of traditional morality while recognizing our deep affection for our self?
In trying to answer this question, we will look at the moral views he presents in
his *Groundwork of the Metaphysic of Morals*[10] as well as the often neglected topic of
the interrelationship of Kant's views of morality and his religious beliefs.

Let us begin with the following question: What qualities do we think it is
good for people to have? Intelligence, discipline, perseverance, and wit would
likely make the list. We might also think it is good to have goods of fortune such
as good looks, power, wealth, and honor. Kant agrees that all of these things are
good, but he says that they are only good with qualification; that is they can be
good or bad, depending on how they are used. Think for example of the intelligence of a saint versus that of a scoundrel. Nothing in the world is good without
qualification, contends Kant, nothing except a *good will*. A good will cannot be
used for ill; it is good unconditionally. Kant analyzes the concept of a good will in
order to obtain the principle upon which such a will acts.

What makes a good will good? It's not the consequences it produces: one
may will something good, but it may not come about because of circumstances
beyond one's control; in such a case, one's will may nonetheless be good. It's the
motive of a good will that makes it good. A good will is a will that acts from the
motive of duty, that is, I do the right thing *because* it's the right thing; I do my duty
simply because it's my duty. We might think of it this way: goodness does not de-

---

[10.] Immanuel Kant, *The Groundwork of the Metaphysic of Morals,* trans. H. J. Paton (New York: Hutchinson's
University Library, 1948); hereafter cited in the text as *Groundwork*.

How can one tell if one can will her maxim to become a universal law? Kant says it is a matter of what one can will without contradiction, and he believes that all persons who apply this test should get the same results, that is, they should arrive at the same moral principles. He asks his readers to consider the following example. May one, when in distress, make a promise with the intention of not keeping it? In order to answer this, one must ask, Could my maxim hold as a universal law, that is, may everyone promise falsely when in difficulty? Kant believes that anyone should conclude that while one can will the lie, one cannot will the universal law 'to lie when in distress' since such a law would entail that no one would then believe one's promise. In willing that lying be universal, one would involve herself in a contradiction: She would will to be believed (so that she can get out of trouble) and she would will not to be believed (since the institution of promise keeping would self-destruct). So, the categorical imperative is supposed to show that we have a duty not to lie. What this example makes clear is that in acting immorally, we are trying to make an exception of ourselves. The categorical imperative test is supposed to prevent this. Kant believes he can derive a number of other duties from this supreme principle of morality as well, but before looking at the list, it would be good to briefly look at two other formulations of the categorical imperative.

Kant goes on to ask, if there is a categorical imperative, what would its end be? Every action has an end; and, since the categorical imperative is supposed to be binding on everyone, its end must be given by reason alone and so equally valid for all rational beings. What is this end? Kant answers that every rational being exists as an end in itself. As ends in themselves, human beings have a value that is unconditional. So, humanity is the objective end required for determining the will by the categorical imperative. This suggests a second formulation: *We ought to treat humanity in ourselves and others as ends and never merely as means* (*Groundwork*, 429). Persons are not instruments to our or other people's happiness; they are valuable in themselves and deserve our esteem and respect.

Kant contends that this means that I must make your ends my ends: "For the ends of any person who is an end in himself, must as far as possible also be my end, if that conception of an end in itself is to have its full effect on me" (*Groundwork*, 430). Because I naturally favor my own ends, in order for me to respect you, I must do all that I can to further your ends. If one treats other people's ends as one's own in a community of like-minded people, one belongs to *the kingdom of ends,* which brings us to the third formulation of the categorical imperative: *Act in such a way that the maxims proceeding from your own legislation can harmonize with a possible kingdom of ends* (*Groundwork*, 436).

In Kant's moral kingdom, citizens are self-legislating or autonomous (*Groundwork*, 441ff). The *principle of autonomy* states that everyone is a law unto him or herself. But, Kant does not mean that each person does just as he or she pleases. He believes that as autonomous legislators in the kingdom of ends, we would choose moral laws. It is in obeying these laws that we are truly free.

What moral laws would we choose? Kant's list is quite traditional. He claims that there are two ends required by the categorical imperative, that is, there are two ends it is our duty to make our ends: our own perfection and the happiness of others. From the duty to have our own perfection as an end, Kant derives various duties to self including duties against suicide, drunkenness, gluttony, self-abuse, self-deceit, avarice, and servility, as well as duties to develop one's powers of mind, soul, and body and one's moral perfection, that is, duties to be holy and perfect. From the duty to make the happiness of others one's end, Kant derives duties to love and respect others including duties of beneficence, gratitude, sympathy, and the duty to cultivate friendships, as well as duties against envy, ingratitude, malicious joy, pride, defamation, and mockery. So, in discovering the supreme moral principle on which a good will acts and deriving a variety of other duties from it, Kant gives traditional morality a purely rational basis.

One of Kant's most famous principles is *"Ought implies can."* This means that if we have an obligation to do *x,* it must be possible for us to do *x.* I am not obligated to fly to the space station and rescue the cosmonauts because I can't fly. It may be a good thing to save cosmonauts whose lives are in grave danger, but as long as we lack the ability to assist them, it is not our duty. If we cannot do something, we have no obligation to do it.

This "ought implies can" principle would appear to pose two significant problems for Kant's moral theory: one having to do with the duty to overcome self-love, the other with the duty to pursue the highest good. Both of these would seem to be impossible. Kant's discussion of these issues raises the necessity of *moral faith.* This topic requires a discussion of some of the religious issues so often neglected in Kant scholarship.

According to Kant's moral theory, we have a duty to overcome our self-love. But, in reality it is impossible for us to do this. When we look deep inside human motivation we always see the "dear self." Our corrupt commitment to self is contrary to the call of duty. We ought not, but we do, favor our self; and our ceaseless devotion to self makes moral progress futile. We are required to will the good of others as our own good, but we cannot. We are moved to act by inclination, not by duty. Kant believes that our original disposition to respect the law has been placed in bondage to "radical evil."

According to the "ought implies can" principle, if we cannot overcome our self-love and will the good of others, then we do not have a duty to do so. But, then the whole of morality is destroyed. There is, however, a way out. We cannot liberate ourselves from this bondage; we require a "divine supplement" for our liberation. So, morality requires that we believe there is a God who has the power to reorient our wills from self to other. It is not possible, on our own, to effect a "revolution of the will"; it is possible, however, God willing. So, Kant concludes, if it is possible, God willing, then we can and, therefore, ought to reorient our wills. This sort of "moral faith" is necessary for us to achieve the revolution of the will that is required by the moral life.

A second sort of moral faith is demanded as well. We ought to seek the highest good, that is, according to Kant, virtue and happiness in accord with virtue. But, if we look around us, we see that too often the virtuous suffer while the vicious prosper. And the demands of morality often seem to run counter to our natural desire for happiness. There is no law in nature that assures a connection between virtue and happiness. So, in order to persevere in the moral life, we must also believe that virtue is not an obstacle to happiness. We must, says Kant, postulate a supreme being who ensures that virtue is rewarded with happiness. But, since this does not occur in this life, we must believe that there is a next life in which our moral progress continues and in which God rewards virtue with happiness. If the moral life requires us to pursue the highest good, then (by "ought implies can") we must be able to pursue it. It is, according to Kant, "morally necessary to assume the existence of God."[11]

Kant's moral philosophy unites his beliefs in humanity's inability, unassisted by God, to will the good of others with his belief in the universal and essential other-regarding nature of morality. Given our devotion to the self, divine assistance is required for the reorientation of our wills toward the moral law. But, even with divine assistance, our natures constrain the enthusiastic embrace of the moral law. There are forces in this world that thwart the reward of happiness to virtuous people. We must believe, therefore, that our moral projects continue into the next life, where they will be rewarded.

Kant is perhaps the most influential moral thinker of the modern era. The views attributed to him, however, are often at variance with his written work. He is often considered an atheist or secular thinker, but he clearly argues that the moral life requires faith in God. He has been portrayed as someone who primarily focuses on rules or actions, but his focus is surely on proper moral motivation as most central to morally good actions. He is often accused of being unconcerned about consequences—we must do our duty regardless of the consequences. But he is eminently concerned that the moral life elicit the right consequences—that wickedness be punished and that righteousness be rewarded with happiness.

Despite Kant's own religious beliefs, his notion of autonomy has often been taken to make possible an ethics without God. Indeed, Kant's insistence that morality derives entirely from reason coupled with his endorsement of self-legislation seems to many to leave little or no room for God. God appears to be neither the source nor the force of the moral law. Kant may have wished to defend his Lutheran moral heritage, but his legacy was to assist the break of morality from religion entirely. And since, according to Kant, God superadds happiness to virtue, and since virtue is to be pursued for its own sake, subsequent moral theories begin to pry morality away from the quest for human happiness.

---

11. This is a summary of Kant's moral argument for the existence of God from Immanuel Kant, *Critique of Practical Reason,* trans. L. W. Beck (New York: The Bobbs-Merrill Company, 1956), Bk. II, Ch. 5.

Mary Wollstonecraft

I wish . . . to set some investigations . . . afloat . . . ; and should they lead to a con-firmation of my principles . . . the Rights of Women may be respected, if it be fully proved that reason calls for this respect, and loudly demands JUSTICE for one half of the human race.

Mary Wollstonecraft (1759–1797) lived during and participated in at least two of the revolutions mentioned in the beginning of this chapter. She was hopeful about the successes of the Enlightenment with its emphasis on reason and its rejection of traditional forms of authority. However, she came to see that for all their talk about reason, Enlightenment thinkers believed that only men were capable of reason. She was also an active participant in the debates concerning political revolutions that were rooted in the rights of man. However, she saw that the rights of man were just that—the rights of *man,* not the rights of woman. Women were considered irrational and men only were endowed with the natural rights to liberty and the pursuit of happiness. Because of their perceived deficiencies, women were degraded as persons and their liberties were restricted. In short, for all of the Enlightenment's promise, women continued to be oppressed members of society. The inferior treatment of women, justified by the exclusion of women from reason and rights, provides the background to Wollstonecraft's *A Vindication of the Rights of Woman* (1792).[12]

Vindication is the most prominent early warning that there is something deeply wrong with the moral theories of the men we've studied so far. These men systematically exclude women from the attainment of virtue and fulfillment. They claim that women lack the properties that are essential for becoming virtuous and fulfilled. Wollstonecraft contends that women are fully rational, so they have the property necessary for virtue and fulfillment. She argues that women are intellectually disadvantaged, "enfeebled," not by nature but by a poor system of education that prevents women from gaining the wisdom necessary to secure virtue and fulfillment. Their meager education cultivates prejudice, equips them for submissiveness, and thereby morally and socially impoverishes and oppresses women. Women have been forced to learn, when permitted to learn, from men who consider women to be less than fully human and perhaps, because they lack reason, not human at all.

The history of Western philosophy is littered with thinkers who view women as deficient. In the West, women were believed to lack reason and to be unduly susceptible to the wiles of emotion and desire. Men, it is claimed, are rational and women are emotional. Emotion, passion, and desire are traits humans share with the animals, while reason is the property humans share with the gods.

[12.]   Mary Wollstonecraft, *A Vindication of the Rights of Woman,* ed. Carol H. Poston (New York: W.W. Norton & Co., 1975); hereafter cited in the text as *Vindication.*

Women are located somewhere on the scale of cosmic value midway between animals and men (women are "the link which unites man with brutes (*Vindication*, 35)"); men are located on the scale midway between women and gods. If women lack rationality, they are incapable of moral goodness. Instead, they should aspire to be all that they can be: polite and submissive. Women "are only taught to . . . acquire manners rather than morals" (*Vindication*, 118).

Wollstonecraft does not deny the importance of reason to a life of virtue; she writes that "every being may become virtuous by the exercise of its own reason" (*Vindication*, 21). Rationality is central to the attainment of virtue for two reasons: to see the good and to do the good. First, reason is required for the perception of moral truth; reason is the lens through which humans see the good clearly; reason helps distinguish the good through the fog of its tempting counterfeits. She writes that reason is "the simple power of improvement; or, more properly speaking, of discerning truth" (*Vindication*, 53). But even if one can see the good, one might not be able to do the good. So, second, reason is essential to acting freely, which is required for a life of virtue. A free action is, minimally, an action that is not coerced or caused by forces outside or even within oneself. To act on the basis of reason is to act freely instead of being a slave to passion, desire, or emotion. Wollstonecraft writes that virtue arises from "the clear conviction of reason" so that "morality is made to rest on a rock against which the storms of passion vainly beat" (*Vindication*, 114).

On the centrality of rationality to morality Wollstonecraft is not much different from many of her male predecessors:

> In what does man's pre-eminence over the brute creation consist? The answer is as clear as that a half is less than the whole; in Reason.
>
> What acquirement exalts one being above another? Virtue; we spontaneously reply.
>
> For what purpose were the passions implanted? That man by struggling with them might attain a degree of knowledge denied to the brutes; whispers Experience.
>
> Consequently the perfection of our nature and capability of happiness, must be estimated by the degree of reason, virtue, and knowledge, that distinguish the individual, and direct the laws which bind society: and that from the exercise of reason, knowledge and virtue naturally flow. (*Vindication*, 12)

Where she profoundly differs from her male predecessors is in her insistence that women and men are equally equipped with reason. She rejects the dichotomy between the impoverished, animal existence that was believed attainable by women and the exalted, godlike existence that was believed attainable by men. There is a single notion of the morally good person, and both men and women are fully equipped by reason to attain it. They are, therefore, equally capable of moral excellence.

Wollstonecraft criticizes the belief that the difference in nature between men and women requires different moral standards for men and women. She writes: "To account for, and excuse the tyranny of man, many ingenious arguments have been brought forward to prove, that the two sexes, in the acquirement of virtue, ought to aim at attaining a very different character: or, to speak explicitly, women are not allowed to have sufficient strength of mind to acquire what really deserves the name virtue" (*Vindication*, 19). Given women's perceived lack of reason—their inability to see and choose the good—they require blind obedience to men (of reason) to guide them. Men should use their superior wisdom to pursue virtue, while women, lacking reason, should cultivate submissive obedience (*Vindication*, 25). Throughout her book, Wollstonecraft notes the many degrading ways women have been conceived of as different from men: women are irrational, dependent, triflers, soft, obedient, polite, weak, docile, morally immature, gentle, sentimental, submissive, and fond of clothing. These misconceptions and prejudices serve to reinforce the notion that women are by nature suited to subservience.

If women are deficient in reason (the foundation of virtue), they can only attain a modicum of the virtue (and, therefore, fulfillment) that men can attain. Men can tap the power of their reason to attain the happiness reserved for the life of virtue; women, if they are lucky, can tap the power of their beauty to attain the impoverished happiness reserved for women. When she becomes beautiful, refined, sweet, and weak, she can use her "sweet attractive grace" to present herself for conquest by and subordination to men. Since she is naturally docile and submissive, she is naturally suited to a life of subservience to men. Men, in full possession of reason and strength, can conquer their emotions and desires, thereby attaining to both moral excellence and full human fulfillment. And they can reflect their light of reason onto their women who depend on them for direction.

Wollstonecraft's immediate target is Jean-Jacques Rousseau, who contends that women should be attractive rather than virtuous.[13] He even states that for women, although not for men, the appearance of virtue is more important than the reality. So the goal of the education of women, according to Rousseau is "to render them pleasing" (*Vindication*, 27). Given their deficiencies and proclivities, a woman should strive to become sexually alluring ("render(ed) . . . insignificant objects of desire" [*Vindication*, 10–11]). Rousseau's view of women, Woll-

---

13. Rousseau's *Emile* (1762) is a classic text on the moral education of children (that is, boys). For Rousseau, moral education involves the cultivation of intellect and independence. At the end of the essay, he considers the proper education for Sophie, who is to become Emile's wife. Wollstonecraft's essay is a sustained critique of Rousseau's views on the moral education of girls. One might think that the moral education of children is a curious topic for Rousseau, who deposited his five infant children, against the protests of his mistress, their mother, in an orphanage that had a mortality rate of over 75 percent. Jean-Jacques Rousseau, *Emile*, trans. Alan Bloom (New York: Basic Books, 1979).

stonecraft devastatingly argues, is contradictory. Curiously, Rousseau believes that men and women are equally rational. However, if women are allowed to develop their rationality, they will not serve men properly. So women should be trained not to think for themselves, not to take initiative, not to lead, etc. But conceding that women are rational entails that women can (and should) become virtuous. Since Rousseau takes rationality (and autonomy) as the foundation of virtue, he cannot consistently maintain that women are rational but should not seek to attain virtue.

Wollstonecraft resoundingly calls women to recognize the degradation and humiliation that results from their education in the "female" virtues: "women are . . . degraded by mistaken notions of female excellence" (*Vindication*, 11). Education becomes a "system of slavery" through which men inculcate inferiority in women who, in turn, internalize submissiveness. Education, not women's nature, has dehumanized women: ". . . men have increased that inferiority till women are almost sunk below the standard of rational creatures" (*Vindication*, 35). Release them from the oppressive strictures of education in beauty and manners, which only serve to reinforce prejudice and produce submissiveness, and see how they exercise reason and attain to virtue: "Liberty is the mother of virtue" (*Vindication*, 37). Wollstonecraft endorsed Rousseau's basic philosophy of moral education, which is similar in some ways to Plato's and Aristotle's: "Consequently, the most perfect education . . . is such an exercise of the understanding as is best calculated to strengthen the body and form the heart. Or, in other words, to enable the individual to attain such habits of virtue as will render it independent" (*Vindication*, 21). "This was Rousseau's opinion respecting men," she writes, "I extend it to women . . ." (*Vindication*, 21). She simply claims that women ought to be permitted equal access to the same training in character. Although Wollstonecraft concedes that men are superior in strength to women, she contends that this is irrelevant to the pursuit of virtue, which requires not muscles but reason. Since men and women are alike with respect to reason, they share a common goal of acquiring virtue. She writes:

> But I still insist, that not only the virtue, but the *knowledge* of the two sexes should be the same in nature, . . . and that women, considered not only as moral, but rational creatures, ought to endeavour to acquire human virtues (or perfection) by the *same* means as men, instead of being educated like a fanciful kind of *half* being—one of Rousseau's wild chimeras. (*Vindication*, 39)

Through proper education, women will cease being the slaves of men and become their friends, which is only possible between equals.

Wollstonecraft grounds her belief in the equal possession of rationality between men and women in her view of God. Human beings, created in God's image, are equipped with reason, "the tie that connects the creature with the

Creator" (*Vindication*, 53). The Creator endowed men and women alike with souls, the seat of reason, which stand in need of moral perfecting. The improvement of the soul can be accomplished only by the power of reason: "Yet it should seem, allowing them to have souls, that there is but one way appointed by Providence to lead *mankind* to either virtue or happiness" (*Vindication*, 19). Possession of a soul also outfits men and women for immortality. A good God would not hinder half of the human race in their pursuit of the moral perfection which is required for immortality. She writes: "If woman be allowed to have an immortal soul, she must have, as the employment of life, an understanding to improve" (*Vindication*, 63). By infusing human beings with souls, God as a good Creator shares the very nature of God—intellect and immortality—with all those who are created in God's image. Immortality is the goal, moral perfection is the means to that goal, and reason is the precondition of moral perfection.

There's a great deal that we've left out of our discussion of Wollstonecraft. We've omitted, for example, her belief that the ethical life should unite both feeling and reason. We've neglected her claim that because of the differences between men and women, "women . . . may have different duties to fulfil" (*Vindication*, 51). And we haven't considered her paradoxical theoretical rejection of marriage coupled with her decision to marry. We've focused instead on her moral theory as it relates to the grand theme of this book: the relationship of human nature to human morality (and, subsequently, to human fulfillment). Wollstonecraft has as clear a discussion of this important issue as any thinker we've discussed so far. But she is keenly aware that the thinkers we've discussed so far downgrade women's nature and restrict their access to modes of moral and intellectual development. They thereby use their power to preclude the flourishing of women.

Suppose these traditional thinkers are right about both women and men. Women are by nature incapable of significant moral development and are by nature suited to submissive obedience to men. Men, by contrast, are fully capable (because fully rational) of moral excellence and are by nature suited to rule. If these assumptions about human nature are correct, then society should be organized in ways that allow women to flourish as women and men to flourish as men: women should stay in the home in docile servitude to men and men should move out into society to conquer and rule. And each should be apportioned the happiness their natures allow. If women are by nature suited to submit while men are suited to dominate, then a culture that restricts women to servitude and encourages men to lead women has done nothing wrong. Similar arguments have been used to justify the oppression of entire classes of people who are considered by nature suited to serve. Slavery, for example, was justified by claiming that a race of people, lacking rationality, was suited to and therefore would find fulfillment in forced servitude.

Wollstonecraft demonstrates the powerful practical consequences of moral theories and the views of human persons that moral theories assume. Her solution is to extend reason and rights to all people, not just to privileged and powerful males. What she says about women, in the following, should be applied to all human beings:

> Reason and experience convince me that that only method of leading women to fulfil their peculiar duties, is to free them from all restraint by allowing them to participate in the inherent rights of mankind. Make them free, and they will quickly become wise and virtuous." (*Vindication*, 175)

Although Wollstonecraft's ideas were largely ignored (by men, the handlers of ideas) for over a century, her arguments in favor of the dignity of half of the human race demand consideration. She reminds us that prejudicial views of persons can, under the guise of virtue, be used by those in power to reinforce and perpetuate injustice.[14]

Conclusion

While they were critical of traditional authorities, thinkers in the early modern period sought to buttress the traditional virtues with a variety of rational means. Hobbes set himself the tough project of grounding the life of virtue in self-interest. His Leviathan has the power both to create morality and to compel obedience. It is in our self-interest to obey him, since in so doing we enjoy peace, our deepest desire. Hume argued that good and bad are not quasi-physical properties in objects outside of us but, rather, sentiments within the human breast. With his sentimentalist moral theory, he attempts to ground morality in what he believes to be an "objective and invariant" human nature. And Kant founded morality in rationality. Rational consideration of duty would show us the universal character of the moral law and the respect we owe to all rational creatures.

The view of the life of virtue that these thinkers sought to buttress was not unlike the one discussed by the medieval thinkers. If Hobbes did not think us capable of good will, he nonetheless thought us capable of willing good things for others (even if, ultimately, for our own sakes). And Hume defended the sentiment of benevolence as the foundation of the moral life. Kant claimed that morality requires us to treat persons as ends in themselves and he argued for the rational necessity of belief in God. And, although her work was radical in its application to women, Wollstonecraft, like the others, adopted a fairly traditional view of morality. Unlike these early modern thinkers, some moral philosophers of the 19th and 20th centuries will no longer feel constrained by the Christian tradition and its other-regarding morality; they will strike out on their own to create radically new moral theories, radically new views of human nature, morality, and fulfillment.

---

14. We are grateful for the helpful suggestions of Ruth Groenhout and Simona Goi for this section.

Suggested Readings

F. A. McNEILLY, *The Anatomy of Leviathan* (New York: St. Martin's Press, 1968).

JONATHAN HARRISON, *Hume's Moral Epistemology* (Oxford: Clarendon Press, 1976).

JOHN HARE, *The Moral Gap* (New York: Oxford University Press, 1996).

J. B. SCHNEEWIND (ed.), *Moral Philosophy from Montaigne to Kant* (New York: Cambridge University Press, 1990).

ROGER J. SULLIVAN, *An Introduction to Kant's Ethics* (New York: Cambridge University Press, 1994).

4

The Late
Modern World

Introduction

The late modern world (roughly the 19th century) has been characterized as the century of progress. In politics, democracies replaced decaying monarchies. In chemistry, the basic elements of the physical world were charted and exploited. In geology, the power of elemental change over vast periods of time was discovered. In technology, steam engines traveled the world and revolutionized factory work, ushering in the Industrial Revolution. Farmers moved into cities and cities boomed. Everything was progressing rapidly, perhaps too rapidly for human beings to cope with the changes. With progress, there was also decline: working conditions deteriorated, children were exploited, pollution and poverty spread.

God was pushed even further out of the picture than he had been in the early modern period. As science progressed, the need for God diminished. Natural processes were considered sufficient to account for the governing of the physical world; God was needed less and less to explain otherwise inexplicable natural phenomena. The last holdouts—the need for God to explain the orderly design of the biological world and the unique nature of human beings—fell to Darwin's attack. His theory of natural selection was a theory of progress that required no appeal to a supernatural designer. God became an unnecessary commodity.

As belief in God declined among intellectuals and as new social forces required new moral insights, radically new theories of morality developed. In this chapter, we will consider the moral theories of Karl Marx, John Stuart Mill, Sören Kierkegaard, and Friedrich Nietzsche. As background to these thinkers, we will consider the influence of Hegel as well as the shift from supernaturalistic worldviews to more naturalistic or materialistic worldviews. Before discussing Nietzsche's views, we will briefly examine Darwin's theory of the origin of species, a theory that makes human beings more animal-like than godlike.

Hegelianism and Materialism

The history of the world is none other than the progress of the consciousness of freedom.

The views of Georg Wilhelm Friedrich Hegel (1770–1831) are monumental and difficult. We will look only briefly at the way one element of his thought influenced the development of moral philosophy, especially the views of Marx. The central Hegelian theme for our purposes is his contention that history has a purpose or a meaning. History is, Hegel contends, the rational outworking of mind or spirit. The rational process through which mind moves is *dialectical*: consisting in thesis, antithesis, and synthesis. Throughout history, there are many ideologies which are dominant—*Thesis*. Since these ideologies are typically partial and one-sided, they are often opposed by other (partial and one-sided) ideas—*Antithesis*. What often results is a new idea that combines the virtues and eliminates the vices of the two opposing ideas—*Synthesis*. The resulting synthesis is an improvement on the original and polarized ideas. The dialectic is a process of rational progress usually toward freedom. This new synthesis becomes a thesis that will eventually be opposed by a new idea (antithesis), which will issue forth a new synthesis. And the process goes on until mind is completely free.

Consider the following example. Take an Oriental despotic society in which only the emperor is free (thesis) and the democratic Greek city-state (antithesis); their (literal) clash (Persia v. Greek city-states) resulted in the free individualism of the Greeks (synthesis). But the Greek version of freedom (thesis) relied heavily on slave labor; so, the stage is set for a new antithesis. Similarly, Hegel thought that the guiding ideas of Greek and Roman civilizations (thesis) were opposed by Christian belief (antithesis), which resulted in the Reformation (synthesis). The crucial point, for our purposes, is that, according to Hegel, history is rationally progressing toward increasing freedom.

Although Hegel's views are idealist (ultimate reality is mind or spirit), there is an increasing tendency among 19th-century philosophers toward materialism. Ludwig Feuerbach (1804–1872) was deeply influenced by Hegel, yet became a sharp critic of Hegel's antimaterialistic views. Feuerbach developed a *materialist philosophy* of religion based on the assumption that all that exists is matter and its various manifestations.

Believing religion to be "illusionistic," Feuerbach reduced theology to anthropology: in studying religion, we learn about human beings, not about some transcendent reality. Humans, he believed, created God in their own image as a projection of human ideals. Compared to this ideal invention, human beings are lowly and wicked. Therefore, the invention of God alienates human beings from their true nature. If we could overcome religion, Feuerbach argued, we would overcome our alienation.

Feuerbach also grounded morality on physiological and anthropological observations rather than on religious or philosophical reflections regarding the spiritual essence of human beings. What makes us distinctively human is not our being image-bearers of the divine, but our desire for community with other human beings. We are essentially social and physical, not spiritual, beings.

Karl Marx innovatively unites elements of Hegel's and Feuerbach's views in his *historical materialism*. He embraces Hegel's view that history is goal-oriented while endorsing Feuerbach's materialistic worldview and his critique of religion as an illusion. He believed human beings are by nature communal rather than individualistic.

Karl Marx

The history of all hitherto existing society is the history of class struggles.

Karl Marx (1818–1883) was born in Prussia, an ethnic Jew who was raised as a Christian. He soon abandoned all religious beliefs, making atheism a foundation of his philosophy. His philosophical studies brought him into contact with the views of Hegel and Feuerbach. He rejected the spiritual and idealistic views of Hegel for the more human-oriented philosophy of Feuerbach. However, he never shook Hegel's contention that history is dialectical and goal-oriented.

Because of his radical political writings and activities, Marx was forced out of Prussia, and then Paris, and then Brussels. He settled in London in 1849, where he remained until his death. Along the way, he was befriended by Friedrich Engels, with whom he collaborated on many writings. Engels financially supported Marx, ironically with profits from his company in Manchester. In spite of Engels's assistance, Marx spent many years in near poverty, totally devoted to his writings. In this section, we will examine Marx's views primarily from *The Communist Manifesto* (1848),[1] which has had an extraordinary influence on the politics of the world. Marx is included in a book on the history of ethics not primarily for his political views but for his views on human nature and human fulfillment.

Marx inherits and merges the historical, dialectical views of Hegel with the materialistic views of Feuerbach. He believes that history is ordered and is moving toward a goal. He does not believe, however, that history is guided by mind or spirit (or God); rather, history is the successive process of weak and impoverished classes of people (antithesis) struggling against powerful classes of people (thesis). He writes: "The history of all hitherto existing society is the history of class struggles" (*Manifesto*, 17). According to Marx, the goal of history is a classless society in

---

[1.] Karl Marx and Friedrich Engels, *The Communist Manifesto* (New York: Bantam Books, 1992). This is a summary of Marx's early views; hereafter cited in the text as *Manifesto*. Marx's views become more nuanced and his critique of capitalism more trenchant over the years.

which there is no longer any domination of classes of people by other classes of people. When there is no oppression, there is no antithesis and, therefore, no need for further synthesis.

Marx's philosophy is, in part, a reaction to the individualism assumed by social contract theories. He believed that society is not simply a collection of individuals; it is an *organic community* within which human beings find mutual fulfillment. Since a society is like a body of interconnected parts (i.e., organic), individuals can meaningfully sacrifice their good for the greater good of society. Society, properly ordered, is not an obstacle to the satisfaction of human desire; it is, rather, necessary for complete human fulfillment. Society can hinder human fulfillment, however, if it is not properly ordered. Marx believed, for example, that the social contract, with its assumption of a natural right to property, serves to protect the interests of the bourgeoisie (the rich, capitalist, property-owning, and monopolizing class) and neglects the legitimate rights of the proletariat (the poor, property-less, and powerless class). He believed that human beings cannot find fulfillment in such a society.[2] Indeed, it is only in the final synthesis of history that human beings can find genuine fulfillment.

Marx's starting point is the 19th-century working conditions of laborers. During the Industrial Revolution, workers often were exploited with menial labor, low wages, and long hours. Children often worked 15 to 18 hours per day and were given just enough food to sustain their existence so that they could continue working. Workers were treated as a commodity. And, according to the law of supply and demand, lots of easily replaced workers (i.e., economically unvaluable people) could be paid little. Marx writes: "These laborers, who must sell themselves piecemeal, are a commodity, like every other article of commerce, and are consequently exposed to all the vicissitudes of competition, to all the fluctuations of the market" (*Manifesto,* 25).

Marx vividly describes the oppression of the proletariat by the bourgeoisie:

> The bourgeoisie, wherever it has got the upper hand, has put an end to all feudal, patriarchal, idyllic relations. It has pitilessly torn asunder the motley feudal ties that bound man to his "natural superiors," and has left remaining no other nexus between man and man than naked self-interest, than callous "cash payment." It has drowned the most heavenly ecstasies of religious fervor, of chivalrous enthusiasm, of philistine sentimentalism, in the icy water of egotistical calculation. It has resolved personal worth into exchange value, and in place of the numberless indefeasible chartered freedoms, has set up that single, unconscionable freedom—Free Trade. In one word, for exploitation, veiled by religious and political illusions, it has substituted naked, shameless, direct, brutal exploitation. (*Manifesto,* 20)

---

[2] Marx's discussion of capitalism is not entirely negative; for Marx, capitalism is a step forward from medieval feudalism.

Marx maintained that human worth is diminished when calculated by the dollar value of one's work. Human beings become the tools of the bourgeoisie. People use these economic relations to value people, and hence, to order and control society: "Capital is therefore not only personal; it is a social power" (*Manifesto,* 35).

Marx believes that exploitative working conditions militate against both our sense of self-worth and meaningful human relationships. He believes that human beings find fulfillment and happiness through the free, productive exercise of their natural powers in cooperation with one another. In a properly ordered society, we put a little bit of our self into each of our products; our products express our nature. Creative, honest work is essential to human fulfillment. Marx argues that instead of building a community that permits satisfaction of our social and productive nature, the modern capitalist society alienates human beings. Because of dehumanizing labor, workers are alienated from the objects they produce, from other human beings, and from their very selves.

Marx is especially critical of factory work as alienating workers from the products of their labor. He says that in factory work there is neither free nor creative self-expression; workers must work, tediously and repetitiously, according to the whims of often domineering owners, just to survive. Assembly line work is dehumanizing and elevates the machine above the worker (the machine is more economically valuable): "Owing to the extensive use of machinery and to the division of labour, the work of the proletarians has lost all individual character, and consequently, all charm for the workman. He becomes an appendage of the machine, and it is only the most simple, most monotonous, and most easily acquired knack, that is required of him" (*Manifesto,* 25–26). Doing the same thing, over and over again, under the threat of starvation, cannot satisfy human nature. Marx believed that the product of one's labor, reflecting one's nature, ought not be forcibly snatched by the capitalist factory owner and sold for a pittance. All such conditions alienate human beings from the products of their labor.

Such conditions also alienate human beings from other human beings. This is clear in the breach between the proletariat and the bourgeoisie. Additionally, when one must work mind-numbingly hard for 18 hours per day, is allowed to sleep briefly, only to return to work, seven days per week, 52 tedious weeks per year (and all this merely to survive), husbands are alienated from wives, children from their parents, and friends from friends. Coworkers are even alienated from each other because they are forced to compete with one another to survive.

Finally, human beings are cut off from their own selves. Much of the workers' activities are designed to frustrate their most fundamental needs. Their human nature, to be free and socially productive, is repressed as they are reduced to the level of animals or even automata. Since they cannot find fulfillment through their work, they must seek it outside of their job. But outside of their job there is time only for sleeping, eating, and procreating. They are self-estranged—little more than laboring, eating, and sleeping beasts.

Marx maintains that the capitalist system is irrational as a means of meeting human needs. Except for the bourgeoisie, humans are denied satisfaction at their most fundamental levels. A better social order is required for human fulfillment. The society to which Marx aspires (and toward which he believes history is invariably yet slowly moving) is organized to avoid alienation. It is outlined in the paragraphs that follow.

First, private property will be eliminated: "The theory of the Communists may be summed up in a single sentence: Abolition of private property" (*Manifesto,* 34). Land, factories, stores, capital, and even people are treated as property in the capitalist system. Marx thinks that in order to treat persons as persons and not as commodities, the entire social system that relegates them to the status of the monetary worth must be removed. In the communist society to which Marx aspires, workers are no longer treated as chattel and valued in dollars.

Second, the system of production for profit will be replaced by intrinsically rewarding labor for the satisfaction of communal needs. When work is no longer done for profit, Marx believed, it can be done for the common good. He endorses the famous utopian phrase: "From each according to his ability to each according to his need." Marx also believed that the abolition of the profit system would produce work that was not monotonous, relentless, tedious, and lacking charm. He believed work would be the intrinsically rewarding, creative expression of the worker. In such a society, Marx claimed, there would be no oppression of any class of people by any other class of people. This would diminish violence created by such oppression. This leads to the third part of the plan.

Third, the need for a state to maintain private property and to protect people from other people will disappear. Marx writes: "When, in the course of development, class distinctions have disappeared, and all production has been concentrated in the hands of a vast association of the whole nation, the public power will lose its political character. Political power, properly so called, is merely the organized power of one class for oppressing another" (*Manifesto,* 43). A strong government will not be needed to keep people in check.

Marx has a highly optimistic view of human nature: when freed from the influences of a wicked and oppressive social structure, people will freely work for the common good. Human nature, it seems, is perfectible. The end of history is nothing less than a social utopia: a classless society of mutually fulfilled people who freely order their activities toward the common good.

The fall of communism has rightly sparked new and renewed criticism of Marxism; it is all too evident, for example, that the communist system itself is horribly oppressive, relying on a naive and even dangerous optimism regarding the perfectability of human nature. Still, Marx's views provide a valuable critique of the excesses of capitalism and its individualism. Apart from a proper moral framework, capitalism promotes selfishness, greed, envy, materialism, all things that greatly degrade the human person. Left unchecked, individualism erodes the forms of community that may be necessary for human flourishing. If Marx is cor-

tions, would not maximize happiness for everyone involved even if it makes the liar and some others happier. The meager happiness that lying occasionally affords is not sufficient to constitute what Mill calls utility "in the largest sense." And so, for the utilitarian, lying will seldom be justified.

But aren't there times when it is clearly right to lie? At times, it looks like we must abandon the rules and apply the principle of utility directly to an action. Consider a second example: you are a utilitarian who determines that everyone ought to tell the truth and to do as much as they can to preserve human life. Now suppose that you are in the following position: you live in Holland during World War II and are harboring Jews in your home. Two Nazi SS officers knock at the door and ask you if you are concealing Jews in your home. Which principle should you honor: truth-telling or life-preservation? Mill argues that you should invoke utility to settle incompatible demands. In this case you ask yourself: "Which action will maximize happiness and minimize unhappiness?" Presumably, utility, when applied to this particular case, will be maximized by lying. In this case, utility will determine that, in this nontrivial instance, the principle of truth-telling ought to be subordinated to the principle of preserving human life. The principle of utility provides an umpire between conflicting duties that no other moral theory has.

In the preceding paragraph, what trumped the general guidelines, in this particular situation, was the fundamental principle of utility. We go into each situation armed with secondary principles, gleaned from past experience, about what, generally, will maximize human happiness. Should these secondary moral principles conflict, the primary moral principle of utility will settle the conflict.

In his final chapter of *Utilitarianism*, Mill addresses an apparent conflict between utility and justice. It appears that the principle of utility can be used to justify various forms of injustice. Suppose, for example, that it could be determined that the pain suffered by slaves was outweighed by the happiness that they created for everyone else involved. Further suppose the net amount of happiness involved in a system involving slavery is greater than the net amount of happiness that would result if the slaves were freed. If so, utilitarianism would endorse a principle that conflicts with our moral intuitions about justice. Surely it is clear that no one ought to own another human being, even if it maximizes happiness and minimize unhappiness. Utility conflicts with justice.

Mill understood the force of this argument and saw fit to respond. He claimed that, although we may *feel* that justice is something different from utility, justice is nonetheless derived from or based on utility. Mill analyzes typical notions of justice and injustice to see if they share any common traits. He examines the justice of protecting people's rights, giving each what he deserves, keeping faith, and being impartial. He also considers the injustice of violating people's rights, not giving people their due, breaking faith, and showing preference to one person over another. Is there a common link that ties all of these ideas concerning justice together? They are rooted in social utility, that is, they promote the interests of everyone. Mill believes that justice is grounded in the principle of utility as one of the highest moral principles; he writes, "It appears from what has been said that justice is a name for certain moral requirements which, regarded collectively, stand higher in the scale of social utility, and are therefore of more paramount obligation, than any others . . ." (*Utilitarianism*, 62). And, Mill observes, the obligations of justice are guarded, fortunately, by strong moral feelings. Mill is confident that when the assessments are actually made, utilitarianism will not justify various injustices like slavery. It will turn out that, however it may first appear, more unhappiness than happiness comes of such things.

But what if it does not turn out this way? Utilitarianism can be used to produce deeply revisionist moralities. While it would be difficult to make the case that more happiness than unhappiness would result if we allowed murder, say, and stealing, it might not be as difficult to argue the case for allowing gambling, prostitution, adultery, homosexuality, and infanticide. While Mill believed his moral theory was not opposed to traditional (often religious) values, utilitarianism has been used to permit or even require deviation from traditional duties. It has been used, for example, to defend such things as abortion and active euthanasia and to allow famine victims to starve to death. Such practices have been condemned by traditional moral thinkers, regardless of their net effect on the happiness of everyone as a whole. While Mill himself may have been opposed to them, it is important to be aware of the deeply revisionist tendencies within the theory of utilitarianism.

The principle of utility is such that it allows the happiness of one person to outweigh the happiness of another person. That second person is (and the rest of us are) supposed to be content with this because the happiness of society as a whole makes up for his own unhappiness. But there seems to be something wrong with this. Utilitarianism treats persons as merely parts of a whole, not as wholes in themselves. It fails to account for the dignity of the individual.

Part of the genius of utilitarianism is that it makes morality good for human beings. The ultimate goal of morality, according to utilitarianism, is human well-being, the greatest happiness for the greatest number. In contrast, some views of morality seem severe—they endorse actions as right and good regardless of the consequences. Morality on these views sometimes seems arbitrary, harsh, and opposed to the deepest satisfaction of human desire. Mill grounds morality in human psychology, in our innate desire for pleasure or happiness, and sees morality as an instrument for human fulfillment.

It is clear that we desire our own happiness, but what about the happiness of others? That is, what could motivate self-interested people to take account of the interests of others? Mill contends that we have feelings of duty to and unity with our fellow creatures that direct us toward the benefit of others; we have a natural affection for our fellow creatures (*Utilitarianism*, Ch. III). Mill believed that we can increase this natural affection through proper education and by removing inequalities between individuals and classes so that we identify with all other human beings. Mill himself fought for the liberation of women, the decent treatment of laborers, and the abolition of slavery. If these other-regarding sentiments are strong enough, we will find personal satisfaction in seeking the welfare of others. We are, Mill believes, happiness-seekers and we find our deepest desires fulfilled in a community of people who seek the greatest happiness for the greatest number.

Kierkegaard

The thing is to understand myself, to see what God really wishes me to do; the thing is to find a truth which is true for me, *to find* the idea for which I can live and die.

Sören Kierkegaard (1813–1855) stands in stark contrast to the nontheistic writers of this period. He considered his task as a philosopher to discover what it means to be a Christian. He lived in Denmark, where the state-sponsored church had reduced Christianity to adherence to external formalities all the while ignoring inward transformation. He revolted against the Enlightenment tyranny of reason, which he thought constrained our ability to freely make significant choices. He thought our most significant choices were criterionless (not dictated by reason), the result of passionate and individual commitments.

Kierkegaard was adamantly opposed to the abstract theorizing of the philosophy of his day, especially the views of Hegel. He thought that philosophy had removed itself from ordinary life. He thought philosophy should be intensely personal reflection on matters of fundamental human concern; he believed that whatever one is committed to must make a difference in one's life. His unique contribution to ethics is his understanding of how one becomes an authentic person, his understanding of the process of deep human satisfaction. His discussion of this process, carried through in a variety of his writings, is often referred to as "the stages on life's way."[7]

The first stage on life's way is *the aesthetic stage*. At this stage, one is committed to the satisfaction of one's own desires, to saturation with sense experience. Hedonism (taking one's own pleasure as a guide to the good life) is probably the best modern term for this stage. The aesthete often acts without constraints and without consideration for the future; she lives in and for the moment and fills her present experience with as much sensation as possible. If she does forgo a present pleasure, it is only for some future pleasure she believes to be greater. She may know the difference between right and wrong, but she does not act accordingly. She may pursue sex, drugs, and rock and roll; or she may more moderately consume

---

[7.] We are primarily drawing from Sören Kierkegaard, *The Journals of Sören Kierkegaard,* ed. and trans. Alexander Dru (London: Oxford University Press, 1938); *Either/Or,* trans. David F. and Lillian Marvin Swenson (Princeton, NJ: Princeton University Press, 1944), I; Sören Kierkegaard, *Journals and Papers,* ed. Howard and Edna Hong (Bloomington: Indiana University Press, 1967); *Stages on Life's Way,* trans. Walter Lowrie (New York: Shocken Books, 1967); and *Fear and Trembling* and *The Sickness unto Death,* trans. Walter Lowrie (Princeton, NJ: Princeton University Press, 1970).

gourmet food, fine wine, and high art. The devotion in either case is to the self and to the satisfaction of one's own desires.

The pursuit of the sensual, however, is rooted in dread and emptiness. The aesthete is driven by desire but, when gratified, only desires more; she is filled with hungers that cannot be satisfied. The emptiness and meaninglessness of her life eventually drive her to melancholy: "Wine no longer makes my heart glad; a little of it makes me sad, much makes me melancholy. My soul is faint and impotent; in vain I prick the spur of pleasure into its flank, its strength is gone, it rises no more to the royal leap. I have lost my illusions. Vainly I seek to plunge myself into the boundless sea of joy; it cannot sustain me, or rather, I cannot sustain myself."[8]

Pain is the obvious enemy of the aesthetic life and the more subtle enemy is boredom. Because of the threat of boredom, novelty is sought: so the aesthete pursues a variety of pleasures. She may begin, for example, by drinking beer; boredom eventually forces a switch to wine and then fortified wine, then hard liquor, and finally drugs. Or the sexual aesthete starts with a single partner but boredom inevitably forces a move to new and perhaps multiple partners, even perfect strangers, and ever more exotic sources of sexual pleasure. The life of the high-culture aesthete is a virtual blur of meetings with fashion and interior designers, dinner parties, exotic vacations, lectures, gallery shows, concerts, and various gala events.

The aesthete believes herself to be free but in reality she is bound by her desires. She lacks both reflectiveness and free choice. Her self is lost, hidden beneath and chained by her desires and social customs. Consider the college student who with the approval of his friends drinks heavily, sleeps late every day, skips many of his classes, and picks up a different woman at the bar each weekend. He considers himself free. After all, he is not bound by "outdated" moralities, the teachings of the church, campus rules, societal pressures, or the opinions of his parents. But, his freedom is an illusion. He is, in fact, a slave to his desires and to the peer pressure of his friends. He has avoided self-conscious reflection on his life and has failed to attain true freedom. The self has disappeared and become merely part of a crowd of friends. In Kierkegaard's words, he has forgotten what it means to exist.

A contemporary analogy to the aesthetic stage is the addiction to crack cocaine. Crack directly stimulates the pleasure centers of the brain and the feelings are so intense that people can become addicted with a single trial. That first rush of pleasure is so overwhelming that people will do anything to repeat it; they want more. But the second time is never as good as the first time. So they try even more. And that time is not as good as the first time. Eventually they give up, go home to sleep and then, as darkness falls on a new day, attempt to recapture that original high. The first high of the night is the best, but never as good as that initial one, and the cycle, of attempting to recapture that original high, repeats itself. Junkies call the quest for recapturing that first overpowering sensation of pleasure "Chasing the ghost." The junkie will do anything—sell her parent's property, her body, even her own child, to capture that elusive ghost.

[8.] *Either/Or*, I, 33.

The aesthete chases what cannot be attained by pleasure—a fulfilled life. We are more than animals, more than bodies; we cannot attain happiness simply by satisfying our animal desires. Human beings are a unique synthesis of body and soul, finite and infinite, temporal and eternal, necessity and freedom. The aesthete develops only part of her nature. She focuses on the bodily, finite, temporal, and necessary side, alienating herself from the other half of her self. The authentic person, in contrast, engages every part of her nature in a creative synthesis. Humans are not constructed to be satisfied simply by the stimulation of their pleasurable nerve endings; they have a higher calling.

Pain and boredom eventually lead the aesthete to the threshold of despair—the moment in which she realizes the emptiness of her life of pleasure. Despair beckons her to the next stage: the ethical. She may peer into the ethical stage, see the moral constraints that it would place on her life, and then retreat to the aesthetic stage, perhaps with the hope that some new source of pleasure will arise that will satisfy her soul. Or, she may seek satisfaction by watching more television or drinking more beer, thereby drugging herself once again into the sleep necessary for her life. Or she may, out of despair, take a leap of faith into the ethical stage.

If there is any single lesson to be learned from Kierkegaard it is that life should not be lived neutrally—it must be embraced with passion. Passion enables one to live decisively in the present; but the passionate person does not settle for the present; she takes responsibility for her choices and does her best to transform reality into the ideal. Passion cuts through the fog of the aesthete and helps her to see life clearly. Passion for life brings with it consideration of the ethical—the way things ought to be. It moves one from the aesthetic stage into the ethical stage.

The ethical stage is entered into and sustained by self-conscious choice. In the act of deliberately choosing, the ethical person sets herself apart from the crowd and begins the process of becoming an individual, a self. In this stage, one accepts responsibility for one's self. Although one's self has been fashioned in part by one's environment, instincts, inclinations, desires, and so on, the ethical person assumes responsibility for that self, self-consciously choosing not to be completely determined by these social and physical conditions. She is free to fashion herself according to the ethical principles that she has recognized. Freedom from necessity of desire, habit, and social custom opens up the self to possibility—to what one ought to be.

The ethical person is marked more by what she is becoming than by what she is. In the aesthetic stage, one revels in what one is—selfish, pleasure-seeking, uncommitted. In the ethical stage, the ideal beckons one beyond what one is to the way one ought to be. Goodness has an attractive quality that moves the ethical person from selfishness to duty.

The ethical stage is the sphere of duty, of universal rules, which are expressed in one's work and in relation to others. Creative work and self-sacrificial relationships lift one above desire and custom into the meaningful world of the universally human; it is here that the self begins to find itself. The self is revealed to others and so to itself in uplifting work and in relations like those of marriage and friendship. Human creativity and love were made to find satisfaction in beings and things beyond the self; exclusive devotion to the self subverts the proper satisfaction of our deepest longings.

But what if, try as we might, we cannot heed the call of duty? "The ethical [sphere]," writes Kierkegaard, "is that of requirement, and this requirement is so infinite that the individual always goes bankrupt."[9] The enemy of the ethical stage is guilt. And guilt leads to despair. One may, at this point, draw back into the ethical stage, determined to try even harder to do one's duties. Or, one may take a leap of faith into the next stage, the religious.

The ethical stage is a passageway into *the religious stage*. In *Fear and Trembling*, Kierkegaard describes the transition from the ethical to the religious in the figure of Abraham. In demanding the sacrifice of Abraham's only beloved son, Isaac, God demands something that, from the standpoint of the ethical, is a transgression of duty. Ethics demands that we not kill our (innocent) children. God, by contrast, demands absolute obedience—to leave family, friends, and country for him. From the standpoint of the ethical, what God demands of Abraham is ludicrous. So the religious calls for *the suspension of the ethical*.

Why might someone make a choice that is, from the standpoint of the ethical (and the aesthetic), absurd? No adequate *reason* can be given. Such a choice is criterionless, that is, no rational argument could convince us to make it; it is an act of will, not of reason. Still, it is in only in making such a choice that one can truly find one's self. The religious stage marks the highest personal transformation of the self—the self can only be fully actualized in relationship to God; only then can it become authentic as the fears of death and guilt drop away.

The first step toward the religious stage is the recognition of one's inability to do what is demanded of one. One must move out of the realm of the purely ethical to seek forgiveness; Kierkegaard writes: "An ethics which disregards sin is a perfectly idle science; but if it asserts sin, it is *eo ipso* well beyond itself."[10] Kierkegaard calls this first step *"infinite resignation"*: the self dies to the world, freely confesses itself to be finite, gives up the pretension involved in the construction of the false self and acknowledges the power of the absolute. The second step of faith is the appropriation of forgiveness. Self-renunciation brings one to the place where further progress, humanly speaking, is impossible. But for God all things are possible: what, from a finite, temporal, conditioned perspective, is impossible, is possible with God.

In the religious stage, the disparate paradoxes of one's character are united into a meaningful whole. One can feel secure in one's finitude if one relates to a God who is infinite and ultimately caring. One can accept responsibility for one's social conditioning if one has the power, granted by God, to overcome one's conditioning and to freely carve one's character in terms of one's calling. One can

9.   *Stages on Life's Way*, 430.
10.   *Fear and Trembling*, 108.

avoid paralysis due to one's sinful nature if there is forgiveness. One can affirm one's bodily nature, if it is ruled by one's spirit since the spirit sees to the proper satisfaction of all of one's desires. One can feel unchained from the necessities of time, if the eternal breaks into the temporal and redeems our wasted time and misspent lives. Finite and infinite, necessity and freedom, sinner and saint, body and spirit, temporal and eternal, are all kept in creative tension by faith in God.

The religious person is not an insensible ascetic, forever renouncing the pleasures of this world. The religious person returns to the feast of life but not as a greedy glutton, not as one driven by an insatiable appetite for sex, fame, wealth, or honor; she enjoys such things in the proper way and accepts them as gifts to her self, not as constitutive of her identity or self-worth. As Kierkegaard writes: "It is a great thing to grasp the eternal but it is greater still to hold fast to the temporal after having given it up."[11]

According to Kierkegaard, human beings are both animal-like and godlike. Human fulfillment can only come through a proper relationship to God, who enables us to satisfy both parts of our nature. The aesthete's sole focus on the animal part of human nature ensures despair since it leaves half of the self unfulfilled. The ethical person's focus on duties ensures despair, since human nature is incapable of living up to the ethical life on its own. Only the religious person, by divine grace, can unite both parts of her nature into a meaningful whole. She can affirm both the animal and the divine—the finite and the infinite—in proper relationship with the sensual world, other people, and God. Only through a passionate faith in God can human beings seek and find human fulfillment.

Kierkegaard's emphasis on the inner transformation of the heart and his rejection of the enlightenment view of reason entail that ethical theory is largely impotent to show persons how to live. We cannot lay out our arguments, expecting all rational persons to recognize and choose a certain way of life as the best for human beings. Reason cannot lead us to fulfillment. It is, rather, by a passionate faith that we discover the fulfilling life. Such a faith is not the conclusion of an argument, but an act of will, a will that at the point of personal despair makes a leap into the unknown. As we shall see shortly, Nietzsche also emphasizes the role of will over reason; it is, however, a will that seeks not to love God, but to be god.

Darwinism

We must acknowledge that man with all his noble qualities, with his godlike intellect which has penetrated into the movements and constitution of the solar system—with all these exalted powers—Man still bears in his bodily frame the indelible stamp of his lowly origin.

[11.] *Fear and Trembling*, 33.

Few words on paper have made such a revolutionary impact on human history as Charles Darwin's *The Origin of Species*.[12] As a result of this work virtually every domain of intellectual endeavor required rethinking: biology, psychology, social science, philosophy, and theology (to name a few). We will look very briefly at his work as it prepared the way for whole new views of human nature, morality, and fulfillment.

The central idea of *Origin of Species* is simple: new species arise as a result of random mutations and the competition for scarce resources. New traits arise in individuals randomly. Some of these are helpful to the individuals, some of them are not. Those individuals possessing traits that increase their ability to secure food and protection from the environment are more likely to survive and pass those traits on to their offspring. Those individuals without the helpful traits die off. Eventually, individuals may acquire enough new traits that they constitute a new species. Given ample time, the new species will face new survival pressures and new traits may develop, which in turn gives rise to a new species, and so on. Each time the defective members of a species die off and are replaced by new members that have substantially different characteristics necessary for continued viability, nature has selected a new species.

"Natural selection" is the term that Darwin used to describe this process of the gradual dying off of unfit individuals and their replacement by individuals better suited to their environment and so capable of surviving. Unfavorable traits are selected out and favorable traits are retained in the new species. "*Natural* selection": the term couldn't have been more polemical. Darwin was writing in response to William Paley who, in his argument from design, argued that the biological realm shows such remarkable instances of design that it must be the product of an intelligent designer. Intricate design—such as the humps of camels, the webbed feet of ducks, and the human eye—cannot be explained by chance. According to Paley, *supernatural* selection is required for the creation of species.

Although, as a young man, Darwin was impressed by Paley's argument, his work was intended to be a decisive refutation of the need to postulate a supernatural designer. Random variations plus competition for scarce resources plus time are sufficient to account for the existence of even the most complex species. All living things are related by common descent from preexisting species.

Darwin's work allegedly knocked down the need for God to explain biological diversity. The inexplicable had been explained. God is not required to explain the intricate design we see in the animal kingdom, but what about human beings? Surely God is necessary to explain the crowning glory of creation—homo sapiens. Darwin, in *The Descent of Man*,[13] argues that human beings were created in the image of apes, not in the image of God. We were not created from the dust, God breathing life into our breasts. We evolved from apes, who were not as good

12. Charles Darwin, *The Origin of Species* (New York: Bantam Classic, 1999).
13. Charles Darwin, *The Descent of Man* (Amherst, NY: Prometheus Books, 1997).

at eating and avoiding predators as we are. There is nothing special about human nature—we are the unexpected result of blind mutations, competition, and time, not the preordained plan of a loving God. We are apes without hair, not angels without wings. This is the crucial point: we are animals not gods. We must understand ourselves from below, not from above. Darwin's views paved the way for radically new views of human nature and so, too, for revolutionary views of morality and fulfillment.[14] We turn now to one of the most revolutionary, the work of Friedrich Nietzsche.

Friedrich Nietzsche

Under what conditions did man devise these value judgments good and evil? and what value do they themselves possess? *Have they hitherto hindered or furthered human prosperity? Are they a sign of distress, of impoverishment, of the degeneration of life? Or is there revealed in them, on the contrary, the plenitude, force, and will of life, its courage, certainty, future?*

Friedrich Nietzsche (1844–1900) was the son of a Lutheran pastor. He was educated in classics and, early on, theology. While in university, Nietzsche was deeply influenced by Schopenhauer's powerful antitheistic worldview.[15] Schopenhauer sparked Nietzsche's interest in philosophy and, subsequently, a turning away from theology. The decisive move away from Christianity occurred when Nietzsche read D. F. Strauss's *Life of Jesus,* an attack on the historicity of the New Testament.[16] In 1868, Nietzsche met the composer Richard Wagner, who, with his wife Cosima, influenced Nietzsche's thought. The moral freedom that surrounded the Wagners and their friends ("Wagnerites") further encouraged Nietzsche's movement away from the Lutheranism of his childhood. Nietzsche's work on Greek and Latin poetry attracted him to the heroic virtues in the Homeric tradition and the Roman empire. He admired those cultures that valued strength, domination, and pride rather than the Christian cultures that valued self-sacrifice, devotion, and humility.

Nietzsche's career as professor at Leipzig was damaged by the poor reception of his radical writings. His books were ignored, students were advised to avoid his classes, and his poor health required long stays for recuperation away from the university. Because of his poor health, he eventually left the university, living only on a small pension. His isolation and suffering affected his moral writings. He became

---

[14.] Darwin offered an evolutionary account of the evolution of moral sentiments, but it is beyond the scope of this chapter to consider it.

[15.] Schopenhauer, *The World as Will and Representation* (New York: Dover Publications, 1969).

[16.] D. F. Strauss, *The Life of Jesus* (Mifflintown, PA: Sigler Press, 1994).

increasingly an outsider and critic of human life, traditions, and institutions. In 1889, Nietzsche collapsed and spent the remainder of his life mentally insane.

Nietzsche's major treatise on ethics is *On The Genealogy of Morals*.[17] Nietzsche's argument is based on what he calls the "physico-psychological." Deeply influenced by Darwin's thought, he speculates on human psychology, always keeping in mind the revolutionary thought that humans are not far removed from the animals. As he puts it in another work, "Formerly one sought the feeling of grandeur of man by pointing to his divine *origin*: this has now become a forbidden way, for at its portal stands the ape, together with other gruesome beasts, grinning knowingly as if to say: no further in this direction."[18] He asks such questions as: Why do descendants of animals develop morality and a conscience? Where do Christianity and morality come from? Although we seek to raise ourselves above nature through morality and religion, we are part of nature; we are hairless apes. Nietzsche peers deep inside our human/animal nature to see what will really satisfy our deepest desires.

Nietzsche's moral philosophy begins, first and foremost, with the death of God. His famous parable of the madman describes Western society's progressive movement away from the intellectual necessity of belief in God:

> Have you not heard of that madman who lit a lantern in the bright morning hours, ran to the market place, and cried incessantly, "I seek God! I seek God!" As many of those who do not believe in God were standing around just then, he provoked much laughter. . . . "Whither is God" he cried. "I shall tell you. *We have killed him*—you and I. All of us are his murderers. . . . God is dead. God remains dead. And we have killed him. . . ."
>
> Here the madman fell silent and looked again at his listeners; and they too were silent and stared at him in astonishment. At last he threw his lantern on the ground, and it broke and went out. "I come too early," he said then; "my time has not come yet. This tremendous event is still on its way, still wandering—it has not yet reached the ears of man. . . .
>
> It has been related further that on that same day the madman entered divers churches and there sang his *requiem aeternam deo*. Led out and called to account, he is said to have replied each time, "What are the churches now if they are not the tombs and sepulchers of God?"[19]

Nietzsche does not contend that God at one time existed, got old, and, neglected by his children, died a lonely death. Rather, he accepts the Enlightenment con-

17.   Friedrich Nietzsche, *On the Genealogy of Morals,* trans. Walter Kaufmann (New York: Random House, 1967); hereafter cited in the text as *Genealogy*.
18.   Friedrich Nietzsche, *Daybreak: Thoughts on the Prejudices of Morality,* ed. Maudemarie Clark and Brian Leiter; trans. R. J. Hollingdale (Cambridge: Cambridge University Press, 1997), § 49, p. 47.
19.   From Nietzsche's *The Gay Science* 125 as found in Walter Kaufman, ed. and trans., *The Portable Nietzsche* (New York: Penguin Books, 1968), 95–96.

clusion that there is no longer any reason to believe in God; Western culture no longer needs to ground science, morality, or knowledge in God's existence. Despite this conclusion, Western culture continued to accept the trappings of Judeo-Christian morality without its metaphysical and theological underpinnings. With the foundation of theism dislodged, Nietzsche believed that Judeo-Christian morality would eventually crumble. But Western society was not ready yet to give up Judeo-Christian morality. That time would come.

If there is no God, then the questions above arise: Where do Christianity, morality, and guilt come from? What, if not God, is the source of good and evil? In answering these questions, Nietzsche looks not only at values themselves, but at the value behind the value. What weight, authority, or power do values have? Are they life-affirming or life-denying? Are they destructive of what is most fundamentally human or are they creative and satisfying? His work is a *genealogy* of morals, what he sometimes calls a "history of morals"—how do moralities arise, become approved, and maintain their power? How is the history forgotten when moralities are charged with an allegedly transhistorical or transcendental legitimation and power?

We say "moralities" here because Nietzsche is a relativist of sorts. There is a variety of standards of good and bad, depending on the cultures from which those moralities have arisen. If one can pick and choose from among these competing systems of morality, why not choose a morality that is life-affirming rather than life-denying? Nietzsche believes that there are two basic moralities: Herd and Master Moralities. *Herd or slave morality* is that of the weak, the infirm, and the enslaved. Herd morality arose in the priestly cultures that denied desire and endorsed the weaknesses of the priest. With the antisensualistic priests, Nietzsche writes, "*everything* becomes dangerous" (*Genealogy*, I, §6). What the priests fear and oppose is the master morality of the noble warrior: "The knightly-aristocratic value judgments presupposed a powerful physicality, a flourishing, abundant, even overflowing health, together with that which serves to preserve it: war, adventure, hunting, dancing, war games, and in general all that involves vigorous, free, joyful activity" (*Genealogy*, I, §7). In contrast to herd morality, *master morality* embraces the values of the strong, hearkening back to the Homeric hero.

Nietzsche argues that herd morality develops out of fear and hatred of the master class. The impotent, unable to conquer their more worthy and physically powerful foes, sought "spiritual revenge." They make everything that is opposed to the master class "good," and they align God—who will punish everyone who violates their moral standards—with their cause. The idea of eternal damnation, the ultimate revenge, shows that Judeo-Christian morality is rooted not in love but in hatred and vengefulness. Christian morality, Nietzsche writes, is grounded in "the vengeful cunning of impotence" in which the weak judge themselves good in comparison to the evil (those who wield power over them) (*Genealogy*, I, §13).

Herd morality arises in opposition to the more ancient and natural (i.e., animal) master morality. It is essentially derivative and dependent on the masters and their morality; that is, it consists of a Nay-saying to the abundant, exuberant, courageous, and noble life of the master class. The weak class, resenting their masters, create a system of morality that embraces and sanctifies the values of the weak. Members of the weak class desire the goods possessed by the master class but are impotent to obtain them. In their envy, they determine to create values that prevent the masters from enjoying what the weak cannot, on their own, possess. There is a "slave revolt" against the master class that

> begins when *ressentiment* [resentment] itself becomes creative and gives birth to values: the *ressentiment* of natures that are denied the true reaction, that of deeds, and compensate themselves with an imaginary revenge. While every noble morality develops from a triumphant affirmation of itself, slave morality from the outset says No to what is "outside," what is "different," what is "not itself"; and this No is its creative deed. (*Genealogy*, I, §10)

Herd morality is essentially negative and reactive, finding definition in relation to its opposite. Nietzsche calls it resentment, hatred, sickness, and impotence seeking revenge. The noble have their own resentments but they immediately react; the weak, since they cannot act, let their resentments fester only to find expression in subterranean revenge on their enemies.

The herd, the race of people of resentment, not only fashions virtues out of master-vices and vices out of master-virtues, they also create a new kind of vice, moral Evil: ". . . picture 'the enemy' as the man of *ressentiment* conceives him— and here precisely is his deed, his creation: he has conceived 'the evil enemy,' 'the Evil One,' and this in fact is his basic concept, from which he then evolves, as an afterthought and pendant, a 'good one'—himself" (*Genealogy*, I, §10).

What are the values of the weak and how do they arise? "Weakness," Nietzsche writes, "is being lied into something meritorious . . . impotence which does not requite into 'goodness of heart'; anxious lowliness into 'humility'; subjection to those one hates into 'obedience' . . . inability for revenge is called unwillingness to revenge, perhaps even forgiveness" (*Genealogy*, I, §14). The virtues of the weak, by which they legitimate their impotence and gain power over the strong, are humility, patience, forgiveness, kindness, generosity, pity, and justice.

These virtues serve two purposes. First, the weak benefit when the powerful are required to be, say, kind or generous. Second, the weak can feel good about their weakness because they have twisted it into a prized virtue. These values enable the weak, in spite of their frailty, to feel strong and to maintain a secure place in the universe and forever. Justice, for example, protects the weak from the strong: the demands of justice bind the strong and benefit the weak. The weak, who "crave to be hangmen," are motivated by their desire to get back at the strong; they are "the vengeful disguised as judges, who constantly bear the word 'justice' in their mouths like poisonous spittle" (*Genealogy*, III, §14). Generosity, another example, redistributes wealth from the enterprising and creative class to the impoverished class. Behind the veil of virtue hides crass yet impotent self-interest. Calling humility, patience, and forgiveness virtues enables those who are too weak to be proud, active, and vengeful to feel superior to those who are truly strong.

Nietzsche despises herd morality partly because of its dishonesty: the "counterfeit and self-deception of impotence" (*Genealogy*, I, §13). Underneath the garb of virtue lies the same lust for power that animates the master class. In the weak, justice conceals the feeble grasping for their "fair share"; patience is nothing more than simmering resentment; and love cloaks hatred. Nietzsche decries the duplicity involved in enshrining humility and selflessness while secretly desiring power. The value beneath the value, beneath the herd virtues, is the nonmoral quest for domination.

Nietzsche rejects the traditional view that altruism (acting for the good of another) is the highest good. Everything, including morality, is viewed from a perspective. From the perspective of the weak, altruism is good because it protects their interests. From the perspective of the strong, however, altruism hinders the pursuit of their interests; altruism unduly binds them in favor of the weak. Nietzsche supplies the following analogy:

> That lambs dislike great birds of prey does not seem strange: only it gives no ground for reproaching these birds of prey for bearing off little lambs. And if the lambs say among themselves: "these birds of prey are evil; and whoever is least like a bird of prey, but rather its opposite, a lamb—would he not be good?" there is no reason to find fault with this institution of an ideal, except perhaps that the birds of prey might view it a little ironically and say: "we don't dislike them at all, these good little lambs; we even love them: nothing is more tasty than a tender lamb." (*Genealogy*, I, §13)

What is called good depends on whose interests are at stake. From the perspective of the weak, domination is wicked; from the perspective of the strong, however, it is good.

We have a good idea of what morality looks like from the perspective of the weak; it is the whole Judeo-Christian moral tradition. What does morality look like from the perspective of the strong? Master morality says "Yes" to life with its possibilities and limitations. Master morality is genuinely creative. "The noble man . . . conceives of the basic concept 'good' in advance and spontaneously out of himself . . ." (*Genealogy*, I, §11). He affirms humanity's bestial nature. He values power, power over himself, subjecting himself to severity and hardness. He values faith in himself, pride in himself, freedom, and self-glorification. He loathes selflessness and humility. Master morality even requires enemies as outlets for envy, arrogance, and quarrelsomeness.

Herd morality, by contrast, tames the human beast by favoring those qualities that alleviate their suffering and elevate their low position (by bringing down the masters). As we saw, they value justice, pity, sympathy, kindness, faith in God, selflessness, and humility. Herd morality levels all distinctions among human beings by reducing everyone to the level of the weak.

The master class views the social contract—the mutual agreement to refrain from injury, violence, and exploitation—as a denial of life. According to them, life involves appropriation, injury, conquest of the strange and weak, suppression, severity, and exploitation. The social contract, the foundation of Western society, simply protects the weak from the strong and removes human beings from life itself.

Rather than celebrating and enshrining impotence, the master class embraces strength and nobly affirms life. Masters let the *Will to Power* well up inside themselves and overflow into creative action. They are the creators of their own values. Since there is no God, the masters rise up to take the place of God as a source of value, purpose, strength, and faith. They create values *ex nihilo*. "Ye shall be as gods," the primal temptation that snared Adam and Eve, is embraced with enthusiasm.

The final essay of *On The Genealogy of Morals* defends the noble ascetic ideal of rigorous self-discipline, austerity, self-denial, and abstinence, which is a celebration of life. Nietzsche contrasts this with the ascetic ideal that, perverted by the priest, tames our natural instincts in a withdrawal from life. The noble form of the ascetic ideal is an expression of power while the priestly version is a manifestation of weakness. Nietzsche relies, once again, on our animal nature: "Every animal . . . instinctively strives for an optimum of favorable conditions under which it can expend all its strength and achieve its maximal feeling of power" (*Genealogy*, III, §7).

The great person lives by instincts that refuse control by reason, conscience, tradition, or the gods, but he practices the ascetic ideal so that he can consolidate his power for a great creative act. The weak dissipate their energies in a variety of unfocused activities (like marriage). The noble person masters himself so that he can marshal his creative powers to a single end. Rigorous self-discipline, the single-minded pursuit of artistic creativity, and the overcoming of oneself, allow one to focus all of one's creative energies. In Freudian terms, the artistic genius lifts the lid off of his id and allows it to spew forth in disciplined expression in art or conquest. Such geniuses who have overcome and created their selves include Napoleon, Goethe, Alexander, and Da Vinci.

While such instinctive striving undergirds the noble person's quest for greatness, its expression is not tantamount to happiness; Nietzsche writes: "I am not speaking of the path to happiness, but its path to power, to action, to the most powerful activity, and in most cases actually its path to unhappiness" (*Genealogy*, III, §7). The world and other people are obstacles to one's goal of greatness, so Nietzsche exalts suffering and hardness; you will suffer if you exercise your instinct to power. Such is the price of greatness.

Nietzsche is often criticized as a nihilist or immoralist. But he clearly defends his own vision of the good and the good life: the Homeric hero who overcomes the world and himself to create and conquer.[20] He opposes traditional,

---

[20.] Not every master, of course, will choose the morality and life of the Homeric hero. Standing against her particular social conventions and traditional morality, each will marshal her creative genius in her own way.

Judeo-Christian values, but he is not opposed to values. Indeed, he favors those values that he believes affirm life and express, rather than repress, our nature. He values honesty, contending that Christians are fundamentally dishonest: they espouse altruism but are as selfish and animal-like as everyone else. He peeks behind the veil of Christian virtue and sees the same instinct to life and power that he sees motivating the Homeric hero. The Christian, too feeble to stand up against the powerful, turns weakness into virtue. Nietzsche affirms the honest yet painful expression of our creative urges. We become like gods, that is, creators of value, when we give honest and creative expression to our animal nature, to our desire for power. While such activity may not make us happy, it can make us great.

Conclusion

We have presented the 19th-century ethical thinkers, with the exception of Kierkegaard, as making a decisive break from the religious traditions that shaped the West. While the early modern thinkers often rejected reliance on revelation, they still attempted to maintain traditional (religious) values, basing them on reason instead. The movement away from revelation, tradition, and authority culminates in the autonomous moral theories of the late modern period. The rejection of belief in God led ultimately to new views of human nature. So it is not surprising that the moral theories of Marx and Nietzsche, and, at times, Mill, are truly revisionist. They no longer preserve the husk of Judeo-Christian morality when the kernel of Judeo-Christian religion has been removed.

Despite their sometimes great differences, all of the thinkers we have examined in this book have based their moral theories to some degree or another on their views of human nature. The question of ethics, insofar as it is also the question of human fulfillment, is integrally related to the question, What makes us essentially human? It is not until the postmodern period that this entire approach to ethics is called into question. We shall see in the next chapter how some 20th-century philosophers have attempted to sever moral theory from views of human nature. Just as the moderns thought moral theory did not require theology, some post modernists think it does not require metaphysics. We don't need a conception of human nature, these thinkers claim, any more than we need the concept of God. We shall see where this turn in the journey takes us, and we will look at some alternative paths.

Suggested Readings

PETER SINGER, *Hegel* (New York: Oxford University Press, 1983).
PETER SINGER, *Marx* (New York: Oxford University Press, 1983).
SUSAN LEIGH ANDERSON, *On Kierkegaard* (Belmont, CA: Wadsworth Publishing Company, 1999).

ALASTAIR HANNAY, *Kierkegaard: A Biography* (Cambridge: Cambridge University Press, 2001).

ADRIAN DESMOND and JAMES MOORE, *Darwin: The Life of a Tormented Evolutionist* (New York: W.W. Norton & Co., 1994).

FRIEDRICH NIETZSCHE, *The Basic Writings of Nietzsche,* trans. Walter Kaufmann (New York: Modern Library, 2000).

R. J. HOLLINGDALE, *Nietzsche: The Man and His Philosophy* (Cambridge: Cambridge University Press, 1999).

5

The Postmodern World

Introduction

In his *Meditations on First Philosophy*, the father of modern philosophy, René Descartes, sought to provide a firm foundation for all of knowledge, including moral knowledge. He hoped that moral knowledge could attain the level of unanimity, precision, and certainty of fields like mathematics. This cartesian optimism is characteristic of much of modern moral philosophy. Early modern moral philosophers believed that all rational persons could come to agree on the truth of moral propositions such as *one ought to keep one's promises* and *suicide is wrong* just as everyone could agree on mathematical truths like *2 + 2 = 4* and *triangles have three sides*. Even the moral reformers of the late modern period were confident that all rational persons could be convinced of their revolutionary views of morality.

Postmodern philosophy typically rejects cartesian optimism. According to postmodern philosophers, the project of justifying morality to the satisfaction of all rational persons is a failure. We cannot know with certainty what human beings are like or how they should live; disagreement about such issues is unresolvable. Giving up the hope for universal agreement, postmodern philosophers focused on responding to disagreement. Rather than see disagreement as the moderns had, as the result of error or prejudice and so something to be lamented and eliminated, postmodern philosophers tend to see it as something to be accepted and possibly even celebrated.

Not all 20th-century philosophers are postmodernists in this sense, however, so 20th-century moral philosophy can be seen as, in part, a debate between modern and postmodern philosophers. In this final chapter, we will look briefly at the philosophical and cultural background to this debate followed by an examination of a few of the key figures.[1]

[1.] Perhaps more moral philosophy has been written during this century than all centuries prior. It is inevitable that in such a short space we can provide only an introduction to but a few of the important figures and debates. We are grateful to David Solomon for inspiration regarding the state of philosophy and culture at the beginning of the century.

105

At the start of the 20th century, moral philosophy was in a crisis. The two most prominent theories, utilitarianism and Kantianism were on uncertain ground. Henry Sidgwick (1838–1900), perhaps the most prominent utilitarian of the late 19th and early 20th century, came to acknowledge an apparently irresolvable conflict within utilitarianism itself. Utilitarianism claims that we have reason to act for the greatest happiness for the greatest number; and, yet, Sidgwick recognized, we are driven toward our own individual happiness. Happiness (one's own) and morality (as promoting the happiness of the greatest number), come apart. It was not clear how they could be put back together.

Kantianism suffered from an external critique. According to Kant, the right action is one that reason prescribes, and it is only in acting in accordance with reason that human beings are truly free. In sharp contrast, Nietzsche claimed that the essential characteristic of human beings is not reason but the capacity to express ourselves and exercise power. Persons can be free apart from morality, so freedom and morality come apart. It was not clear how *they* could be put back together.

As if these philosophical problems were not enough, people began to neglect traditional morality as the result of various cultural movements. As we mentioned in the previous chapter, the end of the 19th century brought a prestige to the natural sciences never before seen; conversely, religion was losing its influence. Science's explanatory power was extended to everything in the universe including human beings, and educated persons began to depend on it as their primary source of knowledge. Because of evolutionary theory, ethical theories that viewed human beings as distinct from animals were threatened. Technology had produced such things as railroads, steam engines, and telegraphs. Compared to the progress of scientific knowledge, ethical knowledge seemed uncertain or even impossible. Because God was no longer considered necessary to explain what science could not and biblical criticism was on the rise, religious belief, at least among the educated, continued to dwindle. As various religious doctrines came to be viewed with disdain, the ethical beliefs that rested on them were threatened. Science and technology, rather than religion and morality, offered the promise of a better life.

Individualism was also on the rise. With mass literacy, newspapers, and the rise of democracies, came a newfound confidence in the judgment of the individual. Corresponding to the rise of individualism was a decrease in respect for established authorities and traditional moralities that were considered threats to individual autonomy and self-creation. Finally, as the world began to shrink, there was increasing awareness of conflicting views of morality that suggested to some that moral codes were merely relative to a given community.

With the psychological, philosophical, religious, and cultural supports beneath traditional morality crumbling, the ties between morality and human fulfillment began to unravel: it seemed that human beings could find happiness, exercise their freedom, and live fulfilling lives without following traditional morality.

Various responses to this crisis developed. Intuitionists and emotivists (and later the pragmatists) attempted to set aside thorny and irresolvable metaphysical issues by separating the realms of fact and value. Existentialists produced an innovative metaphysics and corresponding morality. And there have been revivals of older foundations for morality, for example, those associated with Aristotle, Kant, and Mill. In what follows, we look at a single representative of each of these approaches, discussing the work of G. E. Moore, A. J. Ayer, Jean-Paul Sartre, Alasdair MacIntyre, John Rawls, and R. M. Hare, as well as the work of Elizabeth Anscombe, who helped inspire the return to more traditional moral theory. We will also discuss the challenge posed by feminist ethics and conclude with a slightly longer section on Richard Rorty, a philosopher who explicitly calls into question the very practice of moral philosophy itself.

G. E. Moore

[T]his question, how 'good' is to be defined, is the most fundamental question in all Ethics.

Imagine sitting in a comfortable chair in a lovely room filled with good books and fine art, a fire blazing in the fireplace. Drinking port while eating crackers with Stilton cheese, you share witty and intelligent conversation with your best friends. Now imagine that, in so doing, you are participating in the highest good, thus fulfilling the demands of morality. Remarkably, this view of the excellent life was defended in earnest by the first great ethicist of the 20th century, G. E. Moore (1873–1958). In October 1903, G. E. Moore published his classic work, *Principia Ethica*,[2] and ushered in 20th-century ethical theory. As already outlined in the introduction above, morality was in a precarious position because the factual claims on which it was based—claims about human nature, the world, and God—were being called into question. If it could be shown that morality was not based on such factual claims at all, then it would be immune from the chronic changes in beliefs about the factual (metaphysical) realm.

In the first chapter of *Principia Ethica*, Moore defines ethics as "the general enquiry into what is good" (*Principia*, 54). We must begin, he says, with an inquiry into the concept of "good" before we can discuss any other ethical concept such as good conduct, right, or obligation. Moore's *analysis* of the concept "good" is startling: "good," the central concept of all of ethics, is *unanalyzable!* He writes:

> [T]his question, how 'good' is to be defined, is the most fundamental question in all Ethics. . . . my answer to it may seem a very disappointing one. If I am asked 'What is good?' my answer is that good is good, and that is the end of the matter. Or if I am asked 'How is good to be defined?' my answer

2. G. E. Moore, *Principia Ethica*, rev. ed., ed. Thomas Baldwin (Cambridge: Cambridge University Press, 1993); hereafter cited in the text as *Principia*.

is that it cannot be defined, and that is all I have to say about it. But disappointing as these answers may appear, they are of the very last importance. (*Principia*, 57–58)

"Good" can neither be defined, nor can it be identified with any natural or metaphysical property.[3] Those who attempt to do so commit what Moore calls *the naturalistic fallacy.* Moore believes the fallacy so prevalent that all moral philosophers, with the exception of Plato and Sidgwick, have committed it.

Why can't "good" be defined? Moore argues that a definition can only be given for concepts that are complex since a definition simply enumerates the simpler components of the complex. "Horse," for example is defined by its simpler components "hoofed," "quadruped," "of the genus Equus." "Good" cannot be defined, because it is a simple notion. Since it cannot be broken down into simpler parts, "good" is more like "yellow" than "horse." You cannot explain it to someone who does not already know what it is; you simply point to it.

Moral philosophers run into error not only when they try to define "good" in simpler terms, but also when they attempt to explain it by identifying it with some natural or metaphysical property such as *what is desired* or *the will of God.* "Good" is like "pleasure" in this sense; "pleasure," Moore writes, cannot be defined:

> And if anybody tried to define pleasure for us as being any other natural object; if anybody were to say, for instance, that pleasure *means* the sensation of red, and were to proceed to deduce from that that pleasure is a colour, we should be entitled to laugh at him and to distrust his future statements about pleasure. Well, that would be the same fallacy which I have called the naturalistic fallacy. (*Principia*, 64–65)

"Good," concludes Moore, is a simple, nonnatural property that cannot be defined. Moral philosophy must begin by acknowledging as much.

If the central concept of ethics is unanalyzable, how should ethics proceed? Moore claims that there are two questions ethics must answer. First, what kinds of things ought to exist for their own sakes? In other words, what kinds of things have intrinsic value? Second, what kinds of actions ought we to perform? Again, in other words, what are our duties? Moore maintains that the two questions are related in the following manner: People ought to act in ways that bring about as much intrinsic goodness as possible.

The first question concerns things that are "good as ends," the second, things that are "good as means." In order to determine whether or not something is "good as an end" or is intrinsically valuable, persons must inspect their intuitions to see if the candidate is self-evidently good. Moore holds a kind of *intuitionism*

---

3.   By "metaphysical property," Moore means something having to do with some metaphysical entity, for example, God, although the focus of the discussion is on natural properties.

that claims that we know certain things intuitively because of their obviousness or self-evidence. By contrast, judgments about whether things are "good as means" are not self-evident. While Moore believed that we could simply intuit the good ends of action, he rejected the claim that we could intuit the rules or duties designed to bring those ends about. Our duties are discovered through empirical observation of which actions best enable us to achieve our ends.

So, what things, according to Moore, have intrinsic value? And what are our duties? In the final chapter of *Principia Ethica,* Moore claims that, "By far the most valuable things, which we know or can imagine, are certain states of consciousness, which may be roughly described as the pleasures of human intercourse and the enjoyment of beautiful objects" (*Principia,* 237). He continues, "[P]ersonal affections and aesthetic enjoyments include *all* the greatest, and *by far* the greatest, goods we can imagine" (*Principia,* 238). He goes so far as to claim that "the ultimate and fundamental truth of Moral Philosophy" is:

> That it is only for the sake of these things—in order that as much of them as possible may at some time exist—that any one can be justified in performing any public or private duty; that they are the *raison d'être* of virtue; that it is they—these complex wholes *themselves,* and not any constituent or characteristic of them—that form the rational ultimate end of human action and the sole criterion of social progress: these appear to be truths which have been generally overlooked. (*Principia,* 238)

So, we ought to strive in all our actions to create a world in which there are as many experiences of friendship and beauty as possible. The greatest good is something like this: to sit in a comfy room with good friends, enjoying fine cuisine and talking about Monet while listening to Mozart!

How do we go about creating such a world? Moore's account of our obligations is quite conservative. He maintains that the preservation of civilized society is necessary for the existence of anything intrinsically good and that traditional moral rules are necessary and useful for preserving such a society (*Principia,* 207). But, might there be cases in which breaking an established rule will bring about more intrinsic goodness, for example, more friendship or beauty, than following it? Moore allows that there may be some exceptions in cases in which the general effectiveness of a rule has not been demonstrated. But he is pessimistic about our ability to reasonably make legitimate exceptions. So, Moore maintains, even if it looks like more good will come from breaking a rule, we must nevertheless adhere to generally accepted rules.

Despite his apparent conservatism, the possibility of exceptions to traditional moral rules opened the way to some unfamiliar moralities and allowed great individual freedom. One needs only imagine some of Moore's sophisticated and progressive followers in what was known as The Bloomsbury Group celebrating the values of art and friendship while observing that the institution of marriage no longer seems a very useful one, and, indeed, that many such institutions might inhibit one's enjoyment of those things, friendship and art, which are supremely valuable.

The path to new moralities is also paved by Moore's sharp distinction between "good as ends" and "good as means." Recall that judgments about intrinsic value, "good as ends," are self-evident; if they are true, they are universally true. In contrast, judgments about our duties, "good as means," are not necessary but merely probable and depend on the conditions of a particular society to make certain consequences likely to follow from certain actions. A set of duties will be regarded as true within a given age and society, but, Moore writes,

> when we take other ages into account, in many most important cases the normal circumstances of a given kind of action will be so different, that the generalisation which is true for one will not be true for another. With regard then to ethical judgments which assert that a certain kind of action is good as a means to a certain kind of effect, none will be *universally* true; and many, though *generally* true at one period, will be generally false at others. (*Principia*, 74)

And so, once again, we might imagine some of Moore's followers observing with clever sophistication that while the experiences of beauty and social intercourse are certainly universal, various moral rules are not. That is, while those rules were once effective means for realizing intrinsic value, they no longer are; or, while they may be true for a certain middle class, they are not true for a certain group of elites. While Moore may have intended to preserve traditional morality, his philosophy made traditional morality more vulnerable than it had previously been.

Intuitionism was dominant through the 1920s, but came under increasing attack in the 1930s. One obvious objection to intuitionism is that there appears to be no rational way to settle debates over intrinsic value. How could one decide if friendship and not competition, for example, is self-evidently good? Moral disagreements such as these provided the starting point of moral theory for a group of philosophers called the *emotivists*.

A. J. Ayer

> [S]tatements of value . . . are not in the literal sense significant, but are simply expressions of emotion which can be neither true nor false.

The great scientific advances mentioned in our introduction led some philosophers to reexamine the possibility of ethical knowledge. In his work *Language, Truth, and Logic* (1935),[4] A. J. Ayer (1910–1989) advances what he refers to as a

---

4. A. J. Ayer, *Language, Truth, and Logic* (New York: Dover Publications, 1952); hereafter cited in the text as *LTL*.

radical empiricist hypothesis. Following David Hume, he claims that all genuine statements are of two kinds: the necessarily true statements of logic and mathematics, and matters of fact that are empirically verifiable or falsifiable.[5] If a statement does not belong to one of these two classes, it is, according to Ayer, literally meaningless. He provides an ethical theory consistent with this radical empiricism.

Ayer argues first that statements of ethical value cannot be translated into statements of empirical fact. His claims are consistent with Moore's rejection of naturalism and with his view that value judgments belong not to the world of empirical observation but to a "mysterious" world of "intellectual intuition." But Ayer raises a point Moore seemed to overlook: intuitionism makes statements of value unverifiable, "For," Ayer writes, "it is notorious that what seems intuitively certain to one person may seem doubtful, or even false, to another. So that unless it is possible to provide some criterion by which one may decide between conflicting intuitions, a mere appeal to intuition is worthless as a test of a proposition's validity" (*LTL,* 106). Ayer contends that "in the case of moral judgments, no such criterion can be given" (*LTL,* 106). In other words, there is no *rational* way to settle debates over ethical value. Ayer believes his theory, unlike Moore's, explains why this is the case.

Ayer endorses Moore's contention that the fundamental ethical concepts are unanalyzable; but, the reason why this is the case, claims Ayer, is that ethical concepts are "mere pseudo-concepts." The function of ethical terms is "purely 'emotive.'" They are used merely to express one's feelings. So, "X is good" means something like "I like X" or "Yea!" "X is bad" means "I dislike X" or "Boo!" Such exclamations are unanalyzable. And there can be no criterion for determining the validity of value judgments, "not because they have an 'absolute' validity which is mysteriously independent of ordinary sense-experience," as Moore maintained, "but because they have no objective validity whatsoever"(*LTL,* 108). Since moral judgments "do not say anything," since they are literally meaningless, it makes no sense to ask whether they are true or false (*LTL,* 108). If I say "Stealing money is wrong," Ayer writes,

> I produce a sentence which has no factual meaning—that is, expresses no proposition which can either be true or false. It is as if I had written "Stealing money!!"—where the shape and thickness of the exclamation marks show, by a suitable convention, that a special sort of moral disapproval is the feeling which is being expressed. It is clear that there is nothing said here which can be true or false. Another man may disagree with me about the wrongness of stealing, in the sense that he may not have the same feelings about stealing as I have, and he may quarrel with me on account of my moral sentiments. But he cannot, strictly speaking, contradict me. For in

---

5. These central claims were incorporated into *logical positivism* or *logical empiricism,* an influential, pro-science philosophy developed in the early part of this century.

saying that a certain type of action is right or wrong, I am not making any factual statement, not even a statement about my own state of mind. I am merely expressing certain moral sentiments. And the man who is ostensibly contradicting me is merely expressing his moral sentiments. So that there is plainly no sense in asking which of us is in the right. For neither of us is asserting a genuine proposition. (*LTL*, 107–108)

Not only did Ayer claim that ethical debates could not be rationally resolved, he even went so far as to maintain that, despite appearances, there are no genuine debates over questions of value. Since, he observes, "Thrift is a virtue" and "Thrift is a vice" express no propositions at all, they do not express contradictory ones. Indeed, we may encounter persons who actually approve of theft or adultery or who disapprove of beneficence or loyalty. We may believe that our own moral judgments are superior, but we can employ no arguments to demonstrate this. Again, this is because value judgments (as opposed to factual claims and the claims of logic and mathematics) are not subject to rational argument. Ayer concludes that there can be no moral knowledge, hence no field of ethical science. The job of describing the feelings and actions that ethical terms inspire belongs not to the philosopher but to the psychologist.

Emotivism widened the divide between the realms of fact and value. It sought to remove morality's pretensions to objectivity and to more accurately describe the way ethical language is used, that is, as a vehicle for emotive self-expression. One question to ask is, If a person were to accept emotivism's analysis of moral language, would that have any effect on his or her moral commitments? In light of the conclusion that ethical terms merely express the emotions of the speaker and are not, for example, objectively grounded in the world, would persons be more inclined toward skepticism and amoralism in their daily lives? In other words, do ethical theories have any effect on practical living? Some philosophers answered "No" to these questions. They adopted something we may call *The Neutrality Thesis*,[6] according to which conclusions at the theoretical level, questions about the meaning and justification of ethical terms, have no effect on the way persons actually live. This is an issue to which we will return in our final section.

Ayer assumed that ethical language is emotive in part because no rational justification for morality seemed possible (especially given his radical empiricism). People could not be expressing moral truths, Ayer contended, so they must be expressing nonrational emotions. Is the rational justification of morality impossible as Ayer supposed? During the 1950s, a number of philosophers began to ask this question. These philosophers suggested that the realms of fact and value are not as separate as the intuitionists and the emotivists claimed and that we might be able to provide a rational justification for morality by reviving in creative ways the work of philosophers like Aristotle, Kant, and Mill. Before looking at these arguments, however, we will examine another alternative to emotivism, one that bases

---

6. This term was coined by David Solomon.

its revolutionary morality not in the way we use words but in a revolutionary metaphysics of the person.

Jean-Paul Sartre

Man is nothing else but what he makes of himself. Such is the first principle of existentialism.

Near the middle of the 20th century, science was continuing to increase in prestige, while religion and belief in God were falling into disfavor. In "Existentialism is a Humanism" (1947),[7] Jean-Paul Sartre (1905–1980) identifies existentialism as "nothing else than an attempt to draw all the consequences of a coherent atheistic position" ("Existentialism," 51). Some of these consequences are ethical. Sartre is explicitly critical of the attempts to secularize ethics that took place during the 1880s when philosophers tried to hold onto all of traditional morality without its religious backing. If there is no God, says Sartre, then there are no absolute or universal and necessary values either. If the obligations to be honest, not to lie, not to beat one's wife, to raise one's children and so on, do not exist in the mind of God, they do not exist in some intelligible heaven or in our nature either. Sartre adopts the words of Dostoevsky: "If God didn't exist, everything would be possible." This is, he says, "the very starting point of existentialism" ("Existentialism," 22).

What are the consequences of atheism for views of human nature? Sartre sums up what is unique about existentialist metaphysics in the claim that *"Existence precedes essence."* In making this claim, existentialism stands the long held doctrine, *"essence precedes existence,"* on its head. By way of explanation, Sartre asks his audience to think about manufactured articles such as a paper-cutter. A paper-cutter is produced in a certain way and made for a definite purpose; no one makes it without knowing how to make it and what it is for. Its essence, the *what it is,* or its definition, precedes its existence. In other words, what it means to be a paper-cutter is not up to the paper-cutter. Sartre points out that traditionally human beings have been viewed in the same way. For Christians, God was thought of as the artisan who creates human beings for a specific purpose and according to a conception already in His mind. While their atheistic counterparts discarded the idea of God, they still maintained that human beings come into existence with a fixed nature or predetermined essence. According to nonexistentialists, Christian and atheist alike, human beings can no more determine their purpose than a paper-cutter. The human task is to discover this preestablished human essence and then to order one's life according to it.

---

7. Reprinted as "Existentialism" in Jean-Paul Sartre, *Existentialism and Human Emotions* (New York: Carol Publishing Company, 1993), 9–51; hereafter cited in the text as "Existentialism."

The thesis that *existence precedes essence* follows, says Sartre, from the rejection of belief in God: "[I]f God does not exist, there is at least one being in whom existence precedes essence, a being who exists before he can be defined by any concept, . . . this being is man . . ." ("Existentialism," 15). As a result, existentialists adopt a radical view of human freedom, rejecting two conceptions of human nature. First, they reject human nature as a set of universal drives or motivations. According to the existentialists, we are not necessarily motivated by self-preservation (Hobbes) or by pleasure and sympathy (Mill). We are not primarily rational animals of the sort Aristotle and Kant described. And, contrary to the doctrines of those like Augustine and Aquinás, we do not have a sinful nature. None of these drives or motivations determine or explain our actions. We are free to act independent of them.

Second, existentialists reject the conception of human nature as an end or goal. We are, they maintain, free to choose our own destinies. In order to find fulfillment we need not direct our lives toward any predetermined goal or way of life. We need not seek fulfillment in a life of virtue and contemplation as Aristotle held. Our only rest and happiness is not found in communion with God as Augustine and Aquinás claimed. And Kant was naive to think that we are only truly free if we constrain our actions by our duty. We are, say the existentialists, free to direct our lives and find fulfillment as we see fit.

With no God and no human nature to determine our actions or to guide them, with "no excuse behind us, nor justification before us," we must recognize that we are, in Sartre's words, "condemned to be free." Persons are left to define themselves according to their free choices. To illustrate this point, Sartre tells the story of a young man who, during World War II, must decide whether to stay with his dependent mother or whether to join the resistance; no moral principles, passion, or authority can guide the young man. In the end, he must simply choose his course of action.

Say the student is a Christian, asks Sartre rhetorically, which action is Christian? Say he's a Kantian, which action treats the relevant persons as ends and not as mere means? If moral principles cannot help him make the decision, is the young man left to trust his passions? But if feelings are, in part, the result of actions, they cannot be a guide to action. Must the student simply act on the advice of others? Sartre points out that since the young man knows in advance what advice others will give, he is already committed to a certain course of action when he chooses his advisor. Sartre's conclusion? There are no guidelines for life (if there are, then we must interpret them). At bottom is only freedom of choice . . . and responsibility for that choice. Sartre writes:

> Man is at the start a plan which is aware of itself, rather than a patch of moss, a piece of garbage, or a cauliflower; nothing exists prior to this plan; there is nothing in heaven; man will be what he will have planned to be. . . . But if existence really does precede essence, man is responsible for what he is.

Thus, existentialism's first move is to make every man aware of what he is and to make the full responsibility of his existence rest on him. ("Existentialism," 16)

We are responsible for our own lives. I alone can give my life meaning, and I do so through my free actions.

Responsibility for one's life reaches farther than one might think. Sartre writes, "[W]e do not only mean that he is responsible for his own individuality, but that he is responsible for all men" ("Existentialism," 16). When we make our choices, Sartre claims, we are creating an image of human beings as we think they should be. He gives an example of one who chooses to marry and have children. In making that choice, Sartre says, the man is declaring that monogamy is good not merely for himself but for all: "In choosing myself, I choose man" ("Existentialism," 18). Anguish is the realization of this terrible responsibility. Not only am I the person I choose to be, but I am also a lawmaker who is choosing laws to apply to all of humankind. Because of this, cautions Sartre, we must act is if we were role models for all of humanity. The totality of this responsibility and the anguish it entails are probably best illustrated in the following passages from Sartre's *Being and Nothingness:*

> If I am mobilized in a war, this war is *my* war; it is in my image and I deserve it. . . . [E]verything takes places as if I bore the entire responsibility for this war. . . . [I am] as profoundly responsible for the war as if I had myself declared it. . . . I carry the weight of the world by myself alone without anything or any person being able to lighten it.[8]

Critics of existentialism argue that Sartre's discussion of responsibility is not enough. If we reject a view of morality as God's commandment or as eternal truth, then we are left with nothing but arbitrary choice: each person is permitted to do what he or she wishes and no one is capable of judging the views of others. Sartre denies each of these claims. Just because one chooses without reference to pre-established values, he says, does not mean he chooses out of caprice. He compares a moral choice to the production of a work of art. We do not accuse the artist of not following a set of *a priori* rules. We do not ask, "What painting *ought* he to make?" because there is no definite painting to be made. Still, we do not call a canvas of Picasso's arbitrary. Sartre claims that ethical choices embody the same creative and inventive situation as the production of a piece of art. The student mentioned above could not determine his course of action by consulting some set of *a priori* rules, he had to create his law himself. Still, says Sartre, if he chooses individual affection as his law and remains with his mother or if he chooses to make a sacrifice and go to England, we do not claim that his choice was an arbitrary one.

---

8. As reprinted in Jean-Paul Sartre, *Existentialism and Human Emotions* (New York: Carol Publishing Company, 1993), 54–57.

Sartre denies that existentialism entails the impossibility of passing judgment on others. Existentialists maintain that certain choices are based on error, others on truth, and existentialism enables one to see the difference. One is dishonest and a coward, says Sartre, if he makes excuses for his choice claiming it to have been determined for him or if he claims to be guided by values that exist prior to him. By way of contrast, honest persons recognize their freedom and responsibility and make no excuses for their actions. "[T]he ultimate meaning of the acts of honest men," states Sartre, "is the quest for freedom as such" ("Existentialism," 45). So, if you are in love with an engaged man, you can choose to satisfy that passion or give it up. Either course is fine according to existentialism, so long as you choose freely. Either course is bad if it is made by surrender of freedom. If we make conscious free choices and take responsibility for those choices, then, according to existentialism, we are persons of "good faith." If we hide from free choice, let things simply happen to us, let others tell us how to live, or fail to see our actions as our own, then we are persons of "bad faith."

Existentialism is a humanism not because it bases ethics in a predetermined human nature but because human beings must create themselves and give meaning to their lives. This is, according to existentialism, the responsibility we must assume to be truly human.

We might ask, if there are no preestablished standards, what basis does Sartre have for his picture of the ideal agent? Why couldn't I be a person of good faith by freely choosing to give up my freedom? Why can I not, for example, freely choose to live a life of submission to a particular authority? Perhaps Sartre would maintain that even though such a life would be freely chosen, choosing to relinquish one's freedom would be an act of denying what one is as a human being. But then it appears that we have an essence that precedes our existence after all. So, while Sartre begins by denying that our essence precedes our existence, he ends up claiming something very close to it, that is, that persons are essentially individual choosing agents who must live a life that maximally exercises this freedom in order to be fulfilled. He has simply substituted his own radical view of human nature for the more traditional views.

Existentialism paints an exciting and attractive picture of the ideal moral agent as independent, strong, creative, unashamed, fully autonomous, and authentic. We admire persons with these qualities and disdain those who are passive, weak, unimaginative, relinquish control over their lives, and make excuses for themselves. And yet, we might ask, does freedom require the rejection of so much of traditional morality? The concept of autonomy or freedom has not always been separated from a strict and traditional set of moral precepts (recall our section on Kant). Persons were once believed to be fully autonomous only when freely submitting to the moral law; immorality was attributed to slavery to our desires or passions. Sartre claims that this notion of autonomy fails if there is no God. But perhaps we cannot maintain our old ethical theory if we jettison belief in God because we have not supplied a *substitute* for God. In an article (discussed below), Elizabeth Anscombe makes such an observation and goes on to suggest that a traditional conception of ethics may be justified within an Aristotelian frame-work, that is, apart from a divine command theory. And John Rawls, R. M. Hare, and Alasdair MacIntyre provide fairly traditional accounts of morality that do not rely on belief in God. These projects share the belief that, contra Sartre, whether one believes in God or not, human beings are only truly fulfilled when living a moral life.[9]

Elizabeth Anscombe

[I]t is not profitable for us at present to do moral philosophy. . . . [T]he concepts of obligation, and duty . . . ought to be jettisoned.

Intuitionism, emotivism, and existentialism all share in some way the view that moral judgments are not derivable from the world of fact, from, for example, truths about an essential human nature or God's will. There is, according to these philosophies, an unbridgeable gap between facts and values, summed up in Hume's dictum that "one cannot derive an 'ought' from an 'is.'" This fact/value distinction was dominant in the field of philosophy during the 1930s and 1940s, but its influence was not limited to academia. The distinction found widespread approval and is still pervasive in a variety of areas including the social sciences, ed-ucation, politics, and our culture in general. Just think of how often you have heard the following: "That's just a value judgment." "It's only your opinion." "That's a private matter." These views have seeped so deep into our culture it is nearly a platitude that there is no moral authority except the individual's con-science, and most ethical disagreements are at bottom rationally unresolvable. In the 1950s, this fact/value distinction came under increasing philosophical attack inspiring various attempts to revive rational moral argument.

Elizabeth Anscombe's (1919–2001) "Modern Moral Philosophy" (1958),[10] sparked a return to attempts to provide a rational basis for morality. In that article, Anscombe, Britain's most influential female philosopher, argued that terms like "moral goodness" and "moral duty" have no meaning in this day and age because they have lost the context in which they made sense, specifically, the context of a divine law view of ethics, in which words such as "ought" express the commands of God. It simply does not make sense, Anscombe maintains, to have such a con-ception of law unless you believe in God as the lawgiver. This carries over into

---

9. As heirs of the Enlightenment, most 20th-century philosophers have conducted ethics without refer-ence to God. We regret not having the space to cover the recent revival of promising ethical theories that rely on belief in God. See for example, John Hare, *The Moral Gap* (Oxford: Clarendon Press, 1996) and Robert Merrihew Adams, *Finite and Infinite Goods: A Framework for Ethics* (New York: Oxford University Press, 1999).

10. Elizabeth Anscombe, "Modern Moral Philosophy," *Philosophy* 33.124 (1958), 1–19; hereafter cited in the text as "Modern."

terms such as "right," "wrong," and "ought," which are legal terms that imply the existence of a legal authority. She goes on,

> But if such a conception is dominant for many centuries, and then is given up, it is a natural result that the concepts of "obligation," of being bound or required as by a law, should remain though they had lost their root; and if the word "ought" has become invested in certain contexts with the sense of "obligation," it too will remain to be spoken with a special emphasis and a special feeling in these contexts.
>
> It is as if the notion "criminal" were to remain when criminal law and criminal courts had been abolished and forgotten. ("Modern," 6)

She claims that modern philosophers who deny God's existence cannot coherently use these terms: "And I should be inclined to congratulate the present-day moral philosophers on depriving 'morally ought' of its now delusive appearance of content, if only they did not manifest a detestable desire to retain the atmosphere of the term" ("Modern," 18). She argues further that the various substitutes for a divine legislator—conscience, nature, or social contract—all fail.

Anscombe recommends dropping notions such as "moral obligation" and "moral goodness" altogether. She claims that we can do ethics without them, as, for example, Aristotle once did. She recommends focusing our study instead on particular virtues such as courage, charity, or justice. But since the study of particular virtues and prohibitions cannot take place apart from a study of human nature, moral philosophy requires an account of human persons provided by a philosophy of psychology. She writes: "In present-day philosophy an explanation is required how an unjust man is a bad man, or an unjust action a bad one; to give such an explanation belongs to ethics; but it cannot even be begun until we are equipped with a sound philosophy of psychology" ("Modern," 4). In order to do ethics properly, we need an account of human nature, human action (including an account of motivation and intention), the type of characteristic a virtue is, and human flourishing. Anscombe actually recommends that we take a break from ethics completely until we have a better philosophy of psychology, which informs us of the nature of persons.

One might recall that Ayer, too, called for the aid of psychology in ethics; but, it is important to note that while Ayer thought all of ethics could be reduced to psychology, Anscombe believed ethics ought to be based in, but not reduced to, human psychology. She and Ayer could not be more at odds. Ayer's reduction of ethics to psychology, a result of the fact/value dichotomy, reduced ethics to mere feelings. In stark contrast, Anscombe calls for a rejection of this dichotomy and a return to *naturalism,* that is, to a theory that bases ethics in various facts about human beings and the world in which they live.

Anscombe helped redirect the course of moral philosophy. Her work made clear that one need not respond to the crisis of moral foundations with which this century began by making morality foundationless (as the intuitionists and emotivists had), and one need not jettison traditional morality (as the existentialists had), *if* the foundations for morality could be rebuilt. This time, however, the foundations for morality would be built without what were perceived to be problematic metaphysical assumptions, without, for example, the extravagant Platonic and Kantian views of the person and the world, without the metaphysical biology of Aristotle, without the God of Augustine, Aquinás, and Kant.

In the latter half of the 20th century, moral philosophers have returned, for example, to Kantian, utilitarian, and Aristotelian ethical theories in an attempt to answer the question, "How should one live?" But, while they have appropriated some of the old answers, contemporary philosophers have tried to provide a basis for those answers in accounts of human nature and features of our world they find more acceptable. For example, John Rawls's Kantian inspired moral theory is an attempt to found justice in an account of the way persons in fair conditions would deliberate. R. M. Hare's utilitarian account of morality is based in an analysis of the logic of moral words. And, Alasdair MacIntyre situates his Aristotelian account of virtue within an account of the nature of practices, the unity of a human life, and a tradition. In the following section, we will look briefly at each of these attempts to justify morality and some of the debates that have gone on between them.

John Rawls

. . . the desire to act justly derives in part from the desire to express most fully what we are or can be, namely free and equal rational beings with the liberty to choose . . .

Imagine a large cruise ship shipwrecked on a deserted island. The hundreds of survivors, giving up hope of being found, decide to start their own society. If it were up to everyone in the group to decide what moral principles members of this new society should live by so that they could live together in harmony, what principles would they freely choose? How would they go about their deliberations? In *A Theory of Justice* (1971),[11] John Rawls (1921–) articulates a unique *contract theory of morality*. According to contract theorists, a set of governing principles is chosen by free and equal persons who desire to enter society together for their mutual advantage.[12] Rawls believes that such governing principles are

---

[11.] John Rawls, *A Theory of Justice* (Cambridge, MA: Belknap, Harvard University Press, 1971); hereafter cited in the text as *Justice*.

[12.] The reader may recall the discussion of Hobbes's contract theory from Chapter 3. Contract theorists often talk of a "state of nature" from which persons voluntarily enter society. Rawls admits that we do not in fact enter society voluntarily, but he thinks that "a society satisfying the principles of justice as fairness comes as close as a society can to being a voluntary scheme, for it meets the principles which free and equal persons would assent to under circumstances that are fair. In this sense its members are autonomous and the obligations they recognize self-imposed" (*Justice,* 13).

captured in his conception of "justice as fairness." Those who enter society choose principles that assign basic rights and duties and that determine the division of social benefits. They do so as rational persons under a set of reasonable or fair conditions, in what Rawls calls *the original position.* The original position is supposed to incorporate commonly shared assumptions regarding the conditions under which principles of justice should be chosen.

Parties in the original position are thought to be behind a *veil of ignorance,* that is, they know general facts about human society, about political and economic theory, and about human psychology; however, they do not know their place in society, their natural assets and abilities, their conception of the good, their plan of life, or the historical period to which they belong. Persons are ignorant of all these things behind the veil because it "seems reasonable and generally acceptable that no one should be advantaged or disadvantaged by natural fortune or social circumstances in the choice of principles. It also seems widely agreed that it should be impossible to tailor principles to the circumstances of one's own case" (*Justice,* 18). The original position is designed to set aside those things that seem irrelevant or arbitrary from the point of view of justice. It is also supposed to ensure that the same principles of justice will always be chosen no matter who takes up the perspective of the original position. One should not, for example, be able to choose principles that give the right to vote only to concert pianists, or, to take a less fanciful example, only to white, property-holding men. A Catholic priest, a Zen Buddhist, an atheist, a millionaire, a janitor, a slave, a teacher, an artist, a politician, and a stay-at-home mother should arrive at the same principles of justice because the veil of ignorance removes unfair consideration of a certain class or kind of person.

The parties in the original position also are assumed to be rational in the sense "standard in economic theory, of taking the most effective means to given ends" (*Justice,* 14). The rational person has a coherent set of preferences, ranks options open to him according to how well they satisfy those preferences, and follows the plan that will satisfy more of his desires rather than less and that has the greater chance of being successfully carried out (*Justice,* 143). In choosing the principles of justice, persons in the original position try to advance their own interests. But, the veil of ignorance makes it impossible for them to know what their particular interests and ends are. They do not know their particular plan of life, only that they have some rational plan of life. So, how are they to decide which principles will advance their interests? Here, Rawls introduces what he calls "primary goods."

The *primary goods* are goods it is rational to want *whatever else one wants.* They include basic rights and liberties, freedom of opportunity, the powers and prerogatives of offices and positions of responsibility, income and wealth, and self-esteem. Primary goods may be thought of as all-purpose means toward whatever ends a person may have. So, while persons in the original position do not know their particular ends, they do know that they desire more rather than less of the primary goods, for "With more of these goods," writes Rawls, "men can generally be assured of greater success in carrying out their intentions and advancing their ends, whatever these ends may be" (*Justice,* 92). Persons deliberating in the original position "know that in general they must try to protect their liberties, widen their opportunities, and enlarge their means for promoting their aims whatever these are" (*Justice,* 143); they must try to secure for themselves "the highest index of primary social goods, since this enables them to promote their conception of the good most effectively whatever it turns out to be" (*Justice,* 144).

Which principles would be chosen by persons in the original position? Roughly stated, the principles reflect a liberal conception of rights and liberties. First, Rawls claims that it is rational to deliberate from the perspective of those who are worst off in society. Since the parties do not know what places they occupy in society, and it may turn out that they are low on the totem pole, they need to ask what principles and combination of social goods it is rational for the least advantaged to prefer. Rawls contends that justice as fairness ensures that, in spite of inevitable inequalities of ability, health, social position, family, educational opportunities, wealth, and so on, the least advantaged will be accorded substantial social and economic advantages. It is unfair, Rawls contends, for our lot in life to be determined by the "arbitrariness of fortune." So each person will have rights to secure his or her most basic needs—wealth, opportunity, and power—to a fairly high level. In addition, each person's freedom will be protected so that he or she can pursue, without infringing on the rights of others, his or her own dreams and desires (to freely choose his or her own ends).

Strictly speaking, *A Theory of Justice* is a political work, that is, it is about the justice of society and its various institutions (e.g., justice as the distribution of resources). It is not primarily about personal morality (e.g., justice as righteousness of the individual). Still, Rawls claims that his theory can be expanded into a comprehensive moral theory, and he devotes a number of pages to an explicit account of justice, obligation, and natural duty applicable to the individual as well as to accounts of moral education and virtue.[13] It is worth looking briefly at these accounts before discussing the view of human nature at the base of Rawls's theory.

According to Rawls, in order to identify the virtues we need first to identify the moral principles of right to which they correspond. Virtue is simply the desire to act on principles of right. Rawls's list of principles of right includes the principles of justice and efficiency applied to social systems and institutions as well as the following requirements of individuals: obligations of fairness and fidelity; the natural positive duties of upholding justice, mutual aid, and mutual respect; and the natural negative duties not to injure and not to harm the innocent (*Justice,* 109). One might argue that his list of moral requirements is unduly short.

---

[13]. Throughout *Justice,* Rawls suggests that the original position could be used to obtain a comprehensive theory of right, which, when connected to his theory of the good, could be used to explain all other moral notions (see, for example, 17, 109, 111, 115–116, 191–192, 333, 340, 398, 404, 434–435, 439, and 446). For an explicit account of principles applying to individuals, see sections 18–19 and sections 51–52; for Rawls's account of moral worth including an account of the virtues, see sections 60–68; for his theory of moral education, see Chapter VIII in *Justice.*

Moral prohibitions against suicide and materialism, for example, do not make his list of requirements of right. The list also fails to include principles of right that would correspond to many of the standard virtues; for example, the remaining cardinal virtues of wisdom, temperance, and courage, as well as chastity, cultivating one's talents, engaging in meaningful work, and beneficence. All of these have traditionally been thought to be in some way required of human beings, but Rawls's theory leaves them to each person's subjective conception of the good.

In response to the objection that his theory is hostile to such virtues, Rawls has pointed out that persons in society (i.e., outside the original position) are free to cultivate such virtues. Persons are free to live chaste lives, to act from altruistic motives, to cultivate their talents and engage in meaningful work; they are free to abjure materialism and to abhor suicide; and, given various psychological and sociological principles, and various religious and aesthetic considerations, they are likely to do so. We must not, says Rawls, confuse the motivation of the parties in the original position with a person's motivation in everyday life. This response fails to recognize that Rawls's theory diminishes the status of the virtues when compared with the principles of justice. While the principles of justice are considered to be *obligations* binding on all persons, the virtues are seen as mere (though possibly popular) *options*. The virtues are permitted but not required of human beings.

This treatment of the virtues is a consequence of Rawls's view of human nature: we are essentially *free and equal rational beings*. Free and equal persons are characterized by two capacities: "one for a conception of the good, the other for a sense of justice" (*Justice*, 561). "When realized," Rawls elaborates, "the first is expressed by a rational plan of life, the second by a regulative desire to act upon certain principles of right" (*Justice*, 561). We are fulfilled in acting justly. "[A]cting justly," writes Rawls, "is something we want to do as free and equal rational beings . . . The desire to act justly and the desire to express our nature as free moral persons turn out to specify what is practically speaking the same desire" (*Justice*, 572). While acting according to the principles of justice is necessary for fulfilling our moral personality, cultivating the sorts of virtues mentioned above is not. These virtues may be necessary for some person's pursuit of his chosen good—that is, they may be part of his unique rational plan of life—but they need not be. While Rawls claims that liberty, or autonomy, is acting in accordance with a law we give ourselves, his emphasis on justice and his neglect of the virtues seems to ignore a long tradition of thinkers, including his inspiration, Kant, who conceive of autonomy in quite different terms, specifically, as being best expressed in the exercise of the virtues.

Some critics have argued not only that Rawls's emphasis on justice is detrimental to the virtues, but also that the conception of human nature on which it relies is erroneous. They argue that his view of the person as a being separate from and prior to his or her ends is unduly abstract and individualistic. Rawls fails to see, say critics, that persons' identities are partially given by their commitments, roles, and ends, that these are not to be placed behind a veil of ignorance as irrelevant to morality but constitute a moral starting point.[14] Persons are not abstract, but "concrete" or "situated." Rawls's individualistic account also fails to give enough value to the community and the notion of a common good to which the individual may be subordinate. In addition, the critics continue, we can only deliberate from within concrete communities; there is no point outside of all of them, no original position, from which to choose moral principles.

In deriving the principles of justice as fairness, Rawls does not begin from self-evident principles à la Descartes. Nor does he attempt to define moral concepts in terms of nonmoral ones and then try to show that those nonmoral ones are true (a version of naturalism). He relies instead on a coherentist approach. As he puts it, the justification of his view rests on the entire conception of justice and how it fits with or organizes our considered judgments in something he calls *reflective equilibrium*. Rawls maintains that the conditions of the original position are ones we do in fact accept or can be persuaded to accept (*Justice,* 21). The conclusions produced match our considered judgments or extend them in acceptable ways. If, for example, the conditions of the original position led persons to adopt a principle permitting slavery, something would have gone wrong. In such a case, we must go back and adjust the conditions of the original position and/or our intuitions until we reach reflective equilibrium. Rawls believes his theory of justice achieves this. Critics like R. M. Hare argue that even if Rawls's theory achieves reflective equilibrium, it is not an adequate basis for morality. Hare claims that Rawls's method for selecting moral principles is merely a form of intuitionism (*Moral Thinking,* 12, 75); and, "The appeal to moral intuitions will never do as a basis for a moral system" (*Moral Thinking,* 12). One reason for this is that there is no way to convince those who do not already share your intuitions. There are many who are left to wonder, for example, why they should put themselves in the original position in the first place. Its conditions are not obviously reasonable or intuitive to *them.*

Objections along these lines have led Rawls to modify his later work so that while he maintains the conception of justice found in *Justice,* he says it no longer requires commitment to the particular justification offered there. He moves to what he calls a *political* rather than a *metaphysical* basis for his conception of justice. That is, rather than attempt to derive a system of morality from a particular view of human nature, Rawls describes the sort of morality that goes along with a commitment to a particular form of society, namely a liberal democratic one.[15] We will have the opportunity to examine a similar approach in more detail when

---

14. See for example, Michael Sandel, *Liberalism and the Limits of Justice* (Cambridge: Cambridge University Press, 1998) and Alasdair MacIntyre, *After Virtue,* 2nd ed. (Notre Dame, IN: University of Notre Dame Press, 1984). For a feminist critique of Rawls and similar work, see Carol Gilligan, *In a Different Voice: Psychological Theory and Women's Dependence* (Cambridge, MA: Harvard University Press, 1982); see also Seyla Benhabib, "The Concrete and the Generalized Other: The Kohlberg-Gilligan Controversy and Moral Theory" in *Women and Moral Theory,* ed. Eva Feder Kittay and Diana T. Meyers (Totowa, NJ: Rowman and Littlefield, 1987), 154–177.

15. This pragmatic position is most fully articulated in Rawls's *Political Liberalism* (New York: Columbia University Press, 1993).

we discuss the work of Richard Rorty later in the chapter, but first we will look at the utilitarian and Aristotelian alternatives proposed by R. M. Hare and Alasdair MacIntyre.

R. M. Hare

[I]n preferring what we prefer, morality compels us to accommodate ourselves to the preferences of others . . .

R. M. Hare (1919–2002) first entered moral philosophy shortly after World War II because, as he writes in *Moral Thinking* (1981),[16] "[there are] important practical issues . . . over which people are prepared to fight and kill one another; and it may be that unless some way is found of talking about them rationally and with hope of agreement, violence will finally engulf the world" (*Moral Thinking,* v). He believed, contra the antirationalism of the intuitionists, the emotivists, and the existentialists, that just such a way of talking could be found.

Despite his disagreements with the schools of philosophy just mentioned, Hare embraces their antinaturalism. He cannot accept the naturalist thesis that the nonmoral properties of acts, the factual properties, entitle us to call them right or wrong; a description of the act is not sufficient for its evaluation. He claims that there is something beyond the factual properties of actions that makes them right or wrong. In this Hare considers himself a Humean: he maintains that one cannot go from the description of an act to an evaluation of it, one cannot derive an "ought" from an "is." When faced with a description of an act, one must still make an evaluative choice. Recall an example from our earlier section on Hume: imagine a complete list of the natural properties of a person dying from a shotgun wound. The list of properties would include such things as the size of the shell, quantity of gunpowder, initial explosive forces, site of entry, and amount of blood loss. But even the most complete description of the event in natural terms will leave out a key property: whether or not the action was good or bad. According to Hare, "Good" and "bad," "right" and "wrong," are not purely descriptive words; they have an evaluative or *prescriptive* meaning. Moral statements evaluate, and thereby, guide actions; they instruct people as to how they should act, saying essentially "Do this" or "Don't do that." So Hare's view is called *prescriptivism*.

Hare does not think of the evaluative element in moral judgments as a choice of existentialist will. If we are to think rationally we cannot call just anything we choose "right" or "wrong"; our choice must be constrained by reason, by the rules of moral thinking. Hare believes that everyone can and should come to the same answers regarding evaluative questions if we would but follow these

---

16. R. M. Hare, *Moral Thinking: Its Levels, Method and Point* (Oxford: Clarendon Press, 1981); hereafter cited in the text as *Moral Thinking.*

rules. He claims, however, that we discover the rules not by an investigation into the nature of the world, human beings, or God (all of which attempt to derive "ought" from "is"), but through an analysis of moral language.

Hare argues that an analysis of the logical properties of moral words such as "must" and "ought" produces certain rules we must follow if we are to be rational in our moral thinking. In his discussion, he observes that we come to have an understanding of the logic of words in part by their *misuse*. Examples of the logical misuse of language, that is, of self-contradictory statements, are "This apple is red all over and not red" or "That book was written by Plato, who never wrote any books." Similarly, moral words have logical properties that can be discovered in part through their misuse. It would be a contradiction to say to someone, for example, "You ought to do this, but another person in an identical situation ought not to do this." So, one logical property of moral words like "ought" is *universalizability:* moral judgments apply to every person in the same circumstances. Another logical property of moral words is *prescriptivity,* which we mentioned above. In making a moral judgment, we express a preference or desire that something be done or not done.

Universalizability and prescriptivity lead, Hare contends, to a form of utilitarianism. When thinking about one's actions, it is natural to think in terms of the benefits and costs of one's actions to oneself. That is, one is naturally inclined to think in terms of one's own preferences or desires. How can I satisfy my own preferences or desires? One is inclined to favor oneself and also one's family and friends. In thinking *morally,* however, we ought to consider the preferences of every person affected by our actions. Hare claims that in order to fully take into account the preferences of others, we are required to imagine ourselves in the position of each person affected by the proposed action. We are to imagine ourselves as having his or her preferences to whatever degree he or she has them. And when we make our final judgment as to which action we ought to perform, we need to be impartial; that is, we cannot favor our own preferences (or those of our families and friends); we must give equal weight to the preferences of all involved. We also must make no distinctions based on the content of the preferences; that is, we cannot give more weight to what we might consider "higher" or better preferences, less weight to "lower" ones. All preferences are considered equal. We then calculate the sum of preference satisfaction, and adopt the course of action that maximizes it, that is, the course of action that satisfies the most desires and thwarts the fewest of them.[17]

So far, our discussion of Hare's theory has taken place primarily at the abstract meta-ethical level rather than the normative level; that is, we have outlined how the theory is derived (from the logic of moral words) rather than discussing

---

17. Hare acknowledges that there are difficulties. For example, how do we compare the intensity of the affected persons' desires? Even if my own preferences are less intense, why should they be subordinated to another's? What place is there for partiality in moral thinking? Isn't morality something other than the weighing of preference satisfactions? Can't an amoralist opt out of this whole method? He addresses each of these in *Moral Thinking.*

the content of the theory itself (the moral judgments produced by his form of utilitarianism). Hare divides normative ethics into two levels: *critical* thinking and *intuitive* thinking. He believes the distinction to be of extreme importance and writes: "[I]t is hardly an exaggeration to say that more confusion is caused, both in theoretical ethics and in practical moral issues, by the neglect of this distinction than by any other factor" (*Moral Thinking*, 25).[18]

Roughly, the distinction is as follows. Intuitive moral thinking is a form of *rule utilitarianism*. Intuitive moral principles are relatively general and simple rules, usually passed down through moral education by the community; these intuitive moral principles often include, for example, the prohibitions against lying, stealing, and adultery; and the positive duties to bring up children, to cultivate one's talents, and to come to the aid of those in need. Because persons do not always have the time or ability to assess which action would be for the greatest good, they rely on these rules that promote actions that are, in most cases, for the greatest good. Critical thinking is a form of *act utilitarianism*. If we could employ this form of thinking perfectly, we would act like a character Hare refers to as the *archangel*. The archangel is an imaginary creature who is, among other things, committed to making moral decisions; he has perfect knowledge of the consequences of actions and the preferences of the people affected by human actions. Hare describes the archangel's moral thinking: "When presented with a novel situation, he will be able at once to scan all its properties, including the consequences of alternative actions, and frame a universal principle (perhaps a highly specific one) which he can accept for action in that situation, no matter what role he himself were to occupy in it" (*Moral Thinking*, 44). This form of thinking is used to select or justify intuitive moral principles as well as to resolve conflicts that may arise between them.

Hare maintains that we need both forms of thought; the existentialists and the intuitionists each fail to recognize this. Contra the existentialists, says Hare, we do not need to start fresh each time we are faced with a situation. Instead, we employ our intuitive principles and act out of the dispositions educated by them. "Let anybody who is tempted by [existentialist] doctrines of this kind think what it would be like to drive a car without having *learnt* how to drive a car, or having totally forgotten everything that one had ever learnt—to drive it, that is, deciding *ab initio* at each moment what to do with the steering wheel, brake and other controls" (*Moral Thinking*, 36).

Intuitive principles also help guard against rationalizations in our own self-interest. Hare writes:

> A further reason for relying in much of our moral conduct on relatively general principles is that, if we do not, we expose ourselves to constant temptation to special pleading. . . . In practice, especially when in haste or under stress, we may easily, being human, 'cook' our moral thinking to suit

---

18. Hare claims this distinction exists in both Plato and Aristotle.

our own interest. For example, it is only too easy to persuade ourselves that the act of telling a lie in order to get ourselves out of a hole does a great deal of good to ourselves at relatively small cost to anybody else; whereas in fact, if we view the situation impartially, the indirect costs are much greater than the total gains. It is partly to avoid such cooking that we have intuitions or dispositions firmly built into our characters and motivations. (*Moral Thinking,* 38)

While the existentialsts are wrong to dismiss intuitive moral principles, the intuitionists are wrong to think they are sufficient for moral thinking. We do sometimes encounter situations in which our intuitive principles do not seem appropriate (Should we lie, for example, to Aunt Polly when she asks us if we like her dress? Should we lie to the Nazi at the door?). We may be confronted with a conflict between two intuitive principles (I have promised to help my roomate with her homework and I have a duty to finish my own homework). Or we may wonder what principles to inculcate in our children. In such cases, we need to rely on critical thinking. We must recognize, says Hare, that our intuitions are the product of our moral education and past decisions:

> They are not self-justifying; we can always ask whether the upbringing was the best we could have, or whether the past decisions were the right ones, or, even if so, whether the principles then formed should be applied to a new situation, or, if they cannot all be applied, *which* should be applied. To use intuition itself to answer such questions is a viciously circular procedure; if the dispositions formed by our upbringing are called into question, we cannot appeal to them to settle the question. (*Moral Thinking,* 40)

If we base our moral theory on intuitions alone as the intuitionists do or if we view everything as situational like the existentialists, we are stuck in relativism. Critical thinking, maintains Hare, provides an objective base for our intuitive principles and so provides a way out of relativism by making rational moral discourse possible.[19]

At the beginning of this chapter, we mentioned that utilitarianism was in a crisis which could be summed up in the question, "If morality is acting for the happiness of the greatest number, what's in it for me?" In answering this question, Hare suggests that we consider how we would raise a child if we had only the child's interests in mind. Using this device, he argues that there are nonmoral reasons for adopting the method of moral thinking outlined above. In other words,

---

[19]. When do we engage in intuitive thinking and when in critical thinking? Hare says that it is up to us to know ourselves—our powers of thought and character: "We have to know ourselves in order to tell how much we can trust ourselves to play the archangel without ending up in the wrong Miltonic camp as *fallen* archangels" (*Moral Thinking,* 45).

the world is such that the moral life is in our own interest; morality helps one find fulfillment.

Hare claims that if he were bringing up a child in the child's interest, he "would bring him up on moral prima facie principles of just the same sort as the act-utilitarian archangel would select, so far as I could determine what these were" (*Moral Thinking,* 194). This would be in the child's interest for several reasons. Hare begins by observing that many qualities that contribute to personal success such as courage, self-control, and perseverance are also moral qualities. Also, we cannot predict the future course of a child's life. We ought not, for example, teach him the principle of always doing (without regard for morality) what is to his own advantage because we do not know if he will be lucky enough or "talented" enough to act this way and get away with it. Most societies are organized so that crime—the unfettered pursuit of self-interest—does not pay. Hare observes that "It is better for nearly all of us if social rewards and penalties are attached to socially beneficial and harmful acts; and so it has come about that on the whole they are" (*Moral Thinking,* 196). Should we teach the child merely to *seem* to be good—to be selfish, but appear to be just? Hare responds that being only superficially very respectable requires capacities beyond those most of us have; by far the easiest way to seem to be good is to be good. If we want the child to have the principles most likely to conduce to his own well-being, he must develop firm dispositions of character that accord with moral principles. Hare is confident that if we bring children up to be virtuous it will be in their interests. People so brought up, he observes, are usually happy. He concludes:

> And I myself would bring up any children that I had charge of accordingly. This is the secular equivalent (or not perhaps so secular) of seeing that they are, as the Marriage Service puts it, 'christianly and virtuously brought up'. And if we ought so to bring up our children, even in their own interests, it would seem that the same could be said of what we ought to do to ourselves, so far as we are able. (*Moral Thinking,* 205)

A popular method of objecting to any form of utilitarianism is to claim that it may be used to justify acts most people consider immoral. For example, we can imagine a case in which it is right, on utilitarian grounds, to sacrifice an innocent person in order to save a number of others. But our intuitions are that innocent people should not be made to suffer for the sake of others. In response to such objections, Hare invokes the distinction in levels of moral thinking. If we are talking about the intuitive level, we can expect to have intuitions that occasionally run counter to the utilitarian conclusion, because these intuitions are the product of our moral upbringing and are designed (by utilitarian critical thinking) to deal with cases we are likely to encounter; there is no guarantee that they will be appropriate for unusual cases. And so, he says, such a reaction does not disprove his theory, it merely suggests that we have been brought up correctly. If we are talking about the critical level, says Hare, we cannot use our intuitions to judge the conclusions of critical thinking because it is critical thinking that judges our intuitions. If critical thinking produces counterintuitive results, so be it. But, it is important to note that Hare thinks this will happen very rarely. Typically, despite initial appearances, utilitarian calculations will not produce counterintuitive judgments (*Moral Thinking*, 182).

So, when faced with such far-fetched examples as a sadistic policeman who gains so much pleasure from torturing his victim that it far outweighs his victim's pain, Hare responds that "It is fairly obvious that no real case like this will occur" (*Moral Thinking*, 141). But suppose the case is made more difficult by greatly increasing the numbers of those who enjoy witnessing the suffering of a few victims, as in the case of the Roman arenas; Hare responds that what ought to be done depends on the alternative to doing it, "The right thing to have done from the utilitarian point of view would have been to have chariot races or football games or other less atrocious sports; modern experience shows that they can generate just as much excitement" (*Moral Thinking*, 142). Now, consider the case of the fanatical doctor who has a strong moral aversion to omitting any steps that could prolong his patients' lives even in the face of great suffering. Hare believes that a conversation with the archangel will convince the doctor that he ought to let the patient die since, in real life, the doctor's preferences will mostly likely be weaker than those of the patient (*Moral Thinking*, 178).

In each of these cases, Hare assumes that the world and our preferences are such that utilitarianism will produce a fairly traditional morality. It could be objected, however, that he is too optimistic, that he underestimates the strength of certain undesirable preferences. There are too many like the sadistic policeman, too many sick people with very strong desires. And, sadly, it is possible that the Roman populace may not have gained as much pleasure from a game of football as from torturing Christians. Finally, the doctor's preferences may be very strong; the pain at letting a patient die may haunt him all of his life, outweighing the pain suffered by the patient in his last days.

So perhaps critical thinking produces counterintuitive results more often than Hare would like to admit. Hare himself acknowledges that it happens in some cases. At the end of his discussion of the fanatical doctor, he admits that we may be forced to conclude that the doctor's preferences win out over the patient's. And, while he thinks that with the world as it is, slavery cannot be justified on utilitarian grounds, he recognizes that this judgment is based on his beliefs about the relevant facts; he admits that if these beliefs "were shown to be false, then the same philosophical views about the nature of the moral argument involved might make me advocate slavery and tyranny" (*Moral Thinking*, 167). Nonetheless, Hare contends that despite the sometimes counterintuitive conclusions of critical thinking, "we would normally be acting rationally if we followed the intuitions, because of the dangers inherent in our human situation: our lack of information and our proneness to self-deception" (*Moral Thinking*, 147).

Such a response will not satisfy some critics. Anscombe, for example, claims not only that we should not reach such conclusions, but that we should not even begin the deliberations in the first place. In "Modern Moral Philosophy," she argues that utilitarianism is inherently flawed precisely because it leaves it open to debate whether, for example, procuring the judicial punishment of the innocent or killing the innocent might, in the face of some consequences, be right. She observes that all forms of utilitarianism are incompatible with the Hebrew-Christian ethic that teaches that certain things are forbidden whatever the consequences (She lists, for example, "choosing to kill the innocent for any purpose, however good; vicarious punishment; treachery . . . ; idolatry; sodomy; adultery; making a false profession of faith" ["Modern," 10]). She observes that the point of the strictness of such prohibitions is, after all, *"that you are not to be tempted by fear or hope of consequences"* ("Modern," 10). And, she goes so far as to say, in response to the person who would leave it open to debate whether or not it may sometimes be right, for example, to procure the judicial execution of the innocent, "I do not want to argue with him; he shows a corrupt mind" ("Modern," 17).[20]

Hare himself seems properly averse to such morally counterintuitive judgments, and he goes to great lengths to avoid making them. At one point in the discussion of the fanatical doctor, Hare allows for the sake of argument that the doctor, his colleagues and the nurses are so morally averse to letting the patient die that their suffering would outweigh that of the suffering patient. So, according to critical thinking, it is right to do what the doctor wishes. But, Hare responds that "we must now make a move that has a decisive impact on the argument: that of asking whether these moral attitudes are alterable, in a way in which the patient's sufferings and consequent preferences are not" (*Moral Thinking,* 180). If the preferences of the doctors and nurses in this case are alterable, Hare asks, "Might not our critical thinking, in that case, come out with the result that the best universal prescription to adopt for this case would be that the doctor and all the others should overcome their aversion [to letting the patient die]? The critical thinking itself might help them to do this" (*Moral Thinking,* 180). That is, perhaps critical thinking will show them that their moral aversions can and should be altered, thus making it right to grant the patient's wish to die in peace (and perhaps making it easier for others to do likewise in the future) (*Moral Thinking,* 181).

But why should we alter some preferences and not others? The fact that preferences may be altered seems to make it possible to reach nearly any conclusion one desires. If a straightforward calculation of existing preferences does not produce the desired conclusion, one might suggest that certain preferences be altered. But which preferences should be altered? One might think that one should alter one's preferences so that they accord with what is morally preferable. That is, one might think that some preferences are morally desirable and some are not and

---

20. Alasdair MacIntyre argues that standoffs such as these are to be expected given the state of modern moral philosophy. Inspired by Anscombe's article, he argues that the modern use of moral terms lacks intelligibility and that the possibility of rational moral discourse has been lost. While Hare and others may be correct in their analysis of the way moral terms *are* used, MacIntyre contends, they are wrong to assume it is the way they *should* be used. He claims that rational moral discourse requires a *teleological* framework. We look at MacIntyre's argument in the next section.

those that are not are the ones that should be altered. But this sort of response fits better with nonutilitarian moral theories like Aristotle's or Kant's. Such moral theories have a conception of the good, of the good life, and of human flourishing around which human preferences should be oriented. It is these conceptions, not utilitarian judgments, which determine which preferences should be altered.

One might follow a more consistently utilitarian approach and ask whether a possible alteration will be more beneficial than not. But it is not clear that this can be determined on a utilitarian basis, that is, apart from a conception of what it means for a human being or a society to flourish. Imagine, for example, the archangel describing in every detail a society in which the principle of fidelity has been abandoned. Reformers and conservatives could agree on the description of such a society, but disagree as to whether or not such a society was better off (and recall, this possibility is an integral part of Hare's prescriptivism). The reason for this, the objection might go, is that how we evaluate a harm or a benefit is determined in part by what one thinks counts as human flourishing. The reformer observes the pain involved in denying various desires and counts these as greater than the satisfactions involved in remaining faithful because, according to his ideal, one flourishes in being true to one's desires, particularly erotic ones. The conservative observes the pain involved in denying various desires and counts them as less than the satisfactions involved in remaining faithful because, according to his ideal, one flourishes when his passions are ruled by right reason. The problem for utilitarianism is that, assuming preferences can be altered, it does not seem to be able to answer the question, "How do we know when they should be altered?" If we alter our existing preferences to maximize the satisfaction of some set of preferences, we can always ask, "Should that set be altered?" When does the alteration stop?

Because it lacks a conception of what it means for a human being to flourish, utilitarian critical thinking can be used to justify such practices as infanticide and killing the mentally diminished or physically disabled. We might claim that allowing such acts runs counter to our intuitive moral principles and, because of our strong moral aversions, would cause more pain than pleasure. But, a plausible argument can be made that ultimately more pleasure than pain will result if we alter our current moral aversions to such practices. While Hare would not endorse such conclusions, his most famous student, Peter Singer, has.[21] The debate between these two utilitarians cannot be settled on utilitarian grounds; it requires a conception of human flourishing. According to Anscombe, rational moral theory itself requires just such a conception. Alasdair MacIntyre, to whom we shall now turn, concurs.

21.   See, for example, Peter Singer, *Practical Ethics,* 2nd ed. (Cambridge: Cambridge University Press, 1993).

Alasdair MacIntyre

[T]he whole point of ethics . . . is to enable man to pass from his present state to his true end . . .

Alasdair MacIntyre (1929–) opens *After Virtue* (1981)[22] with "A Disquieting Suggestion." He invites the reader to imagine that the natural sciences have suffered a catastrophe, leaving us with only bits and pieces of the knowledge we once had. People continue to argue about theories and to use scientific terms, but nobody realizes that the context that made these theories and terms intelligible has been lost. What is the point of this imaginary world? MacIntyre's disquieting suggestion is this: "The hypothesis which I wish to advance is that in the actual world which we inhabit the language of morality is in the same state of grave disorder as the language of natural science in the imaginary world which I described" (*After Virtue*, 2). MacIntyre contends that we possess only parts of a conceptual scheme; so, while we continue to use many ethical terms, "we have—very largely, if not entirely—lost our comprehension, both theoretical and practical, of morality" (*After Virtue*, 2). Ethics has suffered a catastrophe. What is that catastrophe? In a few words: The breakdown of the Enlightenment project to justify morality.

MacIntyre provides a history of the succession of failed attempts to provide a secular foundation for morality. Because our predecessor culture failed to provide a rational justification for morality, our own largely emotivist culture has concluded that morality is a matter of individual desire or choice; moral debates cannot be resolved rationally. MacIntyre contends that the Enlightenment project not only failed but was destined to fail because of its rejection of a *teleological framework,* like that present in the work of Aristotle, which views "man" as a functional concept. Within such a framework, persons are viewed as having a *telos,* a final end, goal, purpose, or true nature toward which they naturally tend. Just as an acorn moves toward and flourishes in becoming an oak tree, human beings move toward and flourish in attaining their final end. For Aristotle, ethics teaches us how to move from man-as-he-happens-to-be toward man-as-he-could-be-if-he-realized-his-essential-nature. The precepts of morality tell us how to realize our true nature or *telos.* To act contrary to them frustrates our nature and prevents us from flourishing as human beings. An intelligible account of ethics, contends MacIntyre, requires all three: Human nature-as-it-is, the precepts of ethics, and human nature-as-it-ought-to-be (human nature, human morality, human fulfillment).[23]

Teleological moral arguments take "man" to be a functional concept, defined in terms of people's roles. According to the Aristotelian tradition, "[T]o be

---

[22.] Alasdair MacIntyre, *After Virtue,* 2nd ed. (Notre Dame, IN: University of Notre Dame Press, 1984); hereafter cited in the text as *After Virtue.*

[23.] MacIntyre notes that this scheme, with some modifications, is found in Aquinás as well (see our Chapter 2).

a man is to fill a set of roles each of which has its own point and p⟩
ber of a family, citizen, soldier, philosopher, servant of God" (*Af*
Within this framework, it is possible, contra Hume and others, to mov⌐ ⌐
tual premises to evaluative conclusions. MacIntyre provides the following illus-
trations:

> From such factual premises as 'This watch is grossly inaccurate and irregular
> in time-keeping' and 'This watch is too heavy to carry about comfortably',
> the evaluative conclusion validly follows that 'This is a bad watch'. From
> such factual premises as 'He gets a better yield for this crop per acre than any
> farmer in the district', . . . and 'His dairy herd wins all the first prizes at the
> agricultural shows', the evaluative conclusion validly follows that 'He is a
> good farmer'. (*After Virtue*, 57–58)

When this functional concept of man was rejected moral philosophers began to
consider "man" independently of his roles. This led to the divorce of fact and
value, to the acceptance of the thesis that "ought" cannot follow from "is." In contrast, if one is defined by one's roles, we can make valid value judgments based on
one's factual success at being, say, a husband, mother, doctor, citizen, or friend.

According to MacIntyre, Hume, Kant, and Kierkegaard all rejected a teleological view of human nature. They maintained the moral content of Christianity
but tried to base the authority of these rules in an account of human-nature-as-
it-is, not as a bridge between human-nature-as-it-is and human nature-as-it-
ought-to-be-if-it-realized-its-telos. But, as MacIntyre points out, since these
precepts were designed to *correct and improve* human-nature-as-it-is, they cannot be
deduced from that conception of human nature. In addition, in an attempt to secularize ethics, philosophers rejected the conception of moral judgments as divine
law. If, says MacIntyre, following Anscombe, we take away both contexts, teleology and divine law, then our moral judgments lose their proper status. The individual becomes his own moral authority, and moral judgments are determined by
the desire and will of the self.

In a chapter entitled, "Nietzsche or Aristotle?," MacIntyre suggests that in
light of the failure of the Enlightenment project these are the only two options
now facing us. Nietzsche was correct in his observation that morality had become
mere expressions of a subjective will. This resulted from the failure of the Enlightenment project after its rejection of an Aristotelian scheme. The defensibility
of Nietzsche's position turns, says MacIntyre, on the following question: "Was it
right in the first place to reject Aristotle?" Contending that it was not, he offers
what he takes to be a viable Aristotelian ethical theory. In doing so, MacIntyre
does not suggest a return to the ancient world with its teleological view of the
universe. He argues, rather, that a teleological view of morality should be constructed within small communities. Such communities can establish agreed-on
ends for which ethics is the bridge from persons-as-they-are to persons-as-they-
ought-to-be. It is in this context that he offers his account of virtue.

MacIntyre says that the primary question to ask in ethics is "What sort of person ought I to become?" This is in contrast to modern moral philosophy in which the primary questions are "What rules ought we to follow?" and "Why ought we obey them?" According to Rawls, because persons are free to disagree over views of the good life or ends, the rules of morality cannot be derived from a view of the good for human beings. In addition, qualities of character are valued only insofar as they enable persons to follow the rules. MacIntyre argues that this primacy of rules over qualities of character cannot provide an adequate account of the virtues since a justification of these qualities depends on a prior justification of rules. But, since the modern justifications of the rules are problematic, so is the modern account of the virtues. He proposes reversing this priority, providing an account of virtue first in order to then understand the function and authority of rules.

MacIntyre develops a concept of virtue in three stages. He first articulates the virtues as "qualities necessary to achieve the goods internal to practices" (*After Virtue*, 273). Next, he describes them as "qualities contributing to the good of a whole life" understood in terms of a narrative unity (*After Virtue*, 273). Finally, they are related to "the pursuit of a good for human beings the conception of which can only be elaborated and possessed within an ongoing social tradition" (*After Virtue*, 273).

Practices are, according to MacIntyre, "any coherent and complex form of socially established cooperative human activity" (*After Virtue*, 187).[24] He provides the following examples: Football, chess, architecture, farming, enquiries of physics, the work of historians, painting, music, and, in the ancient and medieval world, creating and sustaining communities (households, cities, nations). The virtues are qualities that enable persons to attain goods internal to practices (*After Virtue*, 191). Goods internal to the game of chess, for example, are analytic skill and strategic imagination (prize money is a good external to the game).

Practices involve standards of excellence and obedience to rules as well as achievement of goods. When one enters into a practice, one must submit his or her own views to the authority of those standards and to the judgments passed on his or her performance when compared to them. It is not, for example, left to the individual to determine for him or herself what counts as playing chess well. "In the realm of practices," MacIntyre writes, "the authority of both goods and standards operates in such a way as to rule out all subjectivist and emotivist analyses of judgment" (*After Virtue*, 190).

[24.] MacIntyre's full definition of a practice is as follows: "By a 'practice' I am going to mean any coherent and complex form of socially established cooperative human activity through which goods internal to that form of activity are realized in the course of trying to achieve those standards of excellence which are appropriate to, and partially definitive of, that form of activity, with the result that human powers to achieve excellence, and human conceptions of the ends and goods involved, are systematically extended" (*After Virtue*, 187).

Some virtues will be required in any practice. For example, says MacIntyre, persons entering a practice must subordinate themselves to others within the practice; they must recognize what is due to whom; they must be prepared to take risks; they must be aware of their inadequacies. If one cheats, one uses the practice only to obtain external goods. So, maintains MacIntyre, justice, courage, and honesty are necessary in any practice with internal goods and standards of excellence; they are genuine excellences whatever our private moral standpoint or society's particular codes.

MacIntyre recognizes that an account of the virtues in terms of a practice is not by itself adequate; this brings him to the second and third stages of his argument. In the second stage, MacIntyre articulates a conception of a *narrative unity of a life* so we can see that the virtues allow one to live one kind of unified life rather than another. He notes that such a view runs contrary to many of our modern tendencies. For example, we tend to divide our life into many parts; we divide it into work and leisure, public and private. We think atomistically about human action, analyzing the complex in terms of the simple. We separate individuals from their roles. It is alien to us, says MacIntyre, to see that particular actions derive their character as parts of larger wholes. But, he contends, we cannot adequately characterize a person's behavior independently of his or her intentions and the settings that make sense of those intentions. He supplies the following example. A man is busy in the garden. We ask him what he is doing. He may be getting his garden ready for winter and incidentally pleasing his wife, or he may be pleasing his wife by exercising. In order to understand what he is doing, we situate the action within a larger setting: in the first case, the setting of a household activity; in the second, the setting of marriage. Until we know which intentions, beliefs, and settings are primary, until we have *a narrative history,* we cannot adequately understand what someone is doing.

MacIntyre maintains that we need to see all of human life as a narrative from birth to death. I can only answer "What am I to do?" he says, if I first know to what stories I belong. The unity of a human life then "is the unity of a narrative embodied in a single life" (*After Virtue,* 218). MacIntyre continues:

> To ask 'What is the good for me?' is to ask how best I might live out that unity and bring it to completion. To ask 'What is the good for man?' is to ask what all answers to the former question must have in common. But now it is important to emphasize that it is the systematic asking of these two questions and the attempt to answer them in deed as well as in word which provide the moral life with its unity. The unity of a human life is the unity of a narrative quest. Quests sometimes fail, are frustrated, abandoned or dissipated into distractions; and human lives may in all these ways also fail. But the only criteria for success or failure in a human life as a whole are the criteria of success or failure in a narrated or to-be-narrated quest. (*After Virtue,* 218–219)

A quest for what? MacIntyre emphasizes two features of a medieval quest. First, a quest requires a partial conception of the final *telos* (the good for man). Looking for a conception of *the* good helps us order other goods. It allows us to go beyond a conception of the virtues limited to practices that each have their own goods. Second, a quest is not a search for something already fully character-ized; it involves growth in understanding what is being sought as well as increased understanding of the self. "The virtues," MacIntyre concludes,

> are to be understood as those dispositions which will not only sustain prac-tices and enable us to achieve the goods internal to practices, but which will also sustain us in the relevant kind of quest for the good, by enabling us to overcome the harms, dangers, temptations and distractions which we en-counter, and which will furnish us with increasing self-knowledge and in-creasing knowledge of the good. The catalogue of the virtues will therefore include the virtues required to sustain the kind of households and the kind of political communities in which men and women can seek for the good together and the virtues necessary for philosophical enquiry about the char-acter of the good. We have then arrived at a provisional conclusion about the good life for man: the good life for man is the life spent in seeking for the good life for man, and the virtues necessary for the seeking are those which will enable us to understand what more and what else the good life for man is. (*After Virtue*, 219)

This brings MacIntyre to the third stage in his account of the virtues. We do not seek the good or exercise the virtues as abstract individuals; we have a partic-ular social identity; *we are part of an ongoing social tradition*:

> I am someone's son or daughter, someone else's cousin or uncle; I am a cit-izen of this or that city, a member of this or that guild or profession; I be-long to this clan, that tribe, this nation. Hence what is good for me has to be good for one who inhabits these roles. As such, I inherit from the past of my family, my city, my tribe, my nation, a variety of debts, inheritances, rightful expectations and obligations. These constitute the given of my life, my moral starting point. This is in part what gives my life its own moral par-ticularity. (*After Virtue*, 220)

Such a position is in stark contrast with one like Rawls's, according to which such roles are inessential to the person and irrelevant to morality. MacIntyre ac-knowledges that this way of thinking is alien to modern individualism, which claims that persons are what they choose to be and that to be a moral agent is to be able to stand back from every situation and pass judgment on it from a purely universal and abstract point of view, with all particulars stripped away. Morality, according to modern individualism, is located in the abstract autonomous self, not in social roles or practices. In premodern, traditional societies, however, the individual identifies him- or herself by membership in a social group. These are not accidental characteristics that need to be placed behind a veil of ignorance in order to get at the essential person; they are, says MacIntyre, part of my substance, defining partially, sometimes wholly, my obligations and duties. They are not irrelevant to morality but constitute its starting point.

In contrast to the modern liberal view of the self that has no history, MacIntyre offers a narrative view of the self. The story of each person's life is part of the story of the communities in which he or she finds her identity. We can never leave these particularities behind in our search for the good. I am, whether I like it or not, a part of a tradition, a tradition that involves argument as to what the good for human beings is and ought to be (*After Virtue,* 222). What extends and strengthens or weakens and destroys traditions? The exercise or lack of exercise of relevant virtues. Thus, MacIntyre concludes the final stage in his articulation of the virtues:

> The virtues find their point and purpose not only in sustaining those relationships necessary if the variety of goods internal to practices are to be achieved and not only in sustaining the form of an individual life in which that individual may seek out his or her good as the good of his or her whole life, but also in sustaining those traditions which provide both practices and individual lives with their necessary historical context. (*After Virtue,* 223)

Such an account enables us to make moral judgments that are subject to truth and falsity. MacIntyre writes: "[A]ssertions of the form 'To do this in this way would be better for X and/or for his or her family, city or profession' are susceptible of objective truth and falsity" (*After Virtue,* 224). He continues:

> The presupposition of this objectivity is of course that we can understand the notion of 'good for X' and cognate notions in terms of some conception of the unity of X's life. What is better or worse for X depends upon the character of that intelligible narrative which provides X's life with its unity. Unsurprisingly it is the lack of any such unifying conception of a human life which underlies modern denials of the factual character of moral judgments and more especially of those judgments which ascribe virtues or vices to individuals. (*After Virtue,* 225)

MacIntyre attempts to spell out an understanding of social life that a tradition of the virtues requires. It differs from the culture of individualism in which conceptions of virtue are private and morality is primarily rule-based, in which there is no shared view of the good for man so no shared view of the virtues. The question, "Nietzsche or Aristotle?" arose because the current state of morality is one of disorder and apparent arbitrariness. Since the rejection of Aristotelian teleology, philosophers have tried to give some rational, secular alternative account of morality. Nietzsche saw that these failed. Nonetheless, MacIntyre claims, we are not stuck with Nietzsche's view because the initial rejection of Aristotelian tele-ology was wrong, and he offers his own teleological account of the virtues. Nietzsche's rejection of modern rule-based morality does not apply to Aristotle because virtues, not rules, are primary. So, MacIntyre maintains, the Aristotelian tradition can be restated in such a way as to provide a rational justification for our moral and social commitments.

MacIntyre and other so-called friends of the virtues are not without their critics. In response to such Aristotelian revivals, Hare, for example, writes that "[S]ettling on an end, like deciding what 'human flourishing' is, is answering an evaluative question. We cannot therefore without circularity answer all evaluative questions by appealing to a *telos* as given."[25] MacIntyre might respond that such circularity is not vicious and, when conducted within a properly functioning tra-dition, perfectly rational. Other critics worry that this justification is not strong enough; they worry that MacIntyre's contention that moral philosophy must al-ways be conducted within a tradition constitutes a form of relativism. If, as Mac-Intyre maintains, we cannot appeal to any rational standards independent of all traditions, there seems to be no rational way to decide between two incompatible traditions. MacIntyre responds to this charge by arguing that one tradition may be judged rationally superior to its rival if it can provide a better account of its rival's defects and of its own than the rival can. So, even though MacIntyre maintains that morality is only intelligible within a tradition, he believes that rational argu-ment can take place between traditions.[26]

While contemporary liberals have been criticized for emphasizing justice to the detriment of the virtues, virtue theorists like MacIntyre have been criticized for emphasizing virtue to the detriment of justice. MacIntyre offers a brief ac-count of justice in *After Virtue,* in which he is critical of liberal conceptions of jus-tice. He objects, in part, to their view of society as "a collection of strangers, each pursuing his or her own interests under minimal constraints" (*After Virtue,* 251) and suggests that judgments about justice and injustice require a moral consensus regarding the good for man and the common good that can only be had within a community. It is not clear, however, how a community-based conception of jus-tice can adequately deal with those outside of one's community or how it can be used to evaluate the activities of particular communities critically.[27] History has

25.   *Hare and Critics: Essays on Moral Thinking,* ed. Douglas Seanor and N. Fotion (Oxford: Clarendon Press, 1988), 214–215.

26.   MacIntyre's account of tradition-based rationality is worked out more fully in *Whose Justice? Which Ra-tionality?* (Notre Dame, IN: University of Notre Dame Press, 1988) and *Three Rival Versions of Moral En-quiry: Encyclopaedia, Genealogy, and Tradition* (Notre Dame, IN: University of Notre Dame Press, 1990). MacIntyre's later work defends and develops the tradition of Thomas Aquinás.

27.   See, for example, the essays by Charles Taylor, David Miller, Elizabeth Frazer, and Nicola Lacey in *Af-ter MacIntyre: Critical Perspectives on the Work of Alasdair MacIntyre,* ed. John Horton and Susan Mendus (Notre Dame, IN: University of Notre Dame Press, 1994). For an insightful discussion of this debate, see Onora O'Neill, *Towards Justice and Virtue: A Constructive Account of Practical Reasoning* (Cambridge: Cambridge University Press, 1996).

shown that particular communities are too often capable of the greatest atrocities toward those "on the outside" and too often blind to their own prejudices. Such a conception of justice seems inadequate for the needs of justice within such large and diverse bodies as our democratic society, let alone for the increasing needs of global justice. Much of the progress made in the area of justice, movements in human rights, rising democracies, the toleration of religion, the abolition of slavery, and the emancipation of women, has been due, say critics, to accounts of justice that are more universal than an account like MacIntyre's. The last of these movements is the focus of our next section.

Carol Gilligan

My goal is to expand the understanding of human development by using the group left out in the construction of theory to call attention to what is missing in its account.

Although feminist ethics can be traced back to the late 18th century to the work of Mary Wollstonecraft,[28] it has not flourished until quite recently. Still, a history of ethics would be deficient if it were to fail to mention this influential movement. Due to the great diversity of views that fall under this heading and the short space we have to discuss them, we will have to limit our discussion to two of the main options found within feminist ethics: Liberal feminism and Difference feminism. While we will look at some of the differences between the two approaches below, it is important to note that, like most forms of feminism, Liberal and Difference feminism are united in their rejection of conceptions of ethics that exclude the experience of women, enshrine methods and values that privilege men, and justify power relationships that disadvantage women. As would be expected, there is a deeply practical side to feminist ethics. Its proponents seek to eliminate the social, economic, and cultural oppression of women found throughout the world. They demand equal rights for women that include full access to all the modes of life required for human flourishing. The practical concerns of feminism force us to ask once again, the more theoretical question "What does it mean to flourish as a human being?"

This book has examined the relationship of human nature to human morality largely ignoring the fact that most thinkers we have considered believed that women are inferior to men and incapable of moral excellence. They claimed that while women may be capable of cultivating the virtues appropriate to their sex, they are incapable of cultivating the virtues necessary for true human fulfillment. The claim that women are by nature inferior to men runs from Plato and Aristotle through the medievals to Kant and Rousseau and well beyond. Women are

---

[28.]   We discuss Wollstonecraft's work in more detail in Chapter 3.

deficient in reason, these men claimed, and are more moved by emotions, passions, and desires. Emotions, passions, and desires are traits human beings share with animals while reason is a property we share with the gods. So, as we observed in our section on Wollstonecraft, women seem to be located somewhere on the scale of cosmic being and value midway between animals and men while men are located between women and gods. Aristotle, for example, concludes that ". . . the female is, as it were, a mutilated male."[29] And Kant contends that since women are trapped in their passions or desires, they lack the reason and freedom necessary for the attainment of virtue and full personhood. Since they cannot become virtuous, Kant encourages women to aspire to be beautiful![30]

In addition to their different capacities for reason, men and women were thought to differ in a number of other ways. While men are autonomous or independent, women are dependent or interdependent. While men are dominant, competitive, aggressive, emotionally detached, and active, women are submissive, cooperative, nurturing, emotionally attached, and passive. Men are leaders, women followers. These differences alone would not justify the moral superiority of men, but the ideal person has typically been defined in terms of these stereotypical male traits. So, for example, the ideal person is the autonomous man of reason who conquers his emotions and desires, sees the moral law, and sets himself to follow it. Women, possessing by nature the "feminine" traits listed above, are not capable of attaining this ideal.

Society, so the story goes, should be ordered in a manner consistent with these essential differences. Women, outfitted for gestation, are suited to nurture and to be submissive. Men are equipped to impregnate, dominate, and to rule. The private life of the home, thought to be inferior to public life, is the only place for which women are fit. Women are to be limited to the "inferior" work of tending the home, raising children, in short, creating domestic tranquility, so that their men can have the leisure to achieve greatness in their community and beyond. Women may flourish *as women* insofar as they perfect their work in the home, but *human* flourishing is to be obtained largely in the activities of the public sphere.

Feminist ethics seeks to unmask the pretensions of male privilege and power found in such models of human flourishing. As we mentioned above, there are two main approaches to this unmasking: Liberal feminism and Difference feminism. *Liberal feminism* often adopts the "male" ideal, but claims that women are capable of achieving it; in effect, making the ideal gender-neutral. There are, according to Liberal feminists, no morally significant differences between men and women. *Difference feminism* allows that there are morally significant differences but claims that these are not grounds for inequality. There may be a "male" ideal and a "female" ideal, but one is not superior to the other.

29.   From Aristotle, "On the Generation of Animals" in *The Complete Works of Aristotle,* ed. Jonathan Barnes (Princeton, NJ: Princeton University Press, 1984), Book II, 737a, 25.

30.   From Immanuel Kant, *Observations on the Feeling of Beauty and Sublime,* as found in Mary Briody Mahowald, ed., *Philosophy of Woman* (Indianapolis, IN: Hackett Publishing Company, 1994), 102–112.

Mary Wollstonecraft's work is representative of Liberal feminism. We covered her work in some detail in Chapter 3, but recall from our discussion, that Wollstonecraft largely adopts the moral ideal of her male predecessors. She agrees, for example, that reason rules in the morally good person: Virtue arises from "the clear conviction of reason" so that "morality is made to rest on a rock against which the storms of passion vainly beat" (*Vindication*, 114). Where she differs from her predecessors is in her conviction that men and women are equally capable of cultivating the reason proper to the life of virtue and human fulfillment. There is a single gender-neutral form of human flourishing, not one superior form of life appropriate to men and one inferior form of life appropriate to women.

Liberal feminists admit that there are obvious differences between men and women. Men and women are biologically different: for example, they have different reproductive organs and, on average, men are stronger than women. But liberal feminists maintain that all of the differences between the sexes are morally irrelevant; they make no more difference to becoming a morally good person than being left-handed, bald, or tall. Women are not different from men in any ways that prevent them from achieving moral excellence and flourishing as human beings.

Furthermore, men and women are not different in any ways that justify limiting women's roles in society. Liberal feminists tend to agree with the model of human flourishing that locates fulfillment primarily in the public sphere. They maintain that the restriction of women to the private sphere as wives and mothers and to limited public roles such as teacher, social worker, and nurse, hinders their ability to flourish as human beings. Women, no less than men, are capable of cultivating those qualities necessary for success in the public sphere and ought to be given the opportunity to do so. So, a prominent goal of Liberal feminism is the eradication of social, political, religious, and economic obstacles that prevent women from equal access to all of the public roles that are open to men. For example, since child-bearing has historically limited women to roles in the home, liberal feminism often endorses the use of contraceptives, access to abortion, and liberal child-care policies to ensure equal access for women to the public sphere.

As the name suggests, a central tenet of Difference feminism is the belief that there are differences between men and women which are morally significant. In her book, *In a Different Voice* (1982),[31] the psychologist and educator Carol Gilligan (1936–) claims that men and women think differently about ethical issues. Men can be said to have an *ethic of justice,* women an *ethic of care.* But, while these two approaches may be different, they are equal. Indeed, Gilligan at times seems to argue, they complement each other in important ways.

Gilligan's book is largely a response to the theory of moral development advanced by Lawrence Kohlberg. It is worth looking briefly at his theory in order to better appreciate the contrast Gilligan wishes to draw with her own theory. In

---

[31.] Carol Gilligan, *In a Different Voice: Psychological Theory and Women's Dependence* (Cambridge, MA: Harvard University Press, 1982); hereafter cited in the text as *Different Voice*.

developing his theory, Kohlberg explicitly relies on and further develops the work of Rawls. In the eighth chapter of *A Theory of Justice*, Rawls suggests a philosophy of moral education that shows the way a sense of justice is acquired by members in a well-ordered society. He outlines three stages of moral development: the morality of authority, the morality of association, and the morality of principles. In his work, *The Philosophy of Moral Development*,[32] Kohlberg further develops each of these for a total of six stages: *stage 1*—heteronomous morality; *stage 2*—individualism, instrumental purpose, and exchange; *stage 3*—mutual interpersonal expectations, relationships, and interpersonal conformity; *stage 4*—social system and conscience; *stage 5*—social contract or utility and individual rights; and *stage 6*—universal ethical principles. Each stage of moral thinking has its own definition of what is right, its own reasons for doing right, and its own social perspective. Like Rawls, Kohlberg thinks education for justice occurs by moving from lower to higher stages of development.

Morality at the highest stage is characterized by an impartial thought process with an emphasis on justice and rights. Persons at the highest level of moral development reason from something like Rawls's original position. Recall from our earlier discussion that one important condition of the original position is the veil of ignorance that requires persons to assume ignorance of various contingencies like one's place in society, one's natural assets or abilities, and one's conception of the good. We place such particulars behind the veil of ignorance because they may tempt us to bias our choice of moral principles in our own favor. Another key characteristic of this standpoint is reversibility, what Kohlberg calls "moral musical chairs." According to Kohlberg, Rawls's original position embodies the idea that a moral judgment must be reversible: we must be willing to accept our judgment even if we found ourselves in someone else's place. Like Rawls, Kohlberg believes that all rational agents who reason from this point of view will arrive at the same objective moral principles, that is, the principles of justice as fairness. According to Kohlberg, persons at the highest stage of development recognize that morality is all about justice. More specifically, justice is largely about resolving conflicts of rights. On Kohlberg's theory, moral obligation is an obligation to respect the rights of another person; moral principles are principles for impartially resolving competing claims.

The problem with Kohlberg's theory of moral education, according to Gilligan, is that while it may work for boys, it does not work for girls. Very few females, it seems, reach the higher stages of moral development according to Kohlberg's scale.[33] This is not an uncommon phenomenon in the social sciences, observes Gilligan. The practice has often been to develop a standard based on a

---

[32]   Lawrence Kohlberg, *The Philosophy of Moral Development: Moral Stages and the Idea of Justice* (San Francisco: Harper, 1981).

[33]   Actually, the theory may not work all that well for boys either. Later research has shown that very few persons, male or female, reach the highest stage on Kohlberg's scale. This has led proponents of the method to focus on education for the lower stages.

study of male development (Kohlberg originally studied 84 boys); when females are compared to it, they end up looking deficient. But, she suggests, if we were to begin with female subjects, we may end up with a very different standard of development. So, the problem may not be with female development, but rather with our (male) standard. Gilligan writes:

> The disparity between women's experience and the representation of human development, noted throughout the psychological literature, has generally been seen to signify a problem in women's development. Instead, the failure of women to fit existing models of human growth may point to a problem in the representation, a limitation in the conception of human condition, an omission of certain truths about life. (*Different Voice*, 2)

In a Different Voice is an attempt to rectify such omissions by developing a standard of female moral development.

Gilligan argues that, in contrast to men who mature by individuating themselves from others, women develop more in relationship to other people. While they are less able to take the impartial perspective of the "generalized" other, they are more empathetic and better able to take the role of the particular other. This is evident in such things as the differences between the mother–child relationship of boys and girls and in the sorts of games children play. Piaget's studies showed that boys tend to play games with much more complicated sets of rules than girls; for boys, resolving conflicts by increasing the set of rules is as much a part of the fun as the game itself. Girls, by contrast, tend to subordinate the rules to relationships: if there is a conflict, the game ends.

In identifying themselves within relationships, women assume responsibility for others; they see themselves as nurturing and caring for others. Their thinking is contextual and narrative rather than formal and abstract. As a result of their empathetic concern and their willingness to include other perspectives in their deliberations, females may be more reluctant to make firm moral judgments. Rather than accept the classification of women on Kohlberg's scale as typically stage-three thinkers (where morality is conceived in relational terms and goodness is defined in terms of helping and pleasing others) and judge them to be too confused to make firm moral judgments, Gilligan outlines her own stages of moral development based on her observations of the reasoning of women.

The first stage is the stage of self-preservation. At this stage, one is quite egocentric in her attempts to survive in the world. When one recognizes this first stage as selfish, she moves to the second stage, where she focuses on caring for others as the good. But, this constant other-focus, this self-sacrifice, can cause one pain. This, coupled with the recognition of what Gilligan calls "the illogic of inequality between the self and others" forces one to the final stage of development. At this stage, the tension between selfishness and responsibility to others (the central moral conflict for women) is resolved through a new understanding of the connectedness between the self and the other. Care, says Gilligan, becomes universal in its condemnation of hurt; a principle of nonviolence (of not hurting) governs all moral judgment and action. Female self-abnegation and moral self-sacrifice are seen to be immoral in their power to hurt. One sees herself and others as interdependent and equal and so includes both as objects of care.[34] The reluctance to hurt brings with it a reluctance to judge. There is, says Gilligan, a "recognition of the limitation of judgment itself" (*Different Voice*, 103). At this highest stage, goodness is defined as honesty or authenticity. One finds fulfillment in being "true to oneself," while at the same time being responsive to others.

In deliberating from the perspective of an ethic of care, as opposed to an ethic of justice, one does not abstract herself from her particular commitments to family and community, placing them behind a veil of ignorance; rather, she assumes her responsibilities as they arise from her concrete relationships. She thinks concretely in narrative terms rather than abstractly in formal terms. Men reason abstractly as they move away from the messy details of a situation to the pristine universal rule; they seek an algorithm or rational principle that elevates them above the personal and particular to the impersonal and universal. They view ethics like geometry: find the axioms or first principles and then apply them to real-world situations. Women, by contrast, tell stories that describe the actual situation in great detail in order to determine the best course of action. Each person's roles, their relationships to each other, how each would be affected by various courses of action, how their relationships would be altered—all of these particulars are morally relevant. Good judgment, rather than universal principle, is required to show one what to do. In addition, feelings such as affection, empathy, and love do not hinder but actually help one to grasp moral truth.

In an ethic of care, morality is not merely about justice and the resolution of conflicts between rights; it is about caring for others, about nurturing and assuming responsibility for them. The moral person does not merely not interfere with others' rights, she actively promotes the good of others. According to care theory, we ought to become the sorts of people who can fully express concern/nurturance for each other and we ought to create the sort of society in which relationships of care are protected, not prevented, devalued, or used for exploitative purposes. An ethic of care takes intimate relationships as its model, relationships that require compassion, empathy, fidelity, love, and trust. In some cases, the character of the mother has become the model of moral excellence. The nurturing care of a mother for her child is both the source of insight and the motivation for moral decisions.

When compared to Kohlberg's standard and its emphasis on impartiality, justice, and rights, the moral reasoning of women appears partial, inconclusive, and

---

34.   There is a perceived conflict in feminism between an ethics of rights (Liberal feminism) and an ethics of care (Difference feminism). The former are sometimes critical of the latter for emphasizing the care of others to the detriment of individual fulfillment. Gilligan thinks including oneself as an object of care resolves the tension.

immature. But, if we turn the tables and compare the moral reasoning of men to Gilligan's standard with its emphasis on empathy, care, responsibility, and tolerance, male thinking looks detached, cold, indifferent, and intolerant. So which is better?

Some proponents of an ethic of care think it is superior to an ethic of justice and ought to replace it. Critics object, however, that the subordination of rules to relationships, the rejection of the universal in favor of the particular, amounts to a form of relativism. If we all strive, as Gilligan would have us, to be true to ourselves, what's to keep us from all sorts of immoral behavior? This sort of view seems to ignore the fact that our selves are often in need of correction rather than affirmation.

In addition, an ethic of justice may be friendly to the female experience, and so not so much in need of replacement, as some feminists think. A Rawlsian decision procedure, for example, would surely endorse a society willing to listen to the "different voice" of women. It would certainly oppose violence against women, the restriction of rights to men, and other forms of female subordination and oppression. It would support equal access for all persons to the various modes of human flourishing. If women are deficient on Kohlberg's scale, a theory of justice might recognize that this is due, not to their nature, but to past oppression and inferior education. Justice would require this to be remedied. The solution may be not to replace an ethic of justice but more explicitly "to extend it to woman."[35]

Gilligan claims that we actually need both moralities: we need an ethic of justice and an ethic of care. It is not clear, however, how these are to be related. What do we do when they seem to conflict? How are children supposed to be educated? Do we educate boys for justice and girls for caring? Or, should we try to overcompensate for their natural tendencies and educate girls for justice and boys for caring? Or, should we educate both sexes in both forms of thought? How exactly would this work?

Some critics of care ethics object that it would simply restrict women to those same roles that have historically disadvantaged them. For example, given the differences between men and women that Gilligan describes, women seem vastly more suited to raise children than men. Add to this an ethics that emphasizes caring for others and women may find themselves limited to traditional roles in the home or as teachers, social workers, and nurses. An ethic of care, the objection goes, leaves women no better off than the antiwomen ethics of Aristotle and Kant. Defenders of care ethics may respond that they do not intend to keep

---

[35]. One might make a related objection that Gilligan's stages of moral reasoning are less representative of female moral reasoning than even Kohlberg's stages. Gilligan drew her conclusions primarily from three studies: interviews with students who elected to take a college course on moral and political choice; interviews with women contemplating having an abortion; and a rights and responsibilities study. Such studies would seem to produce a picture of moral reasoning so limited it could not safely be generalized to cover all women.

women in the home; they wish, instead, to reform the public sphere by making it more like the private sphere. So, for example, more female doctors would make the medical world more caring; more female CEOs would make the corporate world more cooperative; more female professors would make the academic world more tolerant; and more female politicians would make world peace more attainable.[36]

Both forms of feminist ethics we have considered rely on a view of human nature (either gender-neutral or gendered) that appears to be fixed. Ethics involves finding out what it takes to fulfill that essential nature. More radical forms of feminist ethics reject this *essentialism*. They reject the essentialism of Liberal feminism because, they claim, it assumes that women will flourish when they become like men. They reject the essentialism of difference feminism because they view the differences as endorsing traditional stereotypes which they believe oppress women. Anti-essentialist feminists claim that gender differences, and human nature itself, are mere human constructs. The task of moral philosophy, therefore, is not to discover those ways of life that enable our nature to flourish; it is, rather, to make clear a path for radical free self-creation. This is a view Richard Rorty wholeheartedly shares.

Richard Rorty

[T]o fail as a human being—is to accept somebody else's description of oneself . . .

The work of Rawls, MacIntyre, Hare, and Gilligan is part of a number of larger debates. As we have seen, one debate is over the location of the point from which to justify morality. Is there some point outside of all traditions, some version of an original position, a "view from nowhere," a form of critical thinking, from which we can justify morality; or, must all justifications take place within some tradition and from a particular perspective? Another debate is over which should have priority, justice or the virtues? It seems that if we begin with justice we cannot obtain an adequate account of virtue, but if we begin with virtue we cannot obtain an adequate account of justice. Is an ethic of care a substitute or a supplement to an ethic of justice? Is the preeminent form of human flourishing to be found in the activities of justice or in the possession and exercise of the virtues? Which brings us finally to the debate over the nature of the person. Are persons essentially abstract individual choosers who are properly separated from various contingent characteristics or are they situated, concrete members of communities for whom these characteristics are an essential part of their identity and a proper

---

[36]. For more on feminism and responses to critics, see the essays in *Feminist Ethics,* ed. Moira Gatens (Brookfield, VT: Ashgate Publishing Company, 1998) and *Women and Moral Theory,* ed. Eva Feder Kittay and Diana T. Meyers (Totowa, NJ: Rowman and Littlefield, 1987).

moral starting point? These debates continue with various refinements on each of the sides. There are some philosophers, however, who have refused to choose sides, claiming that these irresolvable debates should be abandoned. Because of their challenges to some of the central and long-held assumptions of moral and political theory, writers like Michel Foucault, Bernard Williams, Judith Butler, and Richard Rorty may be viewed in some sense as antiphilosophy philosophers. In this section, we take a look at Rorty's recommendation that it is time we set these topics aside.

As we begin our discussion of the final philosopher in this book, it is worth taking a moment to reflect. Has our survey of the history of moral thought provided us with an answer (or brought us closer to an answer) to the question, "How should one live?" After looking at some of the central debates, could we declare a winner? Does one view look rationally superior to the others? Does it hold the promise of getting things right? Richard Rorty's (1931–) response to these questions is an enthusiastic "No." When he surveys the history of moral thought, he sees a history of interminable disagreements over human nature, morality, human fulfillment, and the nature of truth. At one time, persons may have characterized such disagreements as the clash between truth and error, reason and prejudice. They may have held out the hope that philosophy could eventually provide us with *the* answer to the question of how to live, an answer that all rational persons could come to accept. According to Rorty, that time has passed. In the paragraphs that follow, we will look at Rorty's views of human nature, morality, rationality, and society found in his book *Contingency, Irony, and Solidarity* (1989).[37] We will take the time to examine these in some detail, since they are representative of a radical shift in the practice of moral philosophy, a shift that calls into question much of the work of moral philosophers since the debates between Socrates and Thrasymachus.

As we have seen throughout this book, many philosophers divide human beings into an essential or "higher" part and inessential, contingent, or "lower" parts. Living a moral and fulfilling life is a matter of overcoming or disciplining what is lower by what is higher. So, for example, Plato thought reason ought to rule our passions and desires; Augustine thought we ought to strive to purify our souls and, with God's help, to overcome our sinful nature; and, Kant thought we ought not be tempted in our moral deliberations to make exceptions for ourselves. In addition, many of the thinkers surveyed maintain that a fulfilling life usually requires some measure of altruism. For Plato, Augustine, and Kant respectively, persons are only fulfilled if they are just, if they follow Christ in a life of self-sacrifice, or if they treat others always as ends in themselves. The good life, according to this long tradition, is to some degree a life lived in harmonious community with others.

As we saw, Nietzsche rejected this view. Traditional morality in general and altruism in particular are not as reasonable as philosophers and theologians have

---

37. Richard Rorty, *Contingency, Irony, and Solidarity* (Cambridge: Cambridge University Press, 1989); hereafter cited in the text as *CIS*.

maintained; indeed, the taming of the self by moral strictures is actually antithetical to our need for self-creation. Rorty observes that Nietzsche's ideal is not the just man, the saint, or the dutiful person but, rather, a poet, someone who Rorty says "makes things new." The poet strives to avoid a life in which he is a mere "copy" or "replica." He or she finds fulfillment in creating a self, in describing that self in his or her own terms. Rorty writes: "To fail as a poet—and thus, for Nietzsche, to fail as a human being—is to accept somebody else's description of oneself, to execute a previously prepared program, to write, at most, elegant variations on previously written poems" (*CIS*, 28). In producing new descriptions of one's self and the world, the poet makes all a product of his or her own will (*CIS*, 29).

Rorty points out that despite their differences, both the traditional and Nietzschean views of morality maintain that human nature is fixed, that it involves a higher/essential part and lower/contingent, parts. Both views go on to develop their own, albeit radically different, moral ideals from their conception of human nature. As Rorty observes, Nietzsche simply inverts Plato, placing *will* above all else. So, who is right? Rorty claims that we need not answer this question. We need not choose between Plato's and Nietzsche's views of human nature and morality if we reject the idea of a fixed human nature altogether.

If we adopt a view of persons as having no essential nature, we will not be able to derive a system of moral principles applicable to all human beings in virtue of that nature. On Rorty's view, each person is a poet who must acknowledge and describe his or her contingent history in his or her own way (*CIS*, 35). There are no universal principles to guide this process. Plato's just man, Augustine's saint, Kant's dutiful person, and Nietzsche's superman exemplify but a few strategies for dealing with the contingencies of one's upbringing. "None of these strategies is privileged over others in the sense of expressing human nature better" (*CIS*, 38). Rorty credits Sigmund Freud with helping us to understand this. According to Rorty, Freud helps us overcome a certain blindness we may have by letting us see with a more sympathetic eye "events which exemplify, for example, sexual perversion, extreme cruelty, ludicrous obsession, and manic delusion" (*CIS*, 38). Freud, Rorty continues, "let us see each of these as the private poem of the pervert, the sadist, or the lunatic: each as richly textured and 'redolent of moral memories' as our own life. He lets us see what moral philosophy describes as extreme, inhuman, and unnatural, as continuous with our own activity" (*CIS*, 38). According to Rorty then, the proper response to debates about human nature and morality is not to choose a side but, rather, "benignly to neglect" those debates.[38]

---

[38] Dropping the topic of human nature is part of a larger movement Rorty refers to as "de-divinization." "De-divinization" involves the rejection of all fixed natures in, for example, God, the world, and persons. The idea that anything has a fixed nature is, according to Rorty, "a remnant of the idea that the world is a divine creation" (*CIS*, 21). De-divinization also involves the rejection of religion, science, and philosophy as fields that discover the truth about essences. Rorty recommends "that we try to get to the point where we no longer worship *anything*, where we treat *nothing* as a quasi-divinity, where we treat *everything*—our language, our conscience, our community—as a product of time and chance. To reach this point would be, in Freud's words, to 'treat chance as worthy of determining our fate'" (*CIS*, 22).

Has Rorty truly opted out of the debates? While rejecting the traditional divisions of the self into, for example, reason, passion, desire and will, Rorty claims that each of us is a web of contingent beliefs and desires and each of us has, whether conscious or unconscious, the need to come to terms with these contingencies (*CIS*, 43). On his account, one succeeds as a human being insofar as one breaks free from one's past and creates a unique self; one fails as a human being insofar as one accepts, like Sartre's "bad faith," "somebody else's description of oneself" (*CIS*, 28). It might be argued that insofar as he identifies features common to all and develops a standard of success and failure applicable to all, Rorty has in fact articulated a conception of human nature (albeit a radical one).

Rorty might respond that at least his view is neutral between Nietzschean and more traditional views of human nature and morality since either form of life may represent a break from one's past.[39] Still, it is in stark opposition to a view like MacIntyre's that requires us to see human life as a unity with one's past. It might be pointed out that Rorty's standard of success is MacIntyre's standard of failure. For MacIntyre, the successful person does not see himself as radically breaking with his past but, rather, as part of a tradition. He is not so much concerned with creating something radically new as with carrying on and developing what has been established. His identity is not something to be created on his own but, rather, something to be discovered and molded in relation to others. One fails as a human being, not insofar as he is a copy, but insofar as he is isolated from his community. Rorty is mistaken to think that avoiding the question, "Plato or Nietzsche?" gets him out of the debates on human nature and morality, since we are still left with the question, "Rorty or MacIntyre?"

In response, Rorty would say that the question "Which view is *true*, Rorty's or MacIntyre's?" cannot be answered. He offers his view not as one that is true but, rather, as one that fits best with the institutions and values of a liberal democratic society. In what follows, we will look first at why Rorty does not offer his view as true; then we will examine his claim that a vocabulary that drops talk of human nature and truth fits best with a certain form of free society.

In a chapter on the contingency of language, Rorty advances two main theses: (1) our beliefs can only have relative validity and (2) intellectual history is the product of random forces. He begins by recommending that we give up the idea of "absolute truth." He adopts instead the view that "truth is made, not found." Truth is a human creation, it is the product of our language. What counts as true at a particular time and place is simply a product of how we happen to talk about things (a product of our "vocabularies"); it is not the discovery of "the way the world really is." Our beliefs are therefore only relatively valid. There is no point of view outside of all vocabularies from which to compare, for example, the

---

[39.] It is interesting to note that despite the professed neutrality, there is a decided tendency toward Nietzschean morality on Rorty's account.

scientific vocabularies of Newton to Aristotle or the moral vocabularies of Freud to St. Paul; there is no way to determine which fits the world better than the other.[40]

"Truth" is a product of human vocabularies that are the result, not of argument or of choice, but of random forces. Drawing an analogy to Darwin's theory of evolution, Rorty contends that language developed from "sheer contingencies" and is aimed at survival not truth; indeed particular vocabularies are no more "true" than any other result of evolution, say "anthropoids or orchids." Like anthropoids and orchids, language develops purposelessly, resulting from mutations produced by random firings in the brain and chance events in the world. This analogy allows us to "see language as we now see evolution, as new forms of life constantly killing off old forms—not to accomplish a higher purpose, but blindly" (*CIS*, 19). Language helps us to survive, that is, *cope* with reality, not grasp truth.[41]

Rorty has a unique approach to philosophical debate. Rather than argue against people who criticize his radical views of truth and human nature, he "redescribes"; that is, he tries "to make the vocabulary in which these [his opponents'] objections are phrased look bad, thereby changing the subject, rather than granting the objector his choice of weapons and terrain by meeting his criticisms head-on" (*CIS*, 44). The intent of redescription is not to show his view is true but to show how things might look if we looked at things his way; in so doing, he hopes to make his view look more attractive, exciting, or open to possibility than any alternative way of looking at things. It is difficult to know how to respond to such an approach. One could employ an alternative vocabulary and hope it, rather than Rorty's, catches on. Or, one could look for a way in which to engage Rorty in argument after all. One could meet Rorty on his own pragmatic terrain and evaluate the claim that his views of the self and of truth are more "useful" for us now. One could ask, "Do they 'cohere better with the institutions of a liberal democracy than the available alternatives do'?" (*CIS*, 197). In what follows, we will claim that the answer to this question is "Yes" and "No": It depends on one's

---

[40.] Rorty acknowledges that it may sometimes look like the world determines which sentences are true or false (e.g., "Red wins" v. "Black wins" or "The butler did it" v. "The doctor did it"). But, he says, when we turn from individual sentences to vocabularies as wholes, the situation is different: "When we consider examples of alternative language games—the vocabulary of ancient Athenian politics versus Jefferson's, the moral vocabulary of Saint Paul versus Freud's, the jargon of Newton versus that of Aristotle, the idiom of Blake versus that of Dryden—it is difficult to think of the world as making one of these better than another, of the world as deciding between them. When the notion of 'description of the world' is moved from the level of criterion-governed sentences within language games to language games as wholes, games which we do not choose between by reference to criteria, the idea that the world decides which descriptions are true can no longer be given a clear sense" (*CIS*, 5).

[41.] To see our current vocabulary as the result of argument, free choice, or some other nonrandom criteria is, claims Rorty, "a species of the more general temptation to think of the world, or the human self, as possessing an intrinsic nature, an essence. That is, it is the result of the temptation to privilege some one among the many languages in which we habitually describe the world or ourselves" (*CIS*, 6).

description of democratic society. Rorty's rhetoric fits well with his own ideal form of liberal democratic society, but it fits poorly with a more traditional or classical liberal view of democratic society.

Rorty redescribes liberalism "as the hope that culture as a whole can be 'poeticized,' . . . the hope that chances for fulfillment of idiosyncratic fantasies will be equalized" (CIS, 53). In such a liberal democratic society, Freedom is placed above Truth as the goal of thinking and social progress (CIS, xiii). Freedom, thought of as "the recognition of contingency" is "the chief virtue" of its citizens (CIS, 46). The ideal citizen is a figure Rorty calls the "liberal ironist." "[L]iberals are people who think that cruelty is the worst thing we do" (CIS, xv). An ironist is one "who faces up to the contingency of his or her own most central beliefs and desires . . ." (CIS, xv). The ironist holds that none of anyone's beliefs was acquired because truth or The True attracted them toward true beliefs; rather, one's beliefs were caused within them by one's parents, culture, historical era, and so on. All beliefs are on a par—they are all radically contingent, caused by sociohistorical accident; one cannot make any legitimate claim to the so-called truth. Liberal ironists recognize they have no justifications for their convictions, yet they "stand for them unflinchingly" (CIS, 46, 60). The ideal citizen recognizes the contingency of all her moral beliefs and so is left to create herself anew. The hero of such a society is the strong poet and the revolutionary. An ideal liberal society, Rorty writes, "is one which has no purpose except freedom, no goal except a willingness to see how such encounters [between present and new practices] go and to abide by the outcome. It has no purpose except to make life easier for poets and revolutionaries . . ." (CIS, 60–61).

Rorty's ideal society should be contrasted with a more traditional or classical form of ideal democratic society. It is the hope of classical liberalism that culture as a whole may be "rationalized," that passion and fantasy will be ruled by reason (CIS, 53). Truth is placed above freedom so that society may attain ordered liberty. Free discourse is valued not in itself but so that truth may prevail. Citizens are free not so they may "do as they please," but so they may "do as they ought." The ideal citizen believes a free society is the most moral form of society based on his view of human nature and human dignity. He strives to abide by the ideal of self-discipline rather than self-creation and understands that a free society can only be truly free within a moral framework. The goal of such a society is not to make life easier for poets and revolutionaries (although it may do that), but to make life easier for forms of community life that enable individual human beings to develop and flourish according to their essential nature.

Those who affirm the classical liberal view of society will reject Rorty's redescription of it as degenerate. Since Rorty recommends his views of human nature and truth not as true but as useful to liberal democratic society, those who reject his redescription also may reject those views of human nature and truth designed as the means to obtain it. Still, such critics may seem to have nothing to say to Rorty when they lament the fact that liberalism would make "all the world like

California"[42] and he responds, "Yes. Isn't it wonderful?" They might go on, however, to point to a long tradition, running from Plato to the current Pope, which argues that Rorty's society is one in which even the sort of freedom he admires cannot be sustained.[43]

There are roughly two strands to this form of argument, one concerning the philosophy or philosophies of the citizenry, the other concerning their conduct. The first strand of argument suggests that relativism of the sort Rorty advocates may so erode the public philosophy that democracy is no longer defendable against tyranny. The second strand of argument suggests that such relativism corrupts the moral culture and that the conditions associated with such a culture make it vulnerable to tyrannical influences.[44] In sum, apart from a certain philosophical and moral framework, the pursuit of liberty leads ultimately to demoralization, despair, and disorder.

We begin with the first strand of argument. If, as Rorty thinks, in answer to the question, "Why do we prize democracy and its institutions and values?" we can only respond, "We just do" or "These just are the values *we* (we moderns or we democratic citizens) hold," don't we have reason to fear we might someday stop valuing those things? Rorty seems to bite the bullet on this: If someday our descendants accept fascism, then 'fascism will be the truth of man', and there will be no way to judge them wrong from an objective point of view.[45] Still, he is likely to continue, even though there is no objective way to judge, there is little reason to think we will stop making nonobjective statements of disapproval of, for example, slavery and fascism. Nor will we stop telling ourselves "stories" about why this is the case. Rorty maintains that we do not need philosophical arguments to protect us from tyranny since, so long as we remain heirs to the same historical traditions and are faced with the same problems, our beliefs and commitments are

42. The phrase is Stephen Macedo's, *Liberal Virtues: Citizenship, Virtue, and Community in Liberal Constitutionalism* (Oxford: Clarendon Press, 1990), 278.

43. See, for example, Plato's *Republic* (Indianapolis, IN: Hackett Publishing Company, 1992); Alexis de Tocqueville's *Democracy in America*, abridgement trans. Henry Reeve. The World's Classics ed. Henry Steele Commager (London: Oxford University Press, 1946); Alexander Hamilton and James Madison's *The Federalist Papers* (New York: Bantam, 1989); Edmund Burke's *Reflections on the Revolution in France* (New York: Viking Press, 1982); Fyodor Dostoevsky's *Grand Inquisitor* (Indianapolis, IN: Hackett Publishing Company, 1993); John Courtney Murray's *We Hold These Truths* (New York: Sheed and Ward, 1960); Gertrude Himmelfarb's *On Looking Into the Abyss: Untimely Thoughts on Culture and Society* (New York: Vintage Books, 1995); and Pope John Paul II's *The Gospel of Life* (see footnote 47).

44. Rorty claims that he is not a relativist. It is difficult to see how he could make such a claim given his views that no moral system can be justified, different cultures will engender different moral beliefs which people will stand for unflinchingly, and so on. His argument is very sophisticated; he suggests, for example, that we drop the vocabulary that includes the term "relativism." But, the objection would go, dropping this kind of talk also makes the culture vulnerable to corruption.

45. Charles Guignon and David Hiley, "Biting the Bullet: Rorty on Private and Public Morality," in *Reading Rorty*, ed. Alan Malachowski (Cambridge, MA: Basil Blackwell, 1990), 355, quoting Rorty's *Consequences of Pragmatism*, xlii.

largely settled. Some issues are simply no longer open to debate, he says, so we ought not think certain threats to liberty are real possibilities.[46]

There are a number of problems with this response. First, as the diversity Rorty so admires continues to increase, we cannot assume that our heirs will inherit the same traditions and face the same problems. Second, Rorty's response ignores the fact that as a society some of our important beliefs and commitments are not yet fixed. For example, while they may be largely fixed regarding slavery, they are certainly not fixed regarding abortion, assisted suicide, and racism (which, given time and opportunity, could find expression once again in slavery). We cannot assume that these issues can be settled apart from metaphysical debates. Third, the deeper philosophical issues Rorty would have us ignore are part of the traditions associated with those beliefs and commitments that are largely settled. The story of the abolition of slavery, for example, is unintelligible apart from metaphysical and religious discussions of personhood and who deserves freedom and protection in a democratic society. Rorty's response to such an objection is to claim that while our ancestors may have needed these discussions, we no longer do (CIS, 194). But, it is not clear that we can avoid the push toward these issues; and, it is not obvious that we should try to since there are often important consequences. We cannot begin our political theory with a commitment to democracy without asking some deeper questions. For example, a commitment to a democratic form of government that is justified primarily by a commitment to free-market capitalism would likely leave democracy more vulnerable to oppressive forms of government and the excesses of consumerism than a commitment to democracy justified primarily by a belief in the dignity of the human person. To take another example, at the level of superficial agreement, all, or virtually all, are committed to democracy because it protects liberty. There are, however, very different interpretations of liberty; and, these interpretations have far reaching consequences even for constitutional essentials. One might compare the opposing positions on abortion and assisted suicide derived form "Assisted Suicide: The Philosophers' Brief" (which argues for a right to suicide) and Pope John Paul II's *The Gospel of Life* (which vehemently opposes such a position).[47]

Finally, evils such as tyranny, cruelty, pain, and humiliation often have been overcome by a strong sense of human solidarity, that is, when persons previously viewed as subhuman come to be seen as fellow human beings who possess an inviolable dignity. If we follow Rorty in rejecting such conceptions of human nature, how are we to maintain and foster solidarity and so prevent various atrocities?

[46.] Richard Rorty, "The Priority of Democracy to Philosophy," reprinted in *Reading Rorty*, 288.

[47.] John Rawls, Ronald Dworkin, Thomas Nagel, Robert Nozick, Thomas Scanlon, and Judith Jarvis Thompson, "Assisted Suicide: The Philosophers' Brief," *New York Review of Books*, March 27, 1997, 41–47. Pope John Paul II, *The Gospel of Life: The Encyclical Letter on Abortion, Euthanasia, and the Death Penalty in Today's World*, letter delivered March 25, 1995, Vatican Translation (New York: Random House).

Rorty responds that, for a liberal ironist, a sense of solidarity is "a matter of imaginative identification with the details of others' lives," not the recognition of a shared essence (*CIS,* 190). In order to foster feelings of solidarity even toward those "wildly different from ourselves," we need "the ability to see more and more traditional differences (of tribe, religion, race, customs, and the like) as unimportant when compared with similarities with respect to pain and humiliation—the ability to think of people wildly different from ourselves as included in the range of 'us'" (*CIS,* 192).

Rorty claims that the source of solidarity is found in broadening the category "us" to include "fellow sufferer." There are a couple of problems with this. First, he claims his view fosters a stronger sense of solidarity than the traditional view because "fellow human being" is too large a category for persons to identify with. But "fellow sufferer" is as large a category as "fellow human being" (larger, unless he can exclude animals); and so, we may have an equally difficult time identifying with others in this respect. Second, the category "fellow sufferer" seems to require a prior category. If we do not first recognize another as, for example, a fellow human being, we may not recognize that person's situation as one of suffering. It is very likely that many of the guards at Auschwitz did not recognize the condition of the Jews as one of suffering precisely because they did not recognize them as fellow human beings.

Rorty thinks it is possible for us all to be liberal ironists even when there is no answer to the question "Why be a liberal ironist?" The considerations above suggest that *no answer* is not a good answer; they also suggest that Rorty ought not be so cavalier in his rejection of the long-held view that philosophical justifications are important in maintaining democratic institutions and values. But, even if we were willing to grant that democratic society can get along fine without philosophical justifications, we might still consider the second strand of argument and ask what effect Rorty's way of talking is likely to have on culture. If a free society has "no purpose except to make life easier for poets and revolutionaries," we need to ask, "Would these poets and revolutionaries serve democracy well?" Won't the poet and revolutionary, always looking for new options, creatively redescribe, challenge, undermine, even outright attack the society and values Rorty admires?

Rorty recognizes this tension. He acknowledges that there is no way to reconcile the Nietzschean ideal of self-creation with justice and solidarity in a single comprehensive philosophy (*CIS,* xiv). But, while Rorty thinks such a union cannot be maintained in theory, he thinks it can be maintained in practice. His response is to privatize the ideal of self-creation and "drop the demand for a theory which unifies the public and private" (*CIS,* xv). He writes:

> There is no way in which philosophy, or any other theoretical discipline, will ever let us do that [unite self-creation with justice and solidarity]. The closest we will come to joining these two quests is to see the aim of a just and free society as letting its citizens be as privatistic, "irrationalist," and aes-

theticist as they please so long as they do it on their own time—causing no harm to others and using no resources needed by those less advantaged. There are practical measures to be taken to accomplish this practical goal. But there is no way to bring self-creation together with justice at the level of theory. The vocabulary of self-creation is necessarily private, unshared, unsuited to argument. The vocabulary of justice is necessarily public and shared, a medium for argumentative exchange. (*CIS*, xiv)

Rorty asks the poets to subordinate "sublimity to the desire to avoid cruelty and pain" (*CIS*, 197). But, we might ask, why should they do that? Rorty responds: "In my view, there is nothing to back up such a request, nor need there be. There is no *neutral,* noncircular way to defend the liberal's claim that cruelty is the worst thing we do, . . ." (*CIS*, 197). Despite this, Rorty is optimistic that the poets will listen.

According to the traditional view of liberal democracy, Rorty has little reason to be optimistic. On this view, the public/private distinction Rorty makes cannot be maintained in practice; the health and freedom of the public sphere depend in various ways on the private actions of the citizens. Even if the poets do not explicitly reject free society, pathologies may develop in private lives which threaten public life.[48] Contrary to Rorty's contention, the public sphere cannot be indifferent to the so-called private virtues of responsibility, sacrifice, integrity, social service, moderation, self-discipline, civility, and brotherly love.[49] The lack of these virtues can lead to such things as drunkenness, gluttony, drug abuse, decline in academic and job performance, unemployment, illegitimacy, broken homes, and broken neighborhoods; which, to be overcome, may require limitations on citizens' freedoms. It may seem an obvious point to claim that these problems have roots in private character, but the strict separation of public and private spheres obscures this fact and brings with it a strong tendency to look for merely public solutions to such problems.

---

48. Perhaps Edmund Burke said it best: "Men are qualified for civil liberty in exact proportion to their disposition to put moral chains upon their own appetites—in proportion as their love of justice is above their rapacity—in proportion as their soundness and sobriety of understanding is above their vanity and presumption—in proportion as they are more disposed to listen to the counsels of the wise and good, in preference to the flattery of knaves. Society cannot exist, unless a controlling power upon will and appetite be placed somewhere; and the less of it there is within, the more there must be without. It is ordained in the eternal constitution of things, that men of intemperate minds cannot be free. Their passions forge their fetters." Quoted in John O'Sullivan's Preface to *The Loss of Virtue: Moral Confusion and Social Disorder in Britain and America,* ed. Digby Anderson (London: Social Affairs Unit, 1992), xiv.

49. This particular list is found in Guignon and Hiley ("Biting the Bullet," 361). The "private" virtues mentioned in our section on Rawls, as well as others, could be added. Guignon and Hiley argue that the adoption of Rorty's philosophy would exacerbate various private disorders of the self and undermine society; it will not lead to greater responsibility, commitment, and community, but, rather, to "a 'culture of narcissism' tending towards social fragmentation, lack of sustaining commitment, cynicism, privatism and self-preoccupation" ("Biting the Bullet," 356).

As Bernard Williams writes, "In the general cultural context, he [Rorty] is just as optimistically neglectful as he was in the case of science about the effects of everyone's coming to believe what he has to say—effects which the pragmatist, least of all, can afford to neglect."[50] We might add that Rorty's recommendation that we adopt his philosophy and "just see how things go" demonstrates a kind of reckless disregard for the effects such an experiment may have on persons. It brings to mind the plea of one of the many who suffered under the rule of communism: "Next time, let them experiment on animals. Persons it hurts too much." History should have taught us this much: there is a price to be paid for mistaken views of human nature and truth. There is likely a price to be paid for neglecting these topics as well.

Human Nature, Human Morality, Human Fulfillment?

In this book's survey of some of history's most important ethical philosophies, we have treated the philosophers in many ways as participants in an ongoing debate, a debate that has not only been about how one should live, but also about what it means to be a human being since one's answer to the former question is often determined by one's answer to the latter question. We have seen that most of the philosophers in this book are optimistic that philosophy can discover the truth about these matters, that philosophy can tell us how all persons should live and that it can do so in a way that is convincing even to the skeptic. In other words, philosophy can provide an answer *for* all persons and *to* all persons.[51] Insofar as it fails to do this, relativism and amoralism is likely to abound.

Each part of this approach to ethical theory has been challenged by some of the philosophers we have examined in this final chapter on the postmodern world. While such philosophers may not deny that this is an accurate picture of the way moral philosophy has been done from ancient times, they believe the approach to be no longer viable. We saw, for example, that earlier in the 20th century, analytic philosophers like Moore and Ayer invoked a separation of the realms of fact and value, thereby rejecting the thesis that ethical theory must be based on a theory of human nature. Some came to the conclusion that there can be no genuine moral knowledge, and yet they were optimistic that this conclusion would not lead to widespread relativism or amoralism because, they believed, theoretical conclusions have little effect on persons' actual moral commitments.

Near the middle of the century, Sartre provided his own challenge to the tradition of moral inquiry. With his thesis that existence precedes essence, he rejected the idea of a fixed nature common to all persons and so also the idea of

---

50. Bernard Williams, "Auto-da-Fé: Consequences of Pragmatism," in *Reading Rorty,* ed. Alan Malachowski (Cambridge, MA: Blackwell, 1990), 35.

51. The phrase is Bernard Williams's. He is, however, skeptical of philosophy's ability to do this. See his *Ethics and the Limits of Philosophy* (Cambridge: Harvard University Press, 1985).

universal moral principles derivable from that nature. Philosophy has shown that human beings are radically free to choose their own ways of life even if it cannot show us what lives to choose. "Everything is possible!" insofar as one chooses in the name of freedom.

Around this same time, philosophers such as Anscombe ushered in a return to the method of moral enquiry exhibited throughout the earlier chapters of this book. The work of Rawls and MacIntyre is part of this return to naturalism, to the reunion of fact and value and the quest for moral truth. In *A Theory of Justice,* Rawls derives a set of principles of justice from a view of human nature as free and rational. These principles are supposed to be applicable to all persons and justified in a way all rational persons can come to accept. In *After Virtue,* MacIntyre seeks to justify an Aristotelian virtue theory that grounds ethics in certain facts about the world, specifically in an account of human practices, the unity of life, and traditions such that persons find fulfillment in successfully participating in the activity of particular communities ordered toward a common good. It is only in these sorts of environments that the virtues and human beings may flourish. While MacIntyre maintains that there is no way to step outside the context of all traditions to provide a justification for morality, he argues that it is possible to provide a rational justification from within a tradition that is superior to those justifications provided by competing traditions. In this way, he concludes, it is possible for philosophy to arrive at true moral knowledge.

Hare is part of the return to rationalism even though he rejects basing it in a form of naturalism. As we saw, he maintains that a rational moral theory must be based on the logic of moral words. He maintains that an analysis of moral language will reveal rules of moral thinking that will produce answers to moral questions on which all persons, insofar as they are thinking rationally, may agree. His is an attempt to provide an objective moral theory based in language rather than a view of human nature. And, he maintains, given the way the world is structured, it is a theory we have good reason to adopt: human beings who live moral lives are most often happy.

Gilligan's work is an attempt to give women a distinctive voice in these debates. It is a voice that emphasizes care rather than justice and responsibilities rather than rights. It asks us to be sensitive to the unique details of situations and to the particular relationships in which we find ourselves. It is a voice that claims boldly that women, no less than men, are capable of the highest levels of human fulfillment.

As we saw, Rorty explicitly rejects the long-held view that ethical and political theory require a theory of human nature. He thinks ethics does not need metaphysics any more than it needs religion. He sees the history of moral enquiry as a series of random interminable disagreements over these matters. Since philosophy cannot provide an answer *to* all persons, Rorty concludes, it cannot provide an answer *for* all persons. It is both possible and desirable for persons to recognize "the relative validity of their convictions and yet stand for them unflinchingly." Literature, Rorty observes, is better equipped than philosophy to show us how. If we give up the quest for a unified philosophical theory we may have a better sense that "everything is possible."

As we saw in previous chapters of this book, the ethical debates from ancient through modern times have largely been over what makes human beings essentially human and what sort of life enables that part of our humanity to flourish. Ethics provides the means for turning humans-as-they-find-themselves into humans-fulfilled: human nature, human morality, human fulfillment. In the postmodern world, the debate has taken a radical turn. Some have suggested we abandon all talk of human nature and fulfillment. For them, the question is no longer, "Which view is true?" but, rather, "Does truth exist?" As we have seen, there are philosophers on both sides. As we enter the 21st century, we must ask, "Will the conclusions we reach in our philosophy have an effect on our lives?" In other words, Was Socrates right in trying to answer Thrasymachus or should he have shrugged his shoulders and walked away? Do *we* need to answer him or may he be ignored? Will history judge our decision a benign one?

Suggested Readings

ROBERT BRANDOM (ed.), *Rorty: And His Critics* (Oxford and Cambridge: Blackwell, 2000).

NORMAN DANIELS (ed.), *Reading Rawls* (Stanford, CA: Stanford University Press, 1975).

ELIZABETH FRAZER, JENNIFER HORNSBY, and SABINA LOVIBOND (eds.), *Ethics: A Feminist Reader* (Oxford: Blackwell, 1992).

JOHN HORTON and SUSAN MENDUS (eds.), *After MacIntyre: Critical Perspectives on the Work of Alasdair MacIntyre* (Notre Dame, IN: University of Notre Dame Press, 1994).

MARY JEANNE LARRABEE, *An Ethic of Care* (New York and London: Routledge, Chapman, and Hall, Inc., 1993).

ALAN MALACHOWSKI (ed.), *Reading Rorty: Critical Responses to Philosophy and the Mirror of Nature (and Beyond)* (Oxford and Cambridge: Blackwell, 1990).

DOUGLAS SEANOR and N. FOTION (eds.), *Hare and Critics: Essays on Moral Thinking* (Oxford: Clarendon Press, 1988).

MARY WARNOCK, *Ethics Since 1900,* 3rd ed. (Oxford: Oxford University Press, 1978).

INDEX